Washington's

BEST WILDFLOWER HIKES

TEXT AND PHOTOGRAPHY BY

Charles Gurche

WESTCLIFFE PUBLISHERS
westcliffepublishers.com

ISBN: 1-56579-440-0

TEXT AND PHOTOGRAPHY: Charles Gurche, © 2004. All rights reserved.
MAP ILLUSTRATIONS: Rebecca Finkel, © 2004. All rights reserved.

EDITORS: Suzanne Venino and Jenna Samelson Browning
DESIGNER: Rebecca Finkel, F + P Graphic Design, Inc.; Fort Collins, CO
PRODUCTION COORDINATOR: Carol Pando

PUBLISHER: Westcliffe Publishers, Inc.
P.O. Box 1261
Englewood, Colorado 80150-1261
WESTCLIFFEPUBLISHERS.COM

Printed in China through H & Y Printing, Ltd.

LIBRARY OF CONGRESS CATALOGING-IN-PUBLICATION DATA:

Gurche, Charles.
   Washington's best wildflower hikes / text and photography
by Charles Gurche.
      p. cm.
   Includes bibliographical references and index.
   ISBN: 1-56579-440-0
   1. Hiking—Washington (State)—Guidebooks. 2. Wild
flowers—Washington (State)—Guidebooks 3. Washington
(State)—Guidebooks. I. Title.
GV199.42.W2G87   2004
796.51'09795—dc22   2003060775

For more information
about other fine books and
calendars from Westcliffe
Publishers, please contact
your local bookstore, call us
at 1-800-523-3692, write
for our free color catalog,
or visit us on the Web at
westcliffepublishers.com.

COVER:
*Paradise Meadows,
Mt. Rainier National Park,
with the Tatoosh Range
in the background*

PREVIOUS PAGE:
*Balsamroot, lupine,
and Indian paintbrush,
Columbia Gorge*

PLEASE NOTE:
Risk is always a factor in backcountry and high-mountain travel. Many
of the activities described in this book can be dangerous, especially when
weather is adverse or unpredictable, and when unforeseen events or
conditions create a hazardous situation. The author has done his best to
provide the reader with accurate information about backcountry travel, as
well as to point out some of its potential hazards. It is the responsibility of
the users of this guide to learn the necessary skills for safe backcountry
travel, and to exercise caution in potentially hazardous areas, especially on
glaciers and avalanche-prone terrain. The author and publisher disclaim
any liability for injury or other damage caused by backcountry traveling
or performing any other activity described in this book.

Acknowledgments

I asked for and received quite a bit of assistance in completing this massive project. For sharing their knowledge of flowers, trails, and writing, or for inspiring me to forge ahead day after day, I'd like to thank the following people:

Peggy Bohan, Carrie Lipe, Sarah Conover, Megan McCarthy, Terry Lawhead, Jack Nisbet, Doug Robnet, Sara Devins, Peter Gurche, Jessi Box, Steve Box, Kai Huschke, Alice Nelson, Barbara Samora, Ann Risvold, Bill Sobieralski, Barb Richey, Eli Warren, Darby Moore, Kelly Busch, Don Coats, Terry Halstead, Pam Camp, Tim Foss, Dianne Taugher, Lief Hazelet, Christine Rader, Lori Baker, Sandy Gourdin, Barb Benner, Betsy Carlson, Steve Aker, Peter Frenzen, Charlie Crifafulli, John Wayland, Howard Fergason, Robin Demario, Carolyn Lord, Tom Davis, Mike Ferris, Jack Thorne, Virginia Smoot, Ronnie Sanchez, Glen Paulson, Rich Davis, Roger Marcus, Greg Marsh, Janice Burger, Ann Dunphy, Edan Lira, Bret Alumbaugh, Mike Connolly, and Stan Hinatsu.

Thanks also to Emily Nisbet and Jill Williams for their extensive work on the wildflower profiles, and to the Westcliffe Publishers team: John Fielder, Linda Doyle, Jenna Browning, Suzanne Venino, Martha Gray, Craig Keyzer, Carol Pando, Rebecca Finkel, and Jasmine Star.

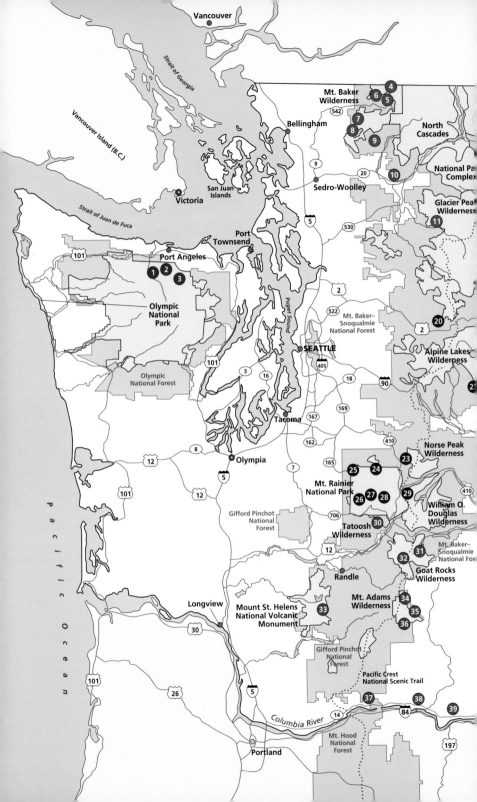

BRITISH COLUMBIA

Pasayten Wilderness

(13)

Okanogan National Forest

(19)

(14)

(16)

(15) (18) (17) **Winthrop**

Lake Chelan–Sawtooth Wilderness

Okanogan National Forest

Okanogan National Forest

Okanogan National Forest

Colville National Forest

Columbia River

Colville National Forest

Kaniksu National Forest

(31)

(395)

Kaniksu National Forest

(20)

(20)

(2)

IDAHO

Lake Chelan

Wenatchee National Forest

Columbia River

Chelan

ALT 97

2/97

(174)

(50)

Banks Lake

(2)

Spokane River

(48)

(90)

Spokane

(21)

(2)

Wenatchee

(97)

Wenatchee National Forest

(28)

(49) **Harrington**

(90)

(47)

(46)

Columbia River

Ellensburg

(82)

(90)

Potholes Reservoir

(395)

(95)

(195) (45)

Pullman

Yakima

Snake River

Richland

(82)

Pasco

(12)

(12)

Kennewick

(82)

Walla Walla

Umatilla National Forest

(12)

Wenaha–Tucannon Wilderness

(129)

(42) (43)

(40) (41)

(44)

(97)

(14)

Yakima River

OREGON

(84)

(395)

N

Contents

Wildflower Profiles Common Name (Latin Name)

Lupine and Indian paintbrush beneath the Tatoosh Range, Mt. Rainier National Park

Introduction

Washington's wide variety of elevations, climates, and soils blesses the state with a diverse collection of wildflowers. Sagebrush areas here host many flowers also commonly found in the deserts of Utah or Nevada. Many species in the Cascades also reside in the Rocky Mountains, British Columbia, and Alaska. The trails in this book represent day hikes in a variety of Washington's ecosystems.

It was a difficult task to choose which hikes to include in a book of Washington's "best" wildflower hikes. I studied piles of books, maps, and plant lists. I spoke with many rangers, hikers, botanists, and flower enthusiasts. I called and visited offices of the U.S. Forest Service, Bureau of Land Management, National Park Service, state parks, and national wildlife refuges. And then I hiked and hiked some more. Although plenty of other trails in the state could qualify as "best" wildflower hikes, my research narrowed the choices down to those appearing in these pages. I hope this book will guide you to many new places to explore.

Flower identification proved another challenge in this project. I began the work as nearly a novice. Although I could identify plants such as lupine, paintbrush, and phlox, little did I know that there are so many kinds of each. This journey took me far beyond, into figworts and saxifrages, buckwheats and parsleys.

I can give you a few hints about flower identification: If you're a beginner, you'll probably want to start with a book that sorts flowers by color, rather than by family, as you'll have no idea what family to look up. *Wildflowers of Washington* by C.P. Lyons is an excellent guide by color, with great photographs, descriptions, and bold type to indicate the best details to differentiate species. Several other good books are mentioned in Appendix C.

The next stage is learning the basic flower parts and terms. Flower identification books refer to parts such as sepals, stamens, and rays. They also use terms such as ovate or basal. Understanding the vocabulary helps in keying out a flower.

My advice is to join a guided wildflower hike or two. In Washington, places such as Paradise and Sunrise at Mt. Rainier National Park, Hurricane Ridge in Olympic National Park, and several districts in the national forests offer guided flower hikes. Ask the ranger to point out the basic parts on some of the flowers. You'll also learn to identify many common flowers that you'll often find in other similar habitats.

Once you have some basic parts down, begin learning about flower families. The great advantage to using a flower-identification book sorted by family

Meadows on Sauk Mountain, Mt. Baker–Snoqualmie National Forest

instead of by color is that it compensates for the fact that many flowers have a wide color range within the same species. For example, thyme-leaved buckwheat, a common plant, can be white, pink, red, or yellow. Certain phloxes can be white, pink, lavender, or blue. Penstemons, daisies, asters, and numerous other flowers also present color variations. If you try to look up these plants by their color, you might not find them because you'll be searching in the wrong color chapter. Looking up these types of flowers by family is much easier.

Another problem you'll encounter is that numerous common names are often used for the same flower, with one guidebook giving a different common name than another. It can get a little confusing when the same plant appears as green hellebore, veratrum, corn lily, swamp veratrum, Indian corn lily, Indian hellebore, or false hellebore. Trying to find it in the index can drive you crazy! Latin names come only one to a species, but who wants to remember *Cryptogramma acrostichoides* for a flower? I have tried to use the most common of the common names, at times giving a second name that is also often used. You might use different common names than the ones I have given and be just as correct.

Lupine meadow on Hurricane Ridge, Olympic National Park

While you're exploring Washington's phenomenal flowered landscapes, please do so with care. Numerous alterations of our natural environment have endangered many plants. Logging, grazing, farming, fire suppression, and the spread of noxious weeds have affected native species across vast swaths of the state. Some of the trails in this book lead to popular places where meadow damage is apparent. Please keep your impact minimal in these fragile locations by leaving them as undisturbed as possible and staying on maintained trails. Practice Leave No Trace ethics while traveling and camping in the backcountry; for more information, visit www.lnt.org.

For those interested in flower photography, here's a bit of information about my equipment and methodology. The close-up wildflower profile images in this book were taken with a Nikon FE and 105mm Nikon lens. For the landscape photographs, I used a Linhoff Technikardan 4x5 and 90mm, 150mm, and 300mm lenses. I used Fujichrome Velvia 50 film and a tripod for all images.

For flower close-ups, I recommend a tripod with spreading legs for low-angle shooting. Close-ups often look great in diffused light, so some type of diffuser panel or umbrella proves quite handy. I employ a white golf umbrella that also blocks the wind. A telephoto close-up lens allows for some working distance from the flower and a narrower range of focus that helps with shooting simple, out-of-focus backgrounds.

The landscape shots were taken under a variety of lighting conditions. Diffused, even foggy conditions work well in small meadows with trees in the background. Backlighting can create a glowing, stained-glass effect with flowers. Mornings often provide the calmer conditions necessary to keep flowers in sharp focus. If flowers are moving, a cable release is helpful to release the shutter during those brief calm moments. With side lighting, a polarizing filter can reduce the reflecting glare on vegetation, thus bringing out brighter colors. A low camera position for wide-angle flower landscapes gives a sense of increased depth and invites the viewer into the photograph.

Good luck, and happy wildflower viewing and shooting!

How to Use This Guide

Each hike gives the following information:

TRAIL RATING: Easy, moderate, or difficult. In general, easy hikes are less than 4 miles and involve less than 500 feet in elevation change. Moderate hikes are typically 4 to 7 miles with 500 to 1,500 feet in elevation change. Difficult hikes are usually more than 7 miles and have over 1,500 feet in elevation change.

TRAIL LENGTH: This is a round-trip distance for an out-and-back hike, or the total distance for a loop hike. Mileages for optional diversions that sometimes appear in the hike description are not included in the total distance. Many trails enter flower areas after little distance, so you could make a shorter hike by turning back early.

LOCATION: Provides the name of any public or private lands on which the hike falls, as well as the nearest town with a gas station, water, and other essential services.

ELEVATION: The minimum to maximum elevations reached on the hike.

BLOOM SEASON: The average time when you'll find at least several wild-flower varieties in bloom.

PEAK BLOOM: The average time when flowers are putting on the best show.

CONTACT: The name and phone number of the managing agency.

DIRECTIONS: Starting in the town mentioned under the Location heading, these driving directions to the trailhead include road numbers, junctions, and distances. It's also often helpful to have a forest service map of the area in which you're traveling.

TRAIL DESCRIPTION: Directions for the hike and descriptions of the flowers most commonly seen on the hike, as well as some less common plants. For easy reference, flower names appear in bold upon first mention in each hike. You'll notice that similar habitats usually host the same set of common flowers and several less common plants more unique to that particular area. The common subalpine species are nearly universally found in every subalpine

Tarn beside meadow with lupine in bloom, William O. Douglas Wilderness

hike from Mt. Adams to Mt. Baker. It is helpful to get to know this group of about 15 to 20 recurrent flowers.

WILDFLOWER PROFILE: Focuses on one species encountered during the hike, depending on bloom time. This section gives the common and Latin name, height, bloom time covering the entire state (not just the hike in which it appears), a photo, and a brief description to enrich your knowledge of the flowers you see along the trail.

MAP: Combined with the trail directions, the maps provided in this book should be adequate for accessing and hiking these trails. However, a more detailed topographic map and the ability to use it will greatly aid hikers in orienting themselves in the backcountry landscape. I highly recommend packing either a Green Trails™ or 7½-minute USGS topographic map of the area where you're hiking, especially for all high-elevation hikes. To access some of the trailheads, you'll need to navigate on forest service roads; a forest service map is useful to supplement the directions given to reach the trailhead.

In picking a flower hike, you'll probably want to consider the season first. In general, flowers peak in eastern Washington from mid-April to mid-June. The Blue Mountains, the first high-elevation hikes accessible after snowmelt, are usually best from June to mid-July. The Cascade and Olympic flowers peak from mid-July to mid-August. Refer to Appendix A for a listing of bloom times that also indicates each hike's difficulty level, another consideration when choosing a hike.

Flowers can vary quite a bit from year to year, depending on winter snowfall amounts, melt-off rates, summer sunshine and rains, and the cycles that many plants undergo. Subalpine meadows can put on a fantastic show in some years, but in others, they might not melt out early enough, resulting in a marginal blooming season. These conditions also affect when flowers will bloom. Every two or three weeks, the same meadow will show quite a different collection of flowers in bloom. I have seen meadows pink with hundreds of grass widow blossoms fade in a few days during an early heat wave. Therefore, don't take this book as gospel, but as a general guide. Call the contact phone numbers listed with each hike to get current flower conditions, especially if you want to see the area at its peak.

Many of the hikes in this book require a usage fee. As of this printing, entry into national parks currently costs $10. An annual national parks pass is available for $50. Most of the hikes in national forests require a Northwest Forest Pass, which must be purchased at a forest service office. These currently cost $5

Arrowleaf balsamroot and lupine, Columbia Hills State Park

for a day pass or $30 for an annual pass. It is frustrating to reach a trailhead where a pass is required and worry about getting a ticket while hiking, so for national forest hikes, plan on obtaining a pass before you head out.

Although most of the hikes in this book are not long, generally 3 to 10 miles, make sure you are prepared for backcountry terrain and weather. Many of the hikes lead into alpine areas where changing weather can be dangerous. Cold fog and rain can enshroud the high country while the lower valleys remain clear and warm. Orientation becomes difficult above tree line in a thick fog. Hypothermia can pose a serious threat throughout the summer. Always carry enough warm clothing for changing conditions. A knife, matches, fire starter, map, compass, flashlight, insect repellant, and first-aid kit are recommended for all higher-elevation hikes. I also recommend carrying a supply of food and water, as well as a water filter and bottle. Many hikes pass streams or lakes

where water may be filtered. I've mentioned the locations of these, and a map can help you to plan where your next water source will be.

A few other hazards are also important to keep in mind. Several trails cross steep snowfields that can be dangerous in June and July. Most of these are melted out by August. Never attempt to cross a steep snowfield. Find a safe way around it or turn back and hike in a safer place. Several of the lower-elevation hikes pass through country where poison ivy and rattlesnakes dwell. Keep an alert eye, and you should have no problem with these. I've also mentioned many plants as edible and some as poisonous. *Never sample any plant without absolute assuredness of its identity. Several edible plants resemble others that can be fatal if ingested. Don't sample plants in national parks.*

The search for flowerlands in Washington has led me to some astounding locales. Everyone finds a few places that are particularly special to them. As people often ask me about my favorite hikes, I'll share some favorites with you. In the spring while the high country lies buried in snow, the beautiful foothills of the Methow Valley brim with balsamroot and lupine. This is also true of the Columbia Gorge hikes. In the high country, try the truly magical hikes near Mt. Baker. Glaciers on Mt. Baker or Mt. Shuksan make a lovely backdrop for meadows. Mt. Rainier also displays this type of majestic scenery; to avoid crowds in the national park, try Spray Park (Hike 25) or Mazama Ridge (Hike 28). I hope these favorite Washington places become a few of your own.

Arrowleaf balsamroot decks a hillside, Columbia Gorge

*Wildflower
Hike 1* # Hurricane Hill

*Lupine and paintbrush on Hurricane Ridge,
Olympic National Park*

Trail Rating	Easy
Trail Length	2.8 miles round trip
Location	Olympic National Park, south of Port Angeles
Elevation	5,100 to 5,757 feet
Bloom Season	July to late September
Peak Bloom	Mid-July to early August
Contact	Olympic National Park, (360) 565-3100
Directions	From US 101 in Port Angeles, turn south on Race Street, following signs to Olympic National Park/Hurricane Ridge. Pass the park visitor center and follow the road up to the Hurricane Ridge Visitor Center. Check in here for current information and to fill water bottles, then proceed west on the Hurricane Ridge Road for 1.3 miles and park at the trailhead at the end of the road.

The paved Hurricane Hill Trail is a short, popular route through mostly open subalpine terrain with fabulous views. Hurricane Hill rises 600 feet near the end of 10- to 12-mile Hurricane Ridge. Through July and often into August, you can have a snowball fight here. At the Hurricane Ridge Visitor Center, ask about guided ranger walks along this trail. If you want to avoid heavy hiker traffic, arrive early or hike up for sunset and bring a headlamp for the hike down. Carry all the water you'll need.

The trail begins by following the narrow crest of Hurricane Ridge. In late July and early August, you'll see a number of white flowers along the beginning of the trail. **Pearly everlasting** has a tight cluster of white, ball-shaped blossoms on each of its many stems. In the same family, **yarrow** shows a lacy white head and feathery leaves. **American bistort** exhibits a single cylindrical head composed of many tiny white blossoms. **Sitka valerian**, also white and made up of tiny blossoms, presents a fuzzy flower head.

Views to the west reveal mountains and valleys that extend to the horizon. To the southwest, across the Elwha River valley, stand the glaciated peaks of Mt. Carrie and Mt. Fairchild.

Several flowers make a striking appearance along the first 0.5 mile of trail. The orange-spotted **tiger lily**, or **Columbia lily**, displays a large, showy, hanging blossom with projecting stamens. Another elegant flower, **larkspur** has blossoms resembling purple butterflies on a stem. In July, **harebell** shows light blue hanging bells.

The trail passes a number of rocky areas where you'll see plants that have adapted to harsh conditions. Growing in stony soil, **woolly sunflower**, or **Oregon sunshine**, exhibits a bouquet of yellow ray flowers, often two-toned. The pink flowers of **dwarf rose** grow low to the ground in the bare rocky soil along the ridge. **Whiteleaf** or **silverleaf phacelia** has a ball of compact blossoms and hairy leaves that are whitish in appearance. Also found in rocky habitats, **Martindale's desert-parsley** is an edible plant that matures carrotlike leaves and a spray of tiny yellow flowers that form an umbrella-shaped head. **Scalloped** or **Olympic onion** produces an edible bulb and round clusters of pale rose-colored blossoms.

Common along this trail and widespread across the Olympic and Cascade Mountains, **broadleaf lupine** displays stems covered with fragrant blossoms of a blue to purple hue. Dotting the meadows with their red bracts, **magenta paintbrush** and **small-flowered paintbrush** often grow near lupine. Both having round heads of many trumpet-shaped purple blossoms, **Cascade penstemon** and **small-flowered penstemon** look similar. They can be differentiated by their leaves, as the leaves on Cascade penstemon have sawtoothed edges.

At mile 0.3 you'll reach a saddle and a junction. Continue straight. (The Little River Trail departs to the right.) Within a half mile you'll enter meadows dotted with several types of yellow ray flower. **Mountain** or **broadleaf arnica** usually generates a single head with 8 to 12 petals on each stem. **Arrowleaf butterweed** shows a cluster of small yellow ray flowers and sawtoothed leaves on 2- to 4-foot stems. Growing from basal leaves, **northern goldenrod** is another yellow composite.

Another family of yellow flowers grows here: cinquefoils, with five-petaled, disk-shaped blossoms. Low-growing **fan-leaved cinquefoil** has three toothed leaflets, almost like a strawberry leaf. **Diverse-leaved cinquefoil** has five to seven large leaves that are deeply serrated. Often growing in rocky soil, **shrubby cinquefoil** sprouts tiny, gray-green leaves like needles on woody stems.

Found along meadow edges, **elegant Jacob's-ladder** has fernlike leaves and light blue petals around a yellow throat. **Subalpine daisy** shows 30 to 40 lavender petals and a yellow center. **Alpine aster** has a similar flower but is smaller, usually 4 to 8 inches high. Endemic to these mountains, **Olympic Mountain aster** displays white rays around a yellow center.

Early in the summer, look for a different group of blossoms in these meadows. Blooming soon after snowmelt, **pasqueflower**, or **western anemone**, puts forth creamy white petals surrounding a cluster of stamens. This plant makes itself more conspicuous in its seed stage in August, when it shows a hairy, football-shaped head. Yellow **glacier lily**, also **fawn lily** or **dogtooth violet**, sprouts draping flower heads with petals arching skyward. **Avalanche lily**, a close relative, displays a white bloom. Small white **spring beauty** is another early bloomer. Also appearing soon after snowmelt, yellow **mountain** or **snow buttercup** blooms in moist soil, showing five-petaled, bowl-shaped flowers. Along forest edges, **Jeffrey's shooting star** exhibits elegant pink blossoms with a ringed anther tube.

A few giant-sized plants dwell on Hurricane Hill. Growing up to 7 feet

SMOOTH DOUGLASIA
Douglasia laevigata

HEIGHT: 1.5" to 2.5"
BLOOMS: July to late August
Shaped like a primrose, the tiny, five-petaled flower of smooth douglasia is pinkish in color. Oval leaves grow in a rosette at its base. When in bloom, smooth douglasia spreads itself in a dense cushion among rocky alpine ridges and talus slopes. Growing in the Cascade and Olympic Mountains, it is quite rare—a real treasure to find.

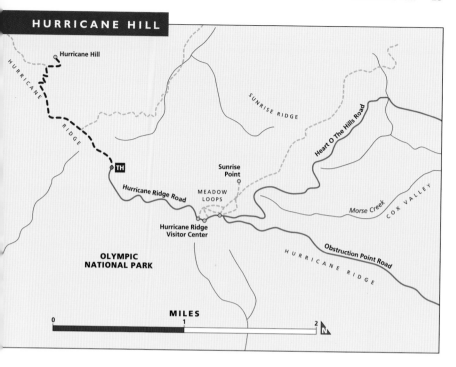

tall, **edible** or **Indian thistle** sports hairy purple heads atop spiky stems. **False hellebore**, or **corn lily**, grows the largest leaves, veined and flame shaped. In moist soil, **cow parsnip** grows huge, presenting an umbrella-shaped white flower head and leaves that may span 10 inches.

Keep an eye out for several smaller plants during peak season in late July and early August. **Cusick's speedwell**, or **Cusick's veronica**, is a small plant with four-petaled purple blossoms. **Mountain owl clover** has showy pink bracts. **Thread-leaved sandwort** bears small, star-shaped white flowers and grassy leaves. **Woolly pussytoes** grows to 6 inches with clustered balls of white flowers and woolly leaves.

The upper trail passes through more rocky areas. Look for **pink mountain heather**, an evergreen shrub with bell-shaped blossoms and needlelike leaves. The flowers of **spreading phlox** may bloom pink, lavender, or white above a mat of spiny leaves. Also found in rocky areas, **Davidson's penstemon** has pink to lavender funnel-shaped flowers, small evergreen leaves, and woody stems. **Smooth douglasia** forms a mat of small symmetrical leaves and five-petaled pink blossoms.

At mile 1.2, Hurricane Hill Trail reaches a junction with the Elwha–Hurricane Hill Trail to the left, a good option to add some extra mileage to the hike. You can follow it along a ridge for 1.5 miles, turning back before the trail drops 4,000 feet to the river below. Fewer people hike this trail.

Continuing on Hurricane Hill Trail, at mile 1.3, a short spur trail on the right leads to an overlook where you can see the trailhead 600 feet below. A plaque identifies many of the features seen from here. Back up the main trail, another sign identifies more landmarks, and on a clear day the panorama at the top of Hurricane Hill is astounding. Nearly 6,000 feet below, Port Angeles looks like a toy town. Across the Strait of Juan de Fuca, the San Juan Islands resemble lily pads. A keen eye may pick out Victoria, British Columbia, or Mt. Baker. If you have lucked into a nice day, you couldn't ask for a better spot to linger.

Cinquefoil and bluebell, Olympic National Park

Cirque Rim

Meadows on Hurricane Ridge, Olympic National Park

Easy	*Trail Rating*
1.5-mile loop	*Trail Length*
Olympic National Park, south of Port Angeles	*Location*
5,240 to 5,471 feet	*Elevation*
June to late September	*Bloom Season*
Mid-July to mid-August	*Peak Bloom*
Olympic National Park, (360) 565-3100	*Contact*
From US 101 in Port Angeles, turn south on Race Street, following signs to Olympic National Park/Hurricane Ridge. Continue to the Hurricane Ridge Visitor Center parking area. Park at the far (west) end of the long parking lot to be near the trailhead.	*Directions*

This short hike through meadowlands and subalpine fir offers many excellent vistas. While the trail is easy enough for children, there are several dangerous drop-offs that demand careful attention. If you wish to add some more mileage to this easy loop hike, you can continue out to Klahhane Ridge, hiking as far as you want.

Stop at the Hurricane Ridge Visitor Center for food, water, and a trail map, which is very helpful in navigating the web of trails and junctions here. This network of trails can get crowded on nice days. More than a dozen trailside signs provide information about many features along these trails.

The trailhead for the Cirque Rim Trail is about 200 feet west of the Hurricane Ridge Visitor Center, on the opposite side of the road. The trail starts out paved and mostly level. Right away you'll see several flowers common to Hurricane Ridge.

Look for the blue stalks of **broadleaf lupine**, a member of the pea family that adds nitrogen to the soil, helping other plants. Several white flowers grow here, including lacy white **yarrow**; **American bistort**, with a cylinder-shaped flower cluster; and **Sitka valerian**, which displays a stamen-fuzzy head. A common sunflower here, **mountain** or **broadleaf arnica** shows 8 to 13 yellow rays. **Olympic Mountain aster**, another composite, has white petals around a yellow center.

The most common tree along the trail is subalpine fir. The narrow, pointed shape of the tree helps to shed snow, a useful adaptation in a region where winters often yield 10 feet of snow, or more. Firs grow in tight clusters, another adaptation that allows the trees to shelter each other from the high winds on the ridge. Growth is slow in this harsh environment: A 5-foot-tall tree can be more than 100 years old. The shorter trees here have spent most of their lives under snow.

PIPER'S OR OLYMPIC BELLFLOWER
Campanula piperi

HEIGHT: 1" to 3"

BLOOMS: August

Piper's bellflower matures a small, bell-shaped blue blossom on a very short stem. The leaves are pointed and perforated. Growing exclusively in the Olympic Mountains, this flower, also called Olympic bellflower, grows in cracks and crevices in high-elevation rock outcroppings. American Indians traditionally used flowers of this family as good luck charms.

CIRQUE RIM

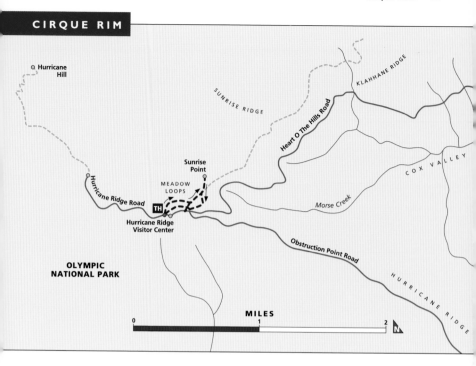

Early, June-blooming flowers here thrive in soil moist with melting snow. One of the first flowers to bloom, **glacier lily**, with its drooping head of arching petals and projecting stamens, sometimes carpets portions of the meadows in yellow. A close relative, **avalanche lily** also puts on a show, producing white blossoms.

At mile 0.1, the trail reaches the edge of a large cirque. Cirques, high basins and bowls carved out by glaciers and rimmed by cliffs, are common in this alpine country. This north-facing cirque often holds snow into September.

At a junction, go left on a spur trail for a little jaunt to an overlook at the end of the path. On a clear day the views to the north make you feel as if you're looking down on the world from an airplane. The northern edge of the Olympic Peninsula runs along the Strait of Juan de Fuca. Across the water lies immense Vancouver Island with the city of Victoria at its southern tip. To the northeast are the magical San Juan Islands.

Follow the spur trail back to Cirque Rim Trail and turn left (east), following the rim of the cirque. Look for **elegant Jacob's-ladder**, presenting a five-petaled blue blossom. The plant's skunklike odor repels ants, making it more inviting for pollinating bees. Just 0.1 mile from the spur trail is an intersection; go straight here. (The right fork leads back to the parking area.) You'll shortly pass an abandoned ski lift. **Indian paintbrush** shows red bracts. **Arrowleaf butterweed** is a yellow composite with many heads. Growing in moist soil, **corn lily**, or **false hellebore**, reveals large, quite elegant veined leaves.

Another junction quickly follows; go left onto an unpaved trail. The path winds beneath subalpine fir with goat's beard lichen hanging on the tree limbs. The trail ascends Sunrise Ridge. Toward the top, the route opens into meadows with lupine, valerian, bistort, yarrow, paintbrush, arnica, and butterweed. An evergreen shrub, **pink mountain heather** bears hanging pink bells.

At a four-way intersection, go left to Sunrise Point. **Spreading phlox** shows pink, lavender, or white star-shaped flowers and a low-growing mat of spiny leaves. The blue blossoms of **Piper's bellflower** poke out of rocky outcrops. From Sunrise Point you can see fabulous views of Mt. Angeles and Klahhane Ridge to the northeast. Hurricane Ridge Road descends below. To the north, the views are similar to those at the Cirque Rim overlook. To the south, dozens of snow-holding peaks extend to the horizon—with the king, Mt. Olympus, thrusting higher than the rest.

Now return to the four-way intersection and proceed straight to complete the loop hike. However, if you want to clock additional miles, a left turn here takes you out to Klahhane Ridge, to more flowers and views.

Continuing on the loop, you'll see **harebell**, with hanging blue bells. **Lousewort**, which comes in a variety of types and colors including yellow, white, pink, and reddish purple, exhibits curved, lobed petals. The trail climbs Alpine Hill, offering up more fine vistas, and then descends back toward the parking lot.

Shrubby cinquefoil yields five-petaled yellow blossoms. **Woolly sunflower**, or **Oregon sunshine**, bears yellow ray flowers; tiny hairs on the plant's leaves give them a sage coloring. Also sage green with hairy leaves, **woolly pussytoes** sprouts ball-shaped white blossoms. **Whiteleaf** or **silverleaf phacelia**, with silvery, hairy leaves, produces small white to lavender flowers with protruding stamens.

At the junction with Big Meadow Loop Trail, take this trail to the right. (If you go straight, you'll reach the east end of the parking lot.) Several edible plants reside along the trail. **Martindale's desert-parsley** hosts a spray of tiny yellow blossoms. Growing close to the ground, **scalloped** or **Olympic onion**, which has an edible bulb, produces a round, clustered, pinkish head. Tall **edible thistle** is a spiny, purple-flowering plant.

Views are so grand that you might miss some of the small flowers in the meadows. **Sandwort** has star-shaped white flower heads and grasslike leaves. Growing 4 to 8 inches tall, **mountain owl clover** produces a flower of purplish pink bracts. **Cusick's speedwell**, also known as **Cusick's veronica**, bears four-petaled, deep purplish blue blossoms with protruding stamens and pistil.

More conspicuous flowers include **tiger lily**, or **Columbia lily**, an orange-spotted flower with large, arching petals. In the pea family, **purple peavine** matures spikes of lobed, deep pink flowers. At the next intersection, turn left to go back to the parking lot—and to your choice of junk food at the visitor center.

Grand Valley

*Elmera
in Badger
Valley,
Olympic
National
Park*

Hurricane Ridge makes a grand place to begin a hike. Just driving the curvy ridge road to the trailhead is exciting, as views open southward to the interior of the mountainous Olympic Peninsula. The end of Hurricane Ridge is called Obstruction Point, where you'll begin this hike at tree line, 6,140 feet. The trail drops into Grand Valley and returns a different way, through Badger Valley. Summer days fluctuate between sparkling sunshine and downright cold fog, mist, and rain. With such fantastic views to enjoy, hopefully you can plan this hike for clear weather.

As storms sweep in off the Pacific with the southwest prevailing winds, parts of the Olympic Peninsula see more than 200 inches of precipitation

Trail Rating	Difficult
Trail Length	9-mile loop
Location	Olympic National Park, south of Port Angeles
Elevation	4,030 to 6,460 feet
Bloom Season	July to late September
Peak Bloom	Mid-July to early August
Contact	Olympic National Park, (360) 565-3100
Directions	From US 101 in Port Angeles, turn south on Race Street, following signs to Olympic National Park/Hurricane Ridge. Pass the park's visitor center and follow the road up toward the Hurricane Ridge Visitor Center. Look for a sign for Obstruction Point. (However, before turning onto Obstruction Point Road—a rocky, mostly one-lane dirt road—you might want to continue 0.2 mile to the Hurricane Ridge Visitor Center for current road and trail information and to fill your water bottles.) Follow Obstruction Point Road for 8.0 miles to its end. An outhouse, but no water, is available near the trailhead.

annually. Obstruction Point, however, lies in a rain shadow, receiving about one-sixteenth of the precipitation of the interior mountains. Plant life in the drier, high-elevation Obstruction Point region is somewhat tundralike.

Make sure you take warm clothing. Even in summer, the weather can turn chilly here. We hiked on a rainy 40-degree day. Water is available along much of the trail, so if you have a filter you won't need to carry much. This area can get a bit populated at times. Early starts on weekdays are your best choice if it's solitude you're seeking.

Two trails depart from the end of the Obstruction Point Road. Take the right (south) trail. (You will return on the left one.) The open trail leads 1.6 miles out to Lillian Ridge, gradually climbing across grassy, rock-strewn slopes where snowfields often linger into August. Along this exposed ridge, flowers are small and sparse, adapted to the rocky soil.

Along the first mile, look for the five-pointed, star-shaped blossoms of **spreading phlox**—pink, lavender, or white—above low mats of needlelike leaves. Also forming mats, **smooth douglasia** generates five-petaled, deep pink flowers above small, rounded basal leaves. **Shrubby cinquefoil** is a woody plant with five-petaled yellow blossoms and spiny leaves. Sometimes growing along with cinquefoil for shelter, **harebell** displays a single, light blue, bell-shaped blossom on each stem.

An uphill traverse leads to the high point of the hike at 6,460 feet. In clear weather, views reveal a vast landscape of high ridges and rocky peaks. Using a topographic map, you can pick out many of the prominent peaks in the park. To the southeast stand the craggy Needles. Mt. Anderson to the south holds glaciers. The Bailey Range rises to the southwest, as does the captain of the peaks, Mt. Olympus. As you gaze across this wilderness, you can easily imagine spending a lifetime exploring these mountains—and still there would be a thousand landscapes never seen.

The trail turns eastward to traverse rocky slopes, and then it drops sharply down switchbacks to a side drainage of Grand Creek. A sheltered valley and richer soils bring forth a new grouping of wildflowers. **Diverse-leaved cinquefoil** shows five notched yellow petals and serrated leaves. Look for Indian paintbrush varieties in several shades of red: **Scarlet**, **magenta**, and **harsh paintbrush** exhibit their color with large bracts. Somewhat similar, pinkish **mountain owl clover** also shows bright bracts.

The trail begins to level out as it enters Grand Valley. At mile 3.4 there is a junction, with the left fork leading down to Grand Lake. You will take this left fork, but first continue straight for a 0.4-mile side trip to Moose Lake. (Don't expect a moose here, or a badger in Badger Valley: The lake was named after Frank Moose and the valley after a ranger's horse.)

Hike along the west side of Moose Lake to a meadow at the southern end. This area hosts an array of wildflowers. **American sawwort** grows 3 to 4 feet tall with violet blossoms and sawtoothed leaves. **Broadleaf lupine** adds clumps of bluish purple. **American bistort**, which often grows near lupine, bears a single cylindrical head of many tiny white blossoms. Fuzzy-looking **Sitka valerian** also has a mass of tiny blossoms. **Cascade** and **small-flowered penstemon**, two penstemons similar in appearance, have ball heads of many trumpet-shaped purple blossoms.

ELMERA
Elmera racemosa

HEIGHT: 6" to 12"
BLOOMS: July to September
A member of the saxifrage family, elmera displays a creamy white flower with five tiny petals; a short fringe on each petal gives them a fuzzy look. Its rounded basal leaves have scalloped edges and silvery hairs. The rare elmera lives in relative obscurity, growing alone on high, rocky slopes in the Cascades and Olympics. This tiny alpine plant is named after the American botanist A. D. E. Elmera.

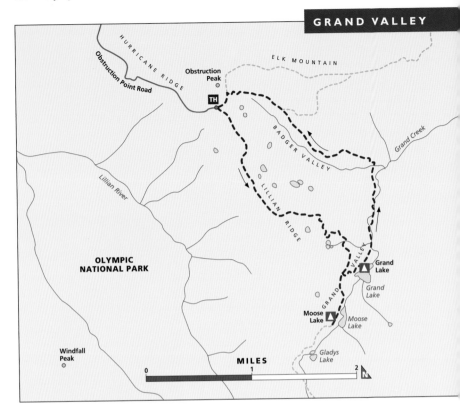

Several composites reside here. Endemic to the Olympic Mountains, **Olympic Mountain aster** has white rays and a yellow center. **Subalpine daisy** shows 30 to 40 lavender petals around a yellow center. **Mountain** or **broadleaf arnica** usually generates a single yellow ray flower on each stem. Clusters of small yellow ray flowers mature on **arrowleaf butterweed**. Growing from basal leaves, **northern goldenrod** is another yellow composite.

Return to the previous junction and turn right (east). The trail drops down 0.2 mile to Grand Lake, which is ringed by forest. The largest of three lakes in the valley, Grand Lake is home to rainbow and eastern brook trout. At the lake, head north on the main trail, following it downstream through Grand Valley. During the next mile, the path crosses Grand Creek twice and passes through several open areas.

Cusick's speedwell, a small plant, exhibits four-petaled purple blossoms; another common name for it is **Cusick's veronica**. Growing around meadow edges and in forest openings, **elegant Jacob's-ladder** generates fernlike leaves and light blue petals around a yellow throat. Large and showy, **tiger lily**, also known as **Columbia lily,** presents a hanging orange-spotted blossom with projecting stamens. Another elegant flower, **larkspur** has blossoms resembling purple butterflies alighting on a stem.

At mile 6.0, the trail crosses Badger Creek and turns westward, beginning its long climb through Badger Valley. Where the path breaks out of the forest, look for **red** or **western columbine** showing a flamboyant blossom with scarlet winged petals and a tuft of yellow stamens.

Several overgrown plants are hard to miss. **Edible thistle**, also called **Indian thistle**, may grow up to 7 feet tall, showing hairy purple heads atop spiky stems. **False hellebore**, or **corn lily**, has very large, flame-shaped, veined leaves and a single stalk of flowers. With an umbrella-shaped white flower head and leaves that can span 10 inches, **cow parsnip** sometimes grows to 6 feet tall, especially in moist soil.

Earlier in the summer, though, much smaller flowers rule these meadows. Soon after the snow melts, **Jeffrey's shooting star** sprouts along forest edges, bearing elegant pink blossoms with a ringed anther tube. Small, white **spring beauty** is another early bloomer. **Glacier lily** displays nodding yellow heads with petals arching skyward. **Snow buttercup** opens five-petaled, bowl-shaped yellow flowers. **Pasqueflower**, or **western anemone**, also blooms early, with creamy white petals surrounding a cluster of stamens. In August, it goes to seed, showing a hairy, football-shaped head.

The path enters a forest where clearings host huckleberry; its fruit ripens in August and makes for a great trailside snack. Where the woods thin, sun-seeking flowers thrive. In addition to many of the species already observed, **old-man's whiskers** show rose-colored globes, which later display plumes of seeds.

At a trail junction at mile 7.8, stay left, keeping on the main trail. (The trail branching right climbs Elk Mountain.) You will cross a couple of streams. Yellow **mountain monkey-flower** and fuchsia **Lewis' monkey-flower** grow in moist soil, displaying lovely, trumpet-shaped blossoms.

Climbing to open slopes, the trail passes **pink mountain heather**, with hanging, bell-shaped blossoms and deep green needles. **Pearly everlasting** grows in clumps, with a tight cluster of ball-shaped white blossoms on each of its many stems. **Thread-leaved sandwort** bears small, star-shaped white flowers and grasslike leaves.

The trail crosses talus slopes where flowers become sparser. With thin, white to pinkish rays, **cut-leaved daisy** grows low to the ground on these rocky slopes. A lavender-rayed composite, **alpine aster** also dwells in this stony soil. Thick patches of **elmera** poke up through scree, showing stalks of cream-colored, hanging crowns. In the mustard family, **western wallflower** sprouts a rounded clump of four-petaled yellow blossoms.

At a T intersection at mile 8.8, you finally reach the more level, east-west Elk Mountain–Grand Ridge Trail. Turn left here and it is less than a quarter mile back to the trailhead. In rocky crevices, **Piper's bellflower**, or **Olympic bellflower**, is a low-growing blue flower with five pointed petals. Forming mats, this flower is endemic to the Olympic Mountains.

Wildflower
Hike 4 **High Pass**

*False hellebore
and wildflowers
in a meadow
near Low Pass,
Mt. Baker
Wilderness*

Beginning at 5,180 feet, this trail passes entirely through subalpine terrain, a definite plus for viewing wildflowers and the surrounding mountains. Mt. Larrabee and the neighboring Pleiades crags are visible much of the way. Plenty of wildflowers border this stretch of trail, and this hike is a good option when the nearby Winchester Mountain Trail (see Hike 5) is too crowded.

To reach High Pass Trail (Trail No. 676), follow Winchester Mountain Trail (Trail No. 685), which begins by traversing between the two Twin Lakes, sometimes still covered with ice in late July or early August. You'll quickly enter the 117,900-acre Mt. Baker Wilderness, which extends from the south side of Mt. Baker to the Canadian border. Climbing uphill, you'll reach a

Trail Rating	Moderate
Trail Length	4.4 miles round trip
Location	Mt. Baker Wilderness, east of Glacier
Elevation	5,180 to 6,750 feet
Bloom Season	July to late September
Peak Bloom	Late July to mid-August
Contact	Mt. Baker–Snoqualmie National Forest, Mt. Baker Ranger District Office, (360) 856-5700
Directions	In the small town of Glacier on WA 542 (the Mt. Baker Highway), stop at the Glacier Public Service Center for road and trail conditions. From the center, drive east on WA 542 for 13.0 miles and keep an eye out for the left turn onto Twin Lakes Road (FR 3065). This road is hard to see because it's close to a maintenance building. Take FR 3065 for 7.0 miles to Twin Lakes. Because the last 2.5 miles are very rough, a high-clearance vehicle is recommended. Park near the lakes.

junction with the High Pass–Mt. Larrabee Trail just a quarter mile past the parking lot. Take the right fork, which goes north toward High Pass. (The left fork leads to the old fire lookout atop Winchester Mountain.)

Blue **broadleaf lupine** and **scarlet paintbrush** are immediately recognizable. With white, stamen-fuzzy blossoms, **American bistort** and **Sitka valerian** round out the patriotic color scheme. In the open meadows, **Cascade penstemon** sprouts sawtoothed triangular leaves and a whorled cluster of tubular purple blossoms. With leaves that resemble carrot greens, **Gray's lovage** puts forth dirty-white compound umbellate heads.

You'll quickly reach a saddle. Soon after, you'll encounter expansive meadows on a steep slope. Look for several types of purple asters and daisies. Preferring open forest and meadow edges, **showy aster** has purple petals, yellow centers, and large sawtoothed leaves. **Leafy bracted aster**, also purple with a yellow center, grows in open meadows. **Cascade aster** has 6 to 15 widely separated lavender rays. The larger **subalpine daisy** can be white, purple, or pink.

A number of yellow composites speckle the meadows. **Mountain arnica**, exhibiting one to three ray flowers on each stem, is quite prevalent. **Arrowleaf butterweed** has several smaller yellow sunflowers on each 20- to 40-inch stem, along with toothed triangular leaves. Also in the sunflower family, **northern goldenrod** has several small ray flowers on each stem.

In late summer, flamboyant **red columbine** produces a scarlet hanging head with long stamens of bright yellow. **Columbia** or **tiger lily** bears arching yellow-orange spotted petals and protruding stamens. **Chocolate lily**, one of the only brownish flowers in the region, has a mottled color.

PEARLY EVERLASTING
Anaphalis margaritacea

HEIGHT: 1" to 6"
BLOOMS: July

Pearly everlasting bears a tight spray of rounded, white flowers in clusters at the top of each stem. Its alternating leaves are long, slender, and woolly. This common flower grows at higher elevations, usually in disturbed areas and along roads and trails.

Traditionally, American Indians tucked pearly everlasting flowers into cradles and clothing to provide a sweet smell. It was also used medicinally, steeped as a tea that had a highly laxative effect and could induce vomiting. Retaining their color and shape when dried, the flowers make long-lasting ornamental bouquets.

The first flowers bloom here earlier in the summer, around the beginning of July. **Pasqueflower**, or **western anemone**, pushes up soon after snowmelt, each blossom opening creamy-white petals surrounding a cluster of stamens. By August, it goes to seed and appears as a hairy football-shaped tuft. **Glacier lily** displays hanging yellow heads with petals arching skyward. Small and white, **spring beauty** is another early bloomer.

The trail heads toward Winchester Creek. Resembling a purple pinecone, **self heal**, which has many medicinal uses, grows in wooded areas. Found in forest clearings, purple **pennyroyal** shows round, fuzzy flowers. A common trailside bloomer, **pearly everlasting** has small white clustered flowers that resemble pearls. White and lacy **yarrow** and tall stalks of pink to purple **fireweed** also dwell in this area. In late summer and early fall, huckleberries are ripe for picking—just make sure you can positively identify them before consuming them.

At about mile 1.0, the trail reaches the headwaters of Winchester Creek. In late summer, **pink** or **Lewis' monkey-flower** forms mats of fuchsia blossoms along seeps. **False hellebore**, also called **corn lily**, sprouts large, veined cabbage-like leaves that dwarf its greenish flowers. Near the beginning of the summer, **early blue violet** displays blossoms that look much like the garden-variety violet. Found in moist areas, **mountain bog**

HIGH PASS

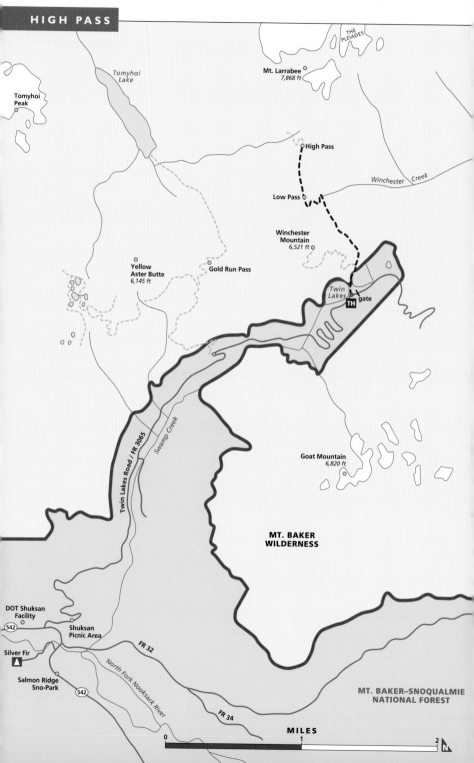

THE PLEIADES

Tomyhoi Lake

Mt. Larrabee
7,868 ft

Tomyhoi Peak

High Pass

Winchester Creek

Low Pass

Winchester Mountain
6,521 ft

Yellow Aster Butte
6,145 ft

Gold Run Pass

Twin Lakes

TH   gate

Goat Mountain
6,820 ft

Twin Lakes Road / FR 3065

Swamp Creek

MT. BAKER WILDERNESS

DOT Shuksan Facility

542

Shuksan Picnic Area

Silver Fir

Salmon Ridge Sno-Park

542

FR 32

North Fork Nooksack River

FR 34

MT. BAKER–SNOQUALMIE NATIONAL FOREST

MILES

0   1   2

N

gentian is an elegant, deep purple flower with five petals often wrapped tightly in a large bud. Also look for the yellow blossoms of **coiled-beak lousewort**.

From the Winchester Creek drainage, the trail switchbacks up a rocky slope. **Davidson's penstemon**, with masses of pink to lavender trumpets, grows here. Bright red **cliff paintbrush** also dwells in high rocky areas, along with **alpine aster**, which has anywhere from 15 to 40 blue to purple rays.

At mile 1.3, you'll reach Low Pass. The trail continues up the ridge for another 0.9 mile to High Pass. Growing close to the ground, **spreading phlox** blooms along the ridge, showing five-petaled pink to lavender blossoms. **Pink mountain heather**, an evergreen shrub with needlelike leaves, generates hanging bells. A beautiful low-growing mountain plant, **alpine golden daisy** displays as many as 70 yellow rays. **Cut-leaved fleabane** shows 40 to 60 thin, pink to lavender rays around a yellow center.

From High Pass, the turnaround point for this hike, the rust red, pyramid-shaped Mt. Larrabee looms large. A faint trail leads left, dropping down to debris scattered around an old mine site. As a diversion, an unmaintained boot path to the right continues to climb 600 feet in 0.7 mile to the flanks of 7,868-foot Mt. Larrabee. Do not attempt this trail if snowfields block the way. The rocky ascent offers fewer flowers, but they are interesting to find in this harsh landscape. Look for low-growing plants such as Davidson's penstemon, which adds splashes of fuchsia in rock crevices. Growing to a height of 1 to 4 inches, **Lyall's** or **alpine lupine** presents clusters of blossoms, blue with a white "eye" in the center of each.

The views from High Pass are nothing short of glorious: To the south stand craggy Mt. Shuksan and cone-shaped Mt. Baker; to the east, you can gaze into North Cascades National Park to see glaciated Mt. Redoubt, Mt. Challenger, and the Picket Range.

Winchester Mountain

Meadow above Twin Lakes on Winchester Mountain

This short, though at times steep, climb up Winchester Mountain leads through flower-filled meadows to an old fire lookout with amazing views. A quick hike to a fantastic location, it can be very popular, so early morning starts or weekday outings are good options for avoiding the weekend crowds. You might even be able to coerce your child up this trail, which is just 1.7 miles one way, by explaining that you are actually going to climb a mountain. But first check with the Forest Service about trail conditions, as snow sometimes lasts well into August on portions of the trail, blocking safe passage.

Trail Rating	Moderate
Trail Length	3.4 miles round trip
Location	Mt. Baker Wilderness, east of Glacier
Elevation	5,180 to 6,510 feet
Bloom Season	July to late September
Peak Bloom	Late July to mid-August
Contact	Mt. Baker–Snoqualmie National Forest, Mt. Baker Ranger District Office, (360) 856-5700
Directions	In the small town of Glacier on WA 542 (the Mt. Baker Highway), stop at the Glacier Public Service Center for road and trail conditions. From the center, drive east on WA 542 for 13.0 miles and keep an eye out for the left turn onto Twin Lakes Road (FR 3065). This road is hard to see because it's close to a maintenance building. Take FR 3065 for 7.0 miles to Twin Lakes. Because the last 2.5 miles are very rough, a high-clearance vehicle is recommended. Park near the lakes.

As usual, flower season often coincides with bug season in the meadowlands, so come prepared. You might want to set up a base camp near Twin Lakes or spend the night on top of the mountain in the lookout, which is available for overnights (contact the Mt. Baker Hiking Club, 360-733-1183). The lookout comes equipped with a single bed, foam pad, kerosene lamp, propane cookstove, and radio. Please bring your own fuel, as well as a sleeping bag.

From the parking area at Twin Lakes, take the signed Winchester Mountain Trail (Trail No. 685) between the two lakes to the base of the hill. Note that ice might still cover the Twin Lakes in late July or early August. You'll quickly enter the 117,900-acre Mt. Baker Wilderness, which extends from the south side of Mt. Baker to the Canadian border. Hike a quarter mile past the parking area to a junction with the High Pass–Mt. Larrabee Trail. Stay left on the Winchester Mountain Trail, hiking through meadows ablaze with color.

The aromatic purple-blue blossoms of **broadleaf lupine** are prevalent here. A member of the pea family, lupine adds nitrogen to the soil. Less abundant but still showy, **magenta paintbrush** displays brilliant scarlet bracts. **Cascade penstemon** pops up in places with clusters of deep blue to purple, trumpetlike flowers in a circular whorl. In late August and September, huckleberries are ripe for harvest if the crowds and bears haven't beaten you to them. Be sure to have a good reference guide on hand before eating any wild plant.

Several white-blossoming species grow on Winchester Mountain. Very common, **Sitka valerian** stands about 2 to 3 feet tall with stamen-fuzzy white blooms. **American bistort**, also white, displays a mass of stamens on cylinder-shaped flowers. **Yarrow** blooms in late summer, bearing feathery leaves and lacy white blossoms. **Pearly everlasting**, another common white flower, has paperlike, ball-shaped flowers in clumps of many stems.

The views just keep getting better as the trail ascends. Yellow blossoms speckle the landscape much of the way. **Arrowleaf butterweed** is the tallest yellow flower here, showing saw-toothed triangular leaves and a cluster of ray heads. Shorter and with fewer yellow flowers, **mountain arnica** has squared-off petals with pointed notches at their tips. Cinquefoils display five-petaled yellow blossoms: **fan-leaved cinquefoil** has leaflets in threes; **diverse-leaved cinquefoil** has five to seven leaflets; while farther up the trail in rocky soil, **shrubby cinquefoil** has needlelike leaves on woody branches.

If you are hiking earlier in the summer, say around early or mid-July, several small blooms will greet you, depending on when the snowpack melts. Among the first to bloom, the elegant, hanging blossoms of **glacier lily** have arching yellow petals and protruding stamens. Another early flower, **shooting star** shows graceful fuchsia blossoms around an anther tube. Maturing a couple of weeks after snowmelt, low-growing **spring beauty** displays five white petals in a star shape. Also white, **pasqueflower**, or **western anemone**, might push up through the snow to bloom. Later in the summer it goes to seed on a tall stalk with a furry mop head.

Toward the top of the mountain, you might encounter a snowfield blocking the trail. This can be a dangerous crossing without an ice ax and the appropriate amount of experience, but you might be able to drop

CASCADE OR COAST PENSTEMON
Penstemon serrulatus

HEIGHT: 8" to 25"
BLOOMS: June to August
A member of the figwort family, Cascade penstemon, also known as coast penstemon, shows deep blue to purple, trumpet-shaped blossoms. It is unusual for a penstemon in that it lacks the typical small hairs that would cover the inner surface of its blossoms. The opposing leaves are egg-shaped and serrated.

American Indians flavored foods with Cascade penstemon. The plant's flowers and leaves were used as eye washes and to disinfect wounds. This familiar flower is common in the open forests and meadows of the Cascades.

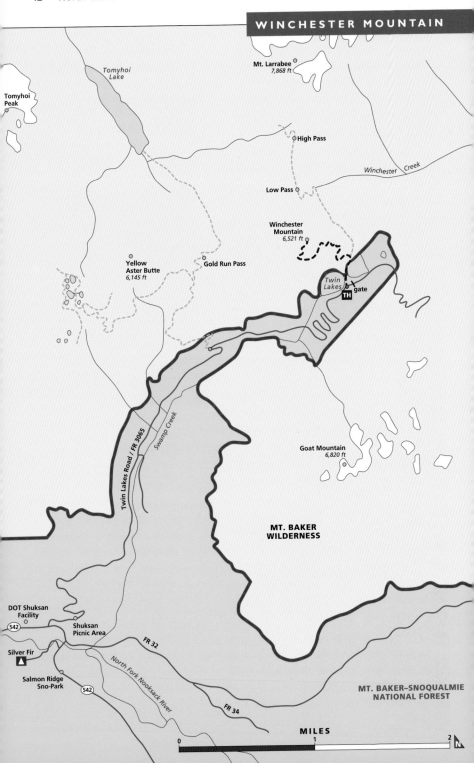

WINCHESTER MOUNTAIN

Tomyhoi Peak

Tomyhoi Lake

Mt. Larrabee
7,868 ft

High Pass

Low Pass

Winchester Creek

Winchester Mountain
6,521 ft

Yellow Aster Butte
6,145 ft

Gold Run Pass

Twin Lakes

TH

gate

Twin Lakes Road / FR 3065

Swamp Creek

Goat Mountain
6,820 ft

MT. BAKER WILDERNESS

DOT Shuksan Facility

542

Shuksan Picnic Area

Silver Fir

FR 32

North Fork Nooksack River

Salmon Ridge Sno-Park

542

FR 34

MT. BAKER–SNOQUALMIE NATIONAL FOREST

MILES

0   1   2   N

down and skirt the base of the snow patch. Hikers not prepared to attempt such a crossing should hike here in August, after snowmelt.

As you approach the summit, **pink mountain heather** exhibits hanging pink bells and evergreen needles. This plant has an amazing ability to survive on windswept ridges and is often covered with snow for eight or nine months of the year. Look for the lavender or pink trumpets of **Davidson's penstemon**, another survivor of harsh conditions, growing low between boulders.

From the old fire lookout atop Winchester Mountain, views extend in all directions. The most conspicuous features are 10,781-foot Mt. Baker to the southwest and 9,127-foot Mt. Shuksan to the southeast. Glaciers drape the flanks of these peaks year-round. Beyond Mt. Shuksan rise a host of crags in North Cascades National Park. To the north, Mt. Larrabee, The Pleiades, and peaks in Canada march across the horizon. This fire tower might well be the finest indoor spot in the state to spend the night!

Snowfield, Mt. Baker Wilderness

*Wildflower
Hike 6* *Yellow Aster Butte*

*Yellow
Aster Butte,
Mt. Baker
Wilderness*

This steady ascent leads to rewarding views, basins with small lakes, and slopes of wildflowers. In late August, you'll also have the treat of ripe huckleberries to munch. The areas around Yellow Aster Butte are very open, so there's plenty to explore, although it's important that you keep impact to a minimum in this fragile alpine zone. This hike gains more than 2,000 feet in elevation, so trekking poles are recommended. If you make this an overnight hike, you'll have views of Mt. Baker or Mt. Shuksan out your tent door.

From the trailhead, follow the Yellow Aster Butte Trail (Trail No. 686) through an old clear-cut. Tall stalks of purple-pink **fireweed** wave in the breeze. **Thimbleberry**, a woody shrub with white blossoms and large leaves

Trail Rating	Difficult
Trail Length	7.5 miles round trip
Location	Mt. Baker Wilderness, east of Glacier
Elevation	3,700 to 5,800 feet
Bloom Season	July to late September
Peak Bloom	Late July to mid-August
Contact	Mt. Baker–Snoqualmie National Forest, Mt. Baker Ranger District Office, (360) 856-5700
Directions	In the small town of Glacier on WA 542 (the Mt. Baker Highway), stop at the Glacier Public Service Center for road and trail conditions. From the center, drive east on WA 542 for 13.0 miles and look for the left turn onto Twin Lakes Road (FR 3065). This road is hard to see because it's close to a maintenance building. Take FR 3065 for 4.5 miles to the trailhead parking area. Note that there once was an older, lower Yellow Aster Butte Trail. The newer trail saves about 600 feet in elevation gain; however, the most recent (1989) USGS topographic map does not show this trail, which was built in 1997.

reminiscent of maples, produces edible raspberrylike berries in late summer. Pink-purple **edible thistle**, also called **Indian thistle**, grows up to 6 feet tall; American Indians at times consumed this plant. (Remember to never eat any wild plant without positive identification.) **Pearly everlasting** sprouts ball-shaped white flowers and sage green leaves. **Foxglove** displays a tall stem with many bell-shaped blossoms of white, pink, lavender, or purple.

The trail climbs and enters forest, where shade-loving flowers grow. Early summer is best for seeing many of these plants in action, although snow will still cover the upper meadows. **Western trillium** is unmistakable with three pointed, tonguelike white petals, which turn purple with age. About 2 feet tall, **Hooker's fairybell** displays hanging cup-shaped white blossoms with long, protruding stamens. Like giant shamrocks, the three large leaves of **vanilla leaf** dwarf its small spike of white flowers, which grows up to 2 inches and is made entirely of stamens.

At mile 1.3, the forest opens to several small meadows cupped in a protected basin. The stalks of **broadleaf lupine**, one of the most common subalpine flowers, grow from a rounded clump and have deep blue blossoms. Often found near lupine, **Sitka valerian** presents clusters of small white flowers with protruding stamens, which create a fuzzy blossom. Also white and fuzzy, **American bistort** has a single cluster of tiny tube-shaped flowers. The bright red of **Indian**

paintbrush is actually the color of its bracts, which hide smaller cylinder-shaped flowers. Huckleberry bushes are thick and ripe with berries, offering provisions for neighborhood bears in late August and September.

Several types of aster reside here. Purple ray flowers with yellow centers, **Douglas' aster** has masses of blossoms on each stem. At least five varieties of leafy bracted aster, also purple with a yellow center, grow in Washington. **Cascade aster**, found in open meadows and on rocky slopes, has 6 to 15 widely separated lavender rays. Higher up, you'll see **alpine aster**, with 15 to 40 blue-purple rays.

The trail reaches a junction at mile 1.5. Take the left fork, Trail No. 686.1, which goes west, traversing the basin. (The right fork, Trail No. 686, continues north to Gold Run Pass and then drops down to Tomyhoi Lake.) Several yellow composites inhabit these meadows. **Arrowleaf butterweed** grows 2 to 3 feet tall, with clustered flower heads and sawtoothed leaves. **Mountain arnica**, a yellow ray flower, can be recognized by its serrated petal tips and coarsely toothed leaves. On dry and rocky slopes, **alpine golden daisy** grows low with as many as 70 ray flowers. Although this butte bears the name "Yellow Aster," it was actually named for alpine golden daisies such as these. Also found in stony soil, **woolly sunflower**, or **Oregon sunshine**, has 8 to 13 yellow rays.

The trail climbs to a saddle where snowfields usually linger late into the summer. Views of the surrounding peaks and glaciers are splendid. Look down and you'll likely spot serpentine, a soft shiny mineral, deep green in color. Marmots make the area their home, and you might hear their high-pitched yips.

Several kinds of yellow cinquefoil are found here, all with five-petaled, disk-shaped flowers. Low-growing **fan-leaved cinquefoil** has three toothed leaflets. **Diverse-leaved cinquefoil** has five to seven larger, deeply

FOXGLOVE
Digitalis purpurea

HEIGHT: 2' to 7'
BLOOMS: June to August
Similar to the domestic flower, foxglove has long, tubular blossoms, ranging in color from white to pink to pink-purple with darker purple spots. The Latin name means "purple digit" or "purple finger." Its oval leaves are serrated and alternating.

Foxglove grows most commonly west of the Cascades, along roadsides, fields, and forest edges at low to middle elevations. The heart medicine digitalis is derived from this plant, which is poisonous to livestock.

YELLOW ASTER BUTTE

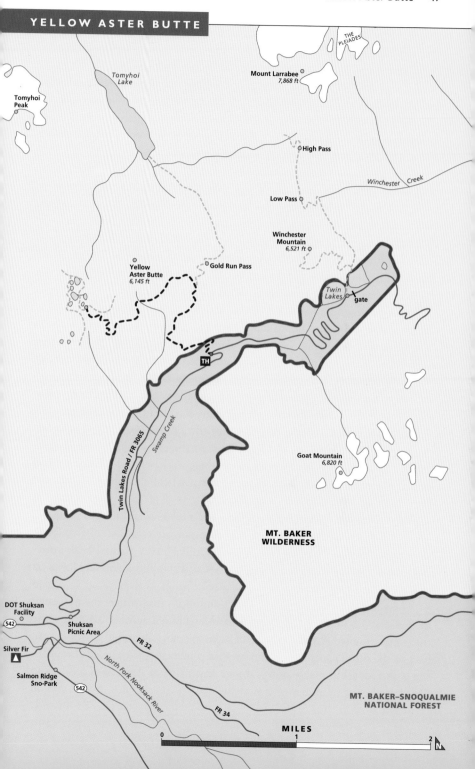

THE PLEIADES

Tomyhoi Lake

Mount Larrabee
7,868 ft

Tomyhoi Peak

High Pass

Winchester Creek

Low Pass

Winchester Mountain
6,521 ft

Yellow Aster Butte
6,145 ft

Gold Run Pass

Twin Lakes

gate

TH

Goat Mountain
6,820 ft

Twin Lakes Road / FR 3065

Swamp Creek

MT. BAKER
WILDERNESS

DOT Shuksan Facility

542

Shuksan Picnic Area

FR 32

Silver Fir

Salmon Ridge Sno-Park

542

North Fork Nooksack River

FR 34

MT. BAKER–SNOQUALMIE
NATIONAL FOREST

MILES

0   1   2

N

serrated leaves. **Shrubby cinquefoil** exhibits tiny, gray-green needlelike leaves sprouting on woody stems.

The rocky soil near the saddle hosts various alpine flowers that bloom in August and usually grow low to the ground. **Pink** and **white mountain heather** bear evergreen leaves and many hanging, bell-shaped flowers. With spiky leaves, **spreading phlox** shows masses of star-shaped flowers, which might be pink, lavender, or white. **Alpine** or **dwarf mountain lupine** grows only 2 to 5 inches tall, a miniature version of its lower-elevation cousins.

The trail rounds the south side of Yellow Aster Butte and once again crosses slopes lush with wildflowers. American bistort and broadleaf lupine grow in profusion, mixed in with paintbrush, arnica, Sitka valerian, and asters. **False hellebore**, or **corn lily**, shows beautiful large, veined leaves.

Easily recognized by their tubular shape, penstemon flowers have two upper and three lower lobes. Bluish purple **Cascade penstemon** reveals sawtoothed leaves, while **small-flowered penstemon** has narrower, smooth-edged leaves. In rocky areas, look for **Davidson's penstemon**, with many pink to lavender trumpets growing in a low mat.

A number of flowers bloom much earlier in the season, in late June or early July, soon after snowmelt. Fields of **avalanche lily** and **glacier lily** often carpet meadows in white and yellow. **Snow** or **mountain buttercup** also blossoms soon after melt-off, with low-growing varnished yellow bowls. **Western anemone**, another early bloomer, is also known as **pasqueflower**; it changes from a low white blossom in early summer to a tall, hairy seed head in late summer.

As the trail wraps around Yellow Aster Butte, a rocky basin filled with tarns comes into view. A trail to the right leads to the top of the butte. Instead, descend into the valley on an unmaintained boot track, which leads to a wonderland of water and smooth stone. Flowers are fewer here, though some interesting varieties dwell in this alpine environment.

Moss campion forms dense cushions of tiny leaves and masses of small five-petaled pink blossoms. Two kinds of lousewort grow here. **Bird's-beak lousewort** has pink beaklike blooms and fernlike leaves. **Coiled-beak lousewort** shows similar white blossoms. Four-petaled white **smelowskia** looks out of place in this rocky landscape.

There is much to explore both north and south from where the trail enters the basin at 3.5 miles; wandering the basin might add another 0.5 mile to the trip's total distance. If you dare, take a swim in a tarn, then find a rock slab and bask in the sun. Debris left behind by gold prospectors is scattered throughout the basin; look but please don't remove any artifacts. Also, be sure to tread lightly in the fragile alpine environment.

Skyline Divide

Mt. Baker looms above a meadow in
Mt. Baker–Snoqualmie National Forest

Moderate	*Trail Rating*
6 to 10 miles round trip	*Trail Length*
Mt. Baker Wilderness, southeast of Glacier	*Location*
4,400 to 6,500 feet	*Elevation*
July to late September	*Bloom Season*
Late July to mid-August	*Peak Bloom*
Mt. Baker–Snoqualmie National Forest, Mt. Baker Ranger District Office, (360) 856-5700	*Contact*

Directions

In the small town of Glacier on WA 542 (the Mt. Baker Highway), stop at the Glacier Public Service Center for road and trail conditions. From the center, drive 1.0 mile east on WA 542. Turn right on Glacier Creek Road (FR 39), go 100 yards, and then turn left onto Deadhorse Road (FR 37). The road climbs, steeply at times. Go 12.5 miles to a parking area on the left. Although sometimes rough, the road is passable in a lower-clearance vehicle.

With exceptional wildflower displays and expansive mountain views accessible after about an hour's walk, this is one of the premier hikes in the North Cascades. Because of its popularity, the Skyline Divide Trail (Trail No. 678) sees much traffic on weekends. Bugs can be nasty, so be armed with repellant. In a year with a heavy winter snowpack, or a cool summer, you'll often be hiking in snow well into July along the upper sections of the trail. August is the best time to explore this area.

From the upper end of the parking lot, the signed trail begins its switchback climb, steep in places, through hemlock and silver fir trees. A standard flower found in wooded areas of the Cascades, **western trillium** is unmistakable with its three tonguelike white petals, which turn purple with age. With long, protruding stamens, the delicate white flowers of **Hooker's fairybell** hide below the leaves of the plant, which grows to about 2 feet tall. The three large leaves of **vanilla leaf** dwarf its tiny flowers, ½- to 2-inch spikes made entirely of stamens.

In the deep forest, look for saprophytes, plants that lack chlorophyll and green leaves; these plants instead get nourishment from decayed organic materials in the soil. The single hanging flower of **Indian pipe** is ghostly in its translucent white to pale pink color. **Pinesap**, another saprophyte, looks similar but with a pale coral hue.

At about mile 1.5, you'll start to see pocket meadows. **Mountain arnica** bears bright yellow sunflowerlike blossoms on 1- to 2-foot stems. Yellow-orange **Columbia** or **tiger lily** is a beautiful plant displaying spotted, hanging blossoms with protruding stamens and large anthers. Sweet-smelling **broadleaf lupine** has blue to purple pod-shaped blossoms along its stem. One of several penstemons in the area, **Cascade penstemon** shows circular whorls of deep purple tubular flowers and toothed leaves.

At about mile 2.0, the trail enters the 117,900-acre Mt. Baker Wilderness. At 10,781 feet, Mt. Baker is Washington's third-highest peak, and its upper elevations often accumulate an average of 18 feet of snow. The runoff provides moisture for the flowers here, but it takes a sunny summer to melt enough snow to produce a good floral show.

You'll soon reach expansive meadows on Skyline Divide with great views of Mt. Baker's north-side glaciers. Flowers are thickest along the first mile of ridge trail. In late July and August, broadleaf lupine and mountain arnica are joined by a multitude of cylinder-shaped **American bistort** and fluffy-looking **Sitka valerian**, two of the most common white flowers in these meadows. **Scarlet** and **magenta paintbrush** add bright splashes of color. The less common **white paintbrush** also grows in the meadows.

Early flowers include yellow **glacier lily** and its white relative, **avalanche lily**, which both bloom soon after snowmelt. So, too, does **snow** or **mountain buttercup**, a small plant showing varnished yellow blossoms. **Western anemone**,

SKYLINE DIVIDE

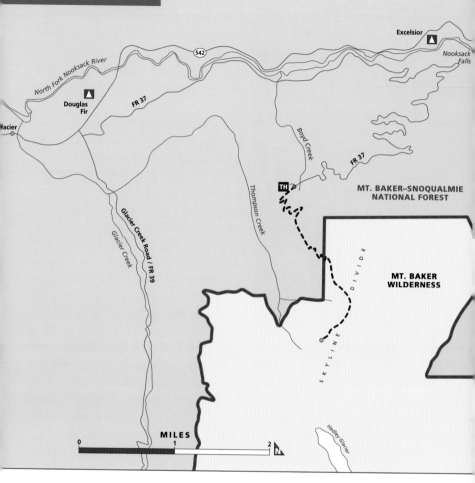

or **pasqueflower**, also blooms early, transforming over the summer from a low-growing white blossom to a dirty-white, tufted seed head on an 18- to 24-inch stem.

In late summer, look for members of the sunflower family. **Alpine aster** is one of several lavender-colored mountain asters. Also lavender, **subalpine daisy** has more rays and grows taller. **Alpine golden daisy**, a yellow composite with 40 to 70 rays, survives in dry, rocky soil at high elevations. Also found in rocky areas, **woolly sunflower** has 8 to 13 petals and sage-green leaves.

A number of cinquefoils grow here, all with five bright yellow petals forming a disk-shaped flower. **Fan-leaved cinquefoil** has toothed leaves in threes, much like large strawberry leaves. **Diverse-leaved cinquefoil** bears five to seven leaflets, while **shrubby cinquefoil** has narrow, almost needlelike leaves on woody branches. **Arrowleaf butterweed**, growing up to 3 feet, shows clusters of small yellow ray flowers and triangular leaves.

At 3.0 miles, the trail ascends Skyline Divide to a knoll where Cascade peaks jut up in just about all directions. To the northeast, look for Tomyhoi Peak and Mt. Larrabee. Surrounded by craggy peaks in North Cascades National Park, Mt. Shuksan dominates the eastern horizon. On a very clear day, you can even see mountains on Vancouver Island, about 70 miles to the west. This spot makes a good turnaround point for a 6-mile round-trip hike, or you can go on for more flower viewing.

As the landscape becomes rockier, the lush meadows give way to plants adapted to the harsher alpine environment. Common at high elevations, **pink mountain heather** has bell-shaped flowers and needlelike evergreen leaves. **Lyall's** or **alpine lupine**, a dwarf lupine found in rocky areas, often grows near **Davidson's penstemon**, which has masses of pink to lavender trumpets. Bright red **cliff paintbrush** adds exclamation points of color.

At about mile 3.5, you'll come to a junction. (The left fork leads down through talus slopes to Chowder Basin, where you can access campsites and water in 0.5 mile.) The right fork climbs up, following the rocky ridge another 1.5 mile to the base of Chowder Ridge. Snow often covers this area, and some years it never melts off. Although you've now left the vibrant meadows behind, there is something wonderful about this land of rocks and snow and the hardy flowering plants that survive here. Sunset turns the nearby glaciers a lovely crimson. This is the turnaround point for a 10-mile round trip. Although the hike back is all downhill, you might just wish you had your sleeping bag.

INDIAN PIPE
Monotropa uniflora

HEIGHT: 4" to 10"
BLOOMS: June and July

Small and waxy, Indian pipe is a white or pinkish perennial. The top of the flower curves over, creating a pipelike shape, hence its name. Oval to lance-shaped, scalelike leaves in the flower's same pale color grow along the stem, camouflaging with the blossom.

Indian pipe, a saprophyte, gathers nutrients from decaying matter. Most commonly found at low to middle elevations in coniferous forests west of the Cascades, it tends to grow in the same areas as mushrooms, often near ferns and moss. Salish and Nlaka'pamux tribes burned the stalks and then rubbed the ash on wounds or sores that would not heal.

Leafy aster, North Cascades National Park

Wildflower
Hike 8 Heliotrope Ridge

Broadleaf
willowherb on
Heliotrope Ridge,
Mt. Baker
Wilderness

This climb passes through an enchanting forest, wildflower meadows, and over mountain streams to superb views of Mt. Baker's glaciated west flank. The third-highest peak in the state, 10,781-foot Mt. Baker is blanketed with more than 10,000 acres of glacial ice—the most heavily glaciated mountain in the Cascades after Mt. Rainier. During the winter of 1998–1999, more than 1,150 inches of snow fell here, at times burying the ski lifts at Mt. Baker Ski Area and closing the slopes.

The Heliotrope Ridge Trail (Trail No. 677) offers the shortest route to the best views of Coleman Glacier, one of 12 named glaciers on Mt. Baker.

Trail Rating	Moderate
Trail Length	6 miles round trip
Location	Mt. Baker Wilderness, southeast of Glacier
Elevation	3,700 to 5,100 feet
Bloom Season	July to late September
Peak Bloom	Late July to mid-August
Contact	Mt. Baker–Snoqualmie National Forest, Mt. Baker Ranger District Office, (360) 856-5700
Directions	In the town of Glacier on WA 542 (Mt. Baker Highway), stop at the Glacier Public Service Center for current road and trail conditions. Continue east on WA 542 for 0.8 mile and turn right on Glacier Creek Road (FR 39). Follow this road for 8.2 miles to a large parking area on the left.

The trail can be busy, especially on weekends as hikers seek the subalpine and climbers seek the summit. However, on a sunny weekday afternoon in late August, I saw only three other people on the trail.

The hike crosses two or three streams that can be potentially hazardous. The depth and power of these streams fluctuate depending on snowmelt, rainfall, and time of day. A stream easily crossed in the morning can become a difficult, dangerous crossing by afternoon. I found trekking poles to be very helpful for rock-hopping across the swift-moving water. You should probably plan on wet feet. On the upside, if you have a filter, you can easily refill your water bottle along the way.

The trail begins by crossing the wild, deep gorge of Grouse Creek and then enters the 117,900-acre Mt. Baker Wilderness. It climbs steadily through old-growth forest where shade-loving flowers are found, often with white blossoms. **Queen's cup** displays a single, six-petaled pure white blossom and shiny lance-shaped leaves. Also with lance-shaped leaves, **false Solomon's seal** bears clusters of cream-colored, star-shaped flowers. Early in the summer, **Indian pipe** has a translucent white or pinkish stem, leaves, and blossom. If you time your trip to see subalpine flowers, however, many of these forest dwellers will already have finished blooming.

Between miles 0.5 and 1.3, look for **pipsissewa**, whose crown-shaped pink flowers hang down from wiry stems. **Woodnymph's** single star-shaped, five-petaled white blossom dangles above evergreen leaves. Also white with hanging flowers, **Hooker's fairybell** grows up to 3 feet tall.

At mile 1.3, you'll reach the first stream crossing. Situated below a small scenic cascade, it is not usually a difficult one. As you switchback up to mile 2.0, you'll pass a few nearly level campsites in close proximity to alpine terrain. The forest begins to open, giving way to huckleberry, which ripens in late August and early September. **Pink mountain heather** is a shrub that bears graceful bell-shaped pink blossoms hanging above evergreen needles.

Several penstemons grow here, all pink to purple in color with five-petaled, funnel-shaped blossoms. In open forest, **woodland penstemon** shows clusters of flowers on leaning stems. In the higher meadows, **Cascade penstemon** produces a whorl-like cluster of tubular blossoms and sawtoothed, triangular leaves. In rocky areas, **Davidson's** and **shrubby penstemon** display pink-purple blossoms and small rounded leaves.

Small meadows host late summer blossoms such as **Sitka valerian**, with stamen-fuzzy white flowers atop nearly leafless stems. Yarrow has a lacy white blossom and featherlike leaves. A type of sunflower, **arrowleaf butterweed** displays yellow ray flower heads above sawtoothed, triangular leaves. Also in the sunflower family, **northern goldenrod** has several small yellow ray flowers on each stem. Indian paintbrush grows in forest clearings and meadows. **Scarlet** and **magenta paintbrush** are named for the brilliant color of their bracts. **Harsh paintbrush**, another variety found in the high country, has red-orange bracts.

BROADLEAF WILLOWHERB
Epilobium latifolium

HEIGHT: 8" to 16"
BLOOMS: July to late August

Broadleaf willowherb hosts blood red to light purple blossoms, wiry stems, and soft pastel green leaves. It gets its name from its willowlike leaves. A slender evening primrose, this plant flourishes in harsh conditions. You can spot it sprouting on hillsides devastated by fire or growing in the bare rocky ground behind a retreating glacier.

Asters and daisies, often difficult to differentiate from one another, display numerous white to purple ray flowers. **Subalpine daisy** is common in mountainous terrain, with ray flowers ranging from white to pink to lavender. **Leafy aster** and **Cascade aster** both display purple rays around yellow disks. Higher up the trail, **alpine aster** grows to about 6 inches tall, showing lavender and yellow heads.

Soon after snowmelt, fields of white **avalanche lily** and yellow **glacier lily** often carpet the slopes with color. Another early blooming flower is **western**

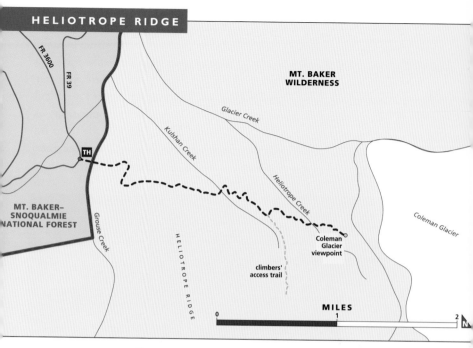

anemone, or **pasqueflower**, which starts out in early summer as a small, five-to eight-petaled white blossom and transforms into a tall, tufted seed head in late summer. **Snow** or **mountain buttercup** also blooms soon after the snow melts, opening low-growing, varnished yellow cups.

Look for several kinds of cinquefoils, all with five-petaled, disk-shaped yellow flowers. Low-growing **fan-leaved cinquefoil** has three toothed leaflets, almost like a strawberry leaf. **Diverse-leaved cinquefoil** has five to seven leaves, larger and deeply serrated. Higher up, in a more rocky landscape, **shrubby cinquefoil** has tiny gray-green needlelike leaves on woody stems.

The next stream crossing is a little trickier. Look carefully for a passage and you just might be able to stay dry. Also look for **Lewis' monkey-flower**, which grows in moist seeps and displays elegant snapdragonlike fuchsia blossoms.

The trail enters a moraine landscape where rock has been deposited from Heliotrope Ridge above. Growing about 10 inches tall, **broadleaf willowherb** bears blossoms with four petals of lavender to deep pink to red. **Pearly ever-lasting** displays packed clusters of papery white bracts. The plant spreads from its roots, and it is often found in disturbed areas.

A third stream crossing can be precarious in high water, so be very careful—or don't attempt it at all if you're unsure. At mile 2.3, the trail comes to a junction. Keep left, which leads to yet another dicey stream crossing. Keep in mind that these streams might rise with melt-off later in the day, making them even higher on the return trip.

Broadleaf willowherb resides here, with blood red to light purple blossoms, pastel green leaves, and willowy stems. The tiny, loosely clustered white blossoms of **small-flowered alumroot** are less apparent than its large maplelike leaves.

Continue east to a ridge that overlooks Coleman Glacier. Here, you can enjoy one of the best glacier views in the state. This massive ice field is difficult to get a scale on until you see a climber, who from here would look as tiny as an ant. This is your turnaround point, 3.0 miles from the trailhead. Don't be tempted to venture onto the glacier: It is extremely dangerous without the proper equipment and experience, and several hikers have died in the area.

Pink mountain heather, North Cascades National Park

Railroad Grade

Wildflower Hike 9

Meadow along Railroad Grade, Mt. Baker National Recreation Area

This is one of several great subalpine Mt. Baker hikes. In just a little over 2.0 miles, you can reach wildflower meadows and incredible vistas of Mt. Baker and the surrounding peaks. Located in the Mt. Baker National Recreation Area, the popular trails to Railroad Grade (Trails No. 603 and 603.2) can get busy on weekends. After a heavy winter snowpack or during a cool summer, you'll likely be hiking through snow on the upper sections of the trail on into July. By late August or September, it's usually possible to hike free of snow.

Pack warm clothes, as the mountain sometimes creates its own cold and cloudy weather. Water is plentiful along the lower stretch of trail, but absent once you reach Railroad Grade ridge. Bugs can be nasty, so

Trail Rating	Difficult
Trail Length	7.0 miles round trip for Railroad Grade; 9.4 miles with Park Butte side trip
Location	Mt. Baker National Recreation Area, north of Concrete
Elevation	3,360 to 5,400 feet
Bloom Season	July to late September
Peak Bloom	Late July to mid-August
Contact	Mt. Baker–Snoqualmie National Forest, Mt. Baker Ranger District Office, (360) 856-5700
Directions	With a full tank of gas, drive west from Concrete on WA 20 to milepost 82.3 and turn right (north) on Baker Lake Road (FR 11). In 12.5 miles, just after the Rocky Creek bridge, turn left on FR 12. In 3.5 miles, turn right on Sulphur Creek Road (FR 13). Follow this road 6 miles to the parking area at the end of the road.

bring repellant. And because this hike gains more than 2,000 feet in elevation, you might want to use hiking poles to ease the strain on your knees.

From the trailhead, where a kiosk shows a map of the area, the Park Butte Trail (Trail No. 603) quickly crosses a bridge over Sulphur Creek, then enters Schriebers Meadow, mostly grassy but with flowers such as white **yarrow** and **pearly everlasting**. Fuzzy clusters of tiny pink flowers bloom on **rosy** or **subalpine spirea**, a fragrant shrub. Another shrub, **pink mountain heather** produces hanging pink bells and needlelike evergreen leaves. Huckleberry yields edible berries in late August and September, but never consume any wild plant without absolute certainty as to its identity. Look for **yellow pond lily** in several small ponds.

The trail winds through forest, where you'll see small white-blooming flowers. **Hooker's fairybell** presents creamy white bells with projecting stamens. **Twinflower**, a creeping vine, has smaller hanging bells that grow in pairs. **Queen's cup** exhibits a six-petaled, star-shaped flower and elegant waxy leaves. **Dwarf dogwood**, or **bunchberry**, also puts forth waxy leaves, as well as four petal-like bracts. These forest flowers usually peak in late June and early July; by August, most of the blooms are gone.

At mile 1.0, you'll cross a suspension bridge over the chill, gray water rushing down from Easton Glacier. The trail continues northwest and begins a long switchback ascent. Near the top of the climb, at mile 2.0, the Scott Paul Trail (Trail No. 603.1) cuts off to the right. Do not take this route yet, but keep it in mind for the return trip. This less-crowded route offers a different way back, if you have the time and energy: It adds an extra 3.5 miles to the total distance, making the hike from here to the trailhead 5.5 miles.

Continue uphill on the main trail and enter lower Morovitz Meadow. Subalpine flowers thrive here, as well as in upper Morovitz Meadow, on into August. You'll find the red, white, and blue standards: **Indian paintbrush**, **American bistort**, and **broadleaf lupine**. Look for deep pink, purple, or blue **Cascade penstemon**, displaying round clusters of funnel-shaped blossoms. Also common here, **Sitka valerian** has clusters of tiny white flowers. **False hellebore**, also known as **corn lily**, sprouts large, veined cabbagelike leaves surrounding greenish flowers.

Several members of the sunflower family grow in both the lower and upper meadows. With toothed leaves, **mountain arnica** speckles the landscape in yellow. Another yellow ray flower, **arrowleaf butterweed** looks similar but grows taller and has more flower heads on each stem. Also common are purple asters, including **leafy** and **Cascade aster**. The purple **subalpine daisy** is often mistaken for an aster but has more rays.

Often preferring moist soils, several unusual-looking members of the figwort family dwell in these meadows. Perhaps the oddest is **elephant's head**, with pink flower heads resembling those of the pachyderms—complete with ears and trunk—on maroon, nonbranching stems 8 to 20 inches tall. **Bracted lousewort**, with a flower head made of several dozen beak-shaped blossoms, displays flowers that vary in color from white to yellow to maroon. With popcornlike white to pink or purplish blossoms, **sickletop lousewort** grows near pockets of trees.

On the showier side, **Columbia** or **tiger lily** seeks the attention of hummingbirds

SUBALPINE OR ROSY SPIREA
Spirea densiflora

HEIGHT: 6" to 18"

BLOOMS: August

An odd but endearing plant, subalpine or rosy spirea has a fuzzy, flat head of dense pink flowers. Its tall, slender stem sprouts alternating dark green leaves that are ovular and toothed. The undersides of the leaves are often a woolly gray.

Spirea grows at higher elevations in open subalpine forests, in moist thickets and meadows, and along stream banks. Traditionally, spirea leaves were boiled for tea and used as a relaxant or to ease stomach pains. Other records indicate the plant was used for making brooms.

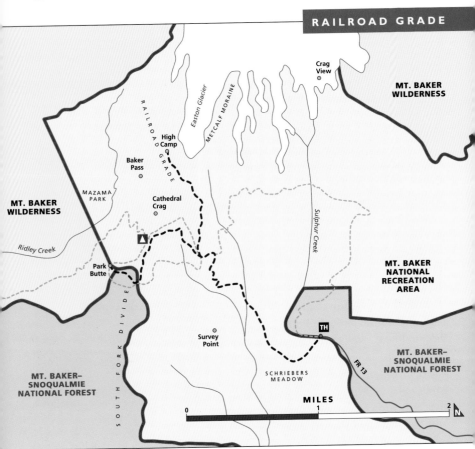

with spotted, yellow-orange arching petals and protruding stamens. Easily notice-able, **fan-leaved** and **shrubby cinquefoil** boast bright yellow five-petaled disks.

In July, soon after snowmelt, a group of early bloomers brightens the meadows. **Sweet coltsfoot** displays white blossoms with a mass of rays and large jagged leaves, which often fill out after the flower blooms. **Pasqueflower**, or **western anemone**, transforms from a simple white-petaled flower in early summer to a hairy moplike seed head in late summer. **Glacier lily**, another early bloomer, has a hanging yellow blossom with six arching tepals. Its relative, the snow-white **avalanche lily**, also grows here.

At mile 2.4, you'll come to a junction. Keep right for the trail to Railroad Grade, Trail No. 603.2. (The path to the left is the continuation of the Park Butte Trail, from here a 1.8-mile round trip that goes to a lovely plateau, then climbs another 0.3 mile to an old lookout cabin with spectacular views. At press time, the cabin was available for use on a first-come, first-served basis; for information, call the Skagit Alpine Club in Mt. Vernon, 360-424-5854. On the large shelf below the lookout there is a tarn, which makes a great spot for lunch, to filter water, and to take pictures. When I was there in late August, a thin layer of ice covered the tarn in the morning.)

On the main trail, continue on toward the moraine called Railroad Grade. Many flowers found in Morovitz Meadow grow here, as well. Especially abundant are broadleaf lupine, mountain arnica, and Indian paintbrush. **Partridgefoot** is common, with cream-colored flower clusters on 3- to 6-inch stems with bright green fringed leaves.

The trail passes several campsites and continues up the moraine. At mile 3.5, your turnaround point, the route dwindles to a path that accesses Easton Glacier. Do not attempt this glacier, popular among climbers, without crampons, ice axes, and climbing experience.

From the top of Railroad Grade, splendid views extend in all directions. The Black Buttes on the western flank of Mt. Baker loom high above. To the south, a multitude of peaks reaches out of the Boulder River, Henry M. Jackson, and Glacier Peak Wilderness Areas. You can also gaze eastward into the 505,000-acre North Cascades National Park, a wilderness extraordinaire.

Mt. Baker at sunset

*Wildflower
Hike 10*

Sauk Mountain

*Meadow on Sauk
Mountain, Mt.
Baker–Snoqualmie
National Forest*

The flanks of Sauk Mountain offer some of the best wildflower displays along the North Cascades Highway corridor. The Sauk Mountain Trail (Trail No. 613) gives fairly quick access to flower-filled meadows and outstanding views. Hike this popular trail on weekdays, if you can, to avoid the weekend crowds. Although it's only 2.0 miles to the top of Sauk Mountain, the trail maintains a steady climb—with nearly 30 switchbacks—and it will take most hikers at least an hour to reach the summit. Hiking poles prove helpful here.

From the signed trailhead, the route immediately enters a subalpine environment. The trail remains in open meadows as it ascends the south

Trail Rating	Moderate
Trail Length	4 miles round trip
Location	Mt. Baker–Snoqualmie National Forest, north of Rockport
Elevation	4,300 to 5,537 feet
Bloom Season	June to late August
Peak Bloom	July
Contact	Mt. Baker–Snoqualmie National Forest, Mt. Baker Ranger District Office, (360) 856-5700
Directions	From the junction of WA 20 and WA 530 in the town of Rockport, drive 1.7 miles west on WA 20 and go right (north) on Sauk Mountain Road (FR 1030). (If you are coming from the town of Concrete, near Baker Dam, drive east on WA 20 for 6.5 miles and turn left onto FR 1030, near milepost 96.) Follow FR 1030 up switchbacks for 7.4 miles to the junction with FR 1036. Turn right onto FR 1036 and go 0.3 mile to the parking area at the road's end.

side of the mountain. You'll see patches of **fireweed**, with purple-pink clusters of four-petaled flowers on tall leafy stems. **Thimbleberry**, a woody shrub with white blossoms and large maplelike leaves, produces edible raspberrylike fruit in late summer. **Indian paintbrush** is commonly found along the trail; its bright red displays are actually the bracts of the flower. A medicinal plant, as its name proclaims, **self heal** has a square stem and a flower head resembling a purple pinecone.

The sunflower family comprises many of the flowers along the trail. Look for **Douglas' aster** with masses of purple ray flowers on stems about 2 to 3 feet tall. Slightly shorter, **Cascade aster** usually has fewer flowers on each stem. **Engelmann's aster** grows up to 5 feet and has a white to pink flower with about 13 rays. **Arrowleaf butterweed** displays several small yellow ray flower heads and toothed, triangular leaves. **Pearly everlasting**, a common trailside flower, has small white clustered ball-shaped blossoms resembling lacy pearls. Also in the sunflower family, **northern goldenrod** has several small yellow ray flowers on each stem.

Several penstemons, all with five-petaled, trumpet-shaped flowers, grow here. Purple **Cascade penstemon**, which prefers moist soil, has circular clusters of many small flowers atop each stem, and tooth-edged, lance-shaped leaves. Found in dry, rocky soil, **Davidson's** and **shrubby penstemon** often have low-growing mats of leaves.

At mile 1.5, you'll reach a junction. Stay left to continue to the summit. (The trail to the right leads to Sauk Lake, an emerald green lake at 4,100 feet. The round trip to Sauk Lake is an additional 3.0 miles, mostly through forest.)

The flowers along the last 0.5 mile of trail put on a show through early August, especially in years following a snowy winter. You'll pass large fields of mountain arnica, a common yellow ray flower with toothed leaves and petal tips. One of the most abundant subalpine flowers, **Sitka valerian** has a fluffy white head of many tiny flowers, blooming on stems up to 40 inches tall. **Common harebell** reveals beautiful hanging blue flowers. It grows up to 2 feet tall at lower elevations, though it might stand only a few inches high in an alpine environment. Blooming in late summer, **American bistort** displays a dense cluster of white blossoms that resembles a thumb. Blue **broadleaf lupine** adds a sweet fragrance to the meadows.

Several flashy flowers brighten the trail. **Red columbine** displays a protruding tuft of stamens and crimson petals arching backward from a yellow center. **Tiger lily**, also known as **Columbia lily**, grows from a bulb, producing hanging orange flowers with maroon spots. **Chocolate lily** is an unusual flower, mottled brown in color and often camouflaged among other plants.

Ranging from lavender to pink to white, **spreading phlox** grows 1 to 3 inches high in a mat of five-petaled flowers. **Pink mountain heather** has dangling floral bells and needlelike leaves. This evergreen shrub is an icon of the subalpine environment and you'll see it as you near the summit.

FIREWEED
Epilobium angustifolium

HEIGHT: 2' to 6'
BLOOMS: June to August
Fireweed shows tall, thin stalks of vibrant pink to purple blossoms and long, willowlike leaves. The four-petaled flowers later turn into seedpods. Common throughout the Pacific Northwest in lowlands as well as in higher elevations, it can grow up to 6 feet tall.

Fireweed is named not for its fiery blaze of color, but for its ability to generate quickly in areas burned by forest fires. It is also well-known for its nutritional value, producing an excellent honey that beekeepers prize.

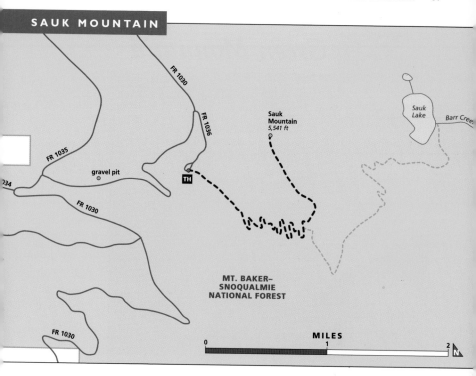

Early in the growing season, you'll see a different variety of flowers. Blooming soon after snowmelt, the delicate hanging blossoms of **glacier lily** can carpet whole areas with yellow. Its relative, the **avalanche lily**, quickly follows the snowmelt, opening a single white blossom on a bare stem. Also an early bloomer, **mountain buttercup** has small shiny yellow disks. **Western anemone**, or **pasqueflower**, begins the summer as a low-growing simple white blossom with five to eight petals. By late summer, it resembles a Dr. Seuss character, sporting a hairy mop top on a tall stem.

From the site of a former lookout at the summit of Sauk Mountain, great views fan out in all directions: the Skagit River Valley to the west; the snowy peaks of Mt. Baker and Mt. Shuksan to the north; the crags of North Cascades National Park to the east; and the confluence of the Sauk and Skagit Rivers to the south, with Glacier Peak and Whitehorse Mountain dominating the southern horizon. If it's a particularly clear day, you can even see Puget Sound and the San Juan Islands. This is a fine place to watch a sunset, so consider packing a flashlight and a picnic dinner for an evening hike.

Wildflower
Hike 11 *Green Mountain*

False hellebore
and Sitka
valerian
adorn Green
Mountain,
Glacier Peak
Wilderness

Green Mountain is, well, green. Even toward the end of summer, the meadows here seem to retain their springtime freshness. The hike to the summit of Green Mountain is a popular one, so weekdays are your best bet if you want to avoid the crowds. With a 3,140-foot elevation gain, the well-maintained Green Mountain Trail (Trail No. 782) proceeds at a steady climb most of the time, so bring your trekking poles.

Starting in forest, the trail then tracks mostly through meadows filled with flowers. Volunteers have been restoring the fire lookout at the summit, which might be available for use. But even without the lookout, the views of Glacier Peak Wilderness are extensive. Water for filtering is available about halfway to the top.

Trail Rating	Difficult
Trail Length	8 miles round trip
Location	Glacier Peak Wilderness, east of Darrington
Elevation	3,360 to 6,500 feet
Bloom Season	June to late September
Peak Bloom	July to mid-August
Contact	Mt. Baker–Snoqualmie National Forest, Darrington Ranger District Office, (360) 436-1155
Directions	From Darrington, drive north on WA 530 for 7.2 miles. Turn right (east) on Suiattle River Road (FR 26). Take this road, which follows the Suiattle River, for 19 miles. Turn left onto FR 2680 and drive 5.8 miles to a parking area, located several hundred yards before the road ends.

From the parking area, the signed Green Mountain Trail passes shade-loving flowers as it climbs through forest for about the first mile. Early summer is the best bloom time for many of these shade-loving plants—however, the upper meadows will usually still be covered with snow. The unmistakable **western trillium** has three pointed white petals that turn purple with age. The hanging bell-shaped white blossoms of **Hooker's fairybell** hide below leaves on 2-foot-tall stems. Looking like giant shamrocks, the three large leaves of **vanilla leaf** dwarf a small spike of white flowers made entirely of stamens. Frontier women used this common plant to scent their clothes and freshen their cabins.

While still in the forest, look for a number of saprophytes, plants that obtain nutrients from decayed organic matter in the soil. With a stem of small scales in place of green leaves, **western coralroot** exhibits narrow leaflike pink flowers that grow on stems up to 20 inches tall. **Pinesap**, another saprophyte, displays pink to yellowish flowers.

At the first clearing, white-flowering **thimbleberry**, pink **fireweed**, and bracken fern dominate the area. **Corn lily** reveals large, elegant, veined leaves and unobtrusive white flowers. **Pearly everlasting** displays ball-shaped white flowers and sage green leaves. Pink to purple **edible thistle**, also known as **Indian thistle**, grows up to 6 feet tall and was consumed by American Indians and early explorers, including Lewis and Clark.

Back in the trees again, look for **queen's cup**, presenting six-petaled white flowers and graceful tonguelike leaves. **Wild strawberry**, with delicate white petals around a yellow center, is very similar to the garden variety. A common forest inhabitant here, **false Solomon's seal** has clusters of cream-colored, star-shaped flowers and lancelike leaves. Vine maple and pink **wild rose** also dwell in this vicinity. These woodland flowers mostly blossom in early summer.

At mile 1.2, the trail breaks out onto open slopes for about a half mile. Ferns prevail, mixed with a number of flowers. Purple asters—**leafy**, **showy**, **Cascade**, and **Engelmann's aster**—are prevalent here and are often difficult to identify without a good reference book. The similar-looking **subalpine daisy** dwells in the higher meadows.

Traversing the slope, you'll pass fireweed, pearly everlasting, thimbleberry, and aster. You'll also see lots of **Canada** or **meadow goldenrod**, which often grows 4 feet tall, sprouting a spray of large yellow heads. A common shrub, **Douglas' spirea** yields fuzzy, cone-shaped pink flower heads. Another common flower, **yarrow** has adapted to varied habitats, and its lacy white flower clusters are found throughout the state. One of the largest flowers of the subalpine, **cow parsnip** can stand 6 feet tall, sporting 10-inch-wide umbrellalike flower heads. **Red columbine** and yellow-orange **tiger lily** generate flamboyant blossoms that hummingbirds find attractive. Ripe huckleberries provide many snack stops in August and September, but just be sure you can positively identify wild plants before consuming them.

At mile 1.7, you enter Glacier Peak Wilderness. At 576,900 acres, it is one of the largest wilderness areas in the Northwest, with 450 miles of trails and more glaciers than any other place in the lower 48 states. The dominant feature is 10,541-foot Glacier Peak, the fourth-highest mountain in the state. Although it last erupted some 12,000 years ago, it is still considered an active volcano.

THIMBLEBERRY
Rubus parviflorus

HEIGHT: Up to 7′
BLOOMS: May

Thimbleberry bears crinkled, tissue-papery, five-petaled white flowers and large maple-shaped leaves. Found in clearings and along roadsides, shorelines, and avalanche chutes, thimbleberry is a plant that is prevalent throughout Washington.

In August, the plant is loaded with juicy, thimble-shaped berries that look like raspberries. American Indians gathered and ate the berries, and they also used the large leaves as short-term containers. Some tribes even lined smoking pits with the leaves to lend extra flavor to their food.

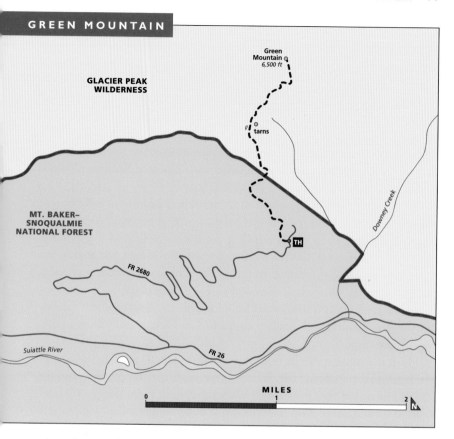

At mile 2.0, the trail rounds a ridge and enters a small valley bursting with wildflowers. **Fan-leaved cinquefoil** shows five-petaled yellow disks and serrated, strawberrylike leaves. A subalpine shrub, **pink mountain heather** boasts evergreen needles and bell-shaped flowers. Prevalent here and in the higher meadows, **Sitka valerian** displays fuzzy white compound heads on nearly leafless stems. Another common white compound, **American bistort** has a cylinder-shaped flower.

Fragrant **broadleaf lupine** produces blue-purple, pod-shaped flowers. **Mountain arnica** bears striking yellow ray flowers. The hanging blue bells of **harebell** closely resemble the garden variety. **Spreading phlox** has five-petaled flowers that grow in low mats of pink, lavender, or white. **American sawwort** puts forth dark purple budlike blossoms. The **Indian paintbrush** in this area might be orange-red, scarlet, or magenta, depending on the species.

At mile 2.5, the trail drops down briefly to two tarns. **White mountain heather** mixes in with pink mountain heather and many of the same flowers seen in the last valley. These tarns are the last reliable water source on the hike, so stop to filter here if your water bottles are low.

The trail climbs, quickly entering a basin. Snow lingers on the north faces well into late summer. Here you'll see the best floral display of the hike. Lupine, bistort, valerian, arnica, aster, cinquefoil, and corn lily all bloom here, thick in places.

Early blooming flowers usually put on a show in June. **Glacier lily**, with elegant arching petals, carpets areas in yellow. **Pasqueflower**, or **western anemone**, begins to bloom soon after snowmelt, showing creamy white petals around a cluster of stamens; in August, the plant goes to seed, sporting a tufted head. Small white **spring beauty** is another early bloomer. **Buttercup** follows the melting snow with varnished yellow bowls.

The trail steepens for the ascent to the summit. Reaching an exposed ridge, you'll see several flowering plants that have adapted to the harsh conditions of higher elevations. These plants usually grow low to the ground to avoid the wind and to gain solar heat from the rocky soil. **Davidson's penstemon** produces masses of pink to lavender trumpet-shaped blossoms. **Alpine aster**, which averages 20 to 30 blue-purple rays, and **alpine golden daisy**, with as many as 70 yellow rays, are two sunflowers found in this challenging environment. **Northern goldenrod** and **shrubby cinquefoil** add splashes of yellow to the big-sky landscape.

From the summit of Green Mountain, at mile 4.0, you can easily see Mt. Baker to the north and Mt. Rainier to the south. To the east rise the glacier-clad mountains of the Glacier Peak Wilderness. Each more than 8,000 feet high, Mt. Formidable, Sentinel Peak, Spire Point, Sinister Peak, and Glacier Peak are popular climbs for mountaineers. The glaciers turn crimson in the waning light of sunset. Hopefully you can stay the night.

Windy Pass

Lupine in a meadow, Pasayten Wilderness

Moderate	***Trail Rating***
7 miles round trip	***Trail Length***
Mt. Baker–Snoqualmie National Forest, northwest of Winthrop	***Location***
6,200 to 6,900 feet	***Elevation***
July to late September	***Bloom Season***
Mid-July to early August	***Peak Bloom***
Okanogan National Forest, Methow Valley Ranger District Office, (509) 997-2131	***Contact***
	Directions

From Winthrop, drive west on WA 20 (North Cascades Highway) for 13.0 miles and turn right (north) at the Mazama sign. Drive 0.4 mile to a T intersection and turn left onto Mazama Road, which parallels the Methow River. Follow this road for 9.0 miles to a signed junction. Stay right and follow Harts Pass Road (FR 5400) 10.0 miles to Harts Pass. (This steep, one-lane road is the highest in the state, and trailers are not allowed. If you drive with care, a 2WD vehicle can make the trip. Check with the Forest Service because the road is sometimes not open all the way until August.) At Harts Pass, turn right onto Slate Peak Road (FR 600) toward Slate Peak. Proceed 1.3 miles to a hairpin switchback where there are several parking options.

At 6,800 feet, this is one of the highest trailheads in the state. (Hike 13, Gold Ridge, is the highest.) Gold was discovered on the west side of Harts Pass in 1893, which was the incentive for building a road this high. The mining settlement of Chanceller, its townsite located on Slate Creek west of the pass, once bustled with more than 1,000 people.

Although the 7-mile distance, for the purposes of this book, earns this hike a moderate rating, this hike is amazingly easy with a very gentle grade. It's a great hike for kids. Most of the route travels through subalpine meadows with fine views of both near and distant peaks. This hike follows the Pacific Crest Trail (Trail No. 2000), so you can easily lengthen or shorten the hike by just turning back whenever you choose. If you're lucky, you might even meet up with some thru-hikers, intrepid trekkers who are tackling the full length of the trail from the Mexican border to the Canadian border.

From the parking area at the road's (FR 600) first switchback, the Pacific Crest Trail heads north, skirting the west flank of Slate Peak. Here you'll see a number of quite common plants. In late July or August, blue **broadleaf lupine** blooms abundantly. This sweet-smelling flower might be the showiest in the state's subalpine meadows. **American bistort** is prolific as well, showing cylinder-shaped white flower heads.

Usually dwelling with lupine and bistort, **Sitka valerian** bears stamen-fuzzy white blossoms on 2-foot-tall stems. Also common, **thread-leaved sandwort** exhibits small five-petaled white flowers and grasslike leaves. **Yarrow**, found in many habitats throughout Washington, has lacy white blossoms and feathery leaves. Also white, the ball-shaped clusters of **pearly everlasting** grace forest clearings and meadow edges.

Look for several kinds of Indian paintbrush, which brighten forest clearings and open meadows. **Scarlet** and **magenta paintbrush** are named for their colorful bracts. **Harsh paintbrush** has red-orange bracts. Paintbrush generally bloom in mid- to late summer.

Many yellow flowers speckle the landscape. **Arrowleaf butterweed** is the tallest, showing a cluster of ray heads and sawtoothed triangular leaves. **Elmer's butterweed** has similar ray flowers. Shorter and with fewer blossoms than butterweeds, **mountain arnica** shows yellow petals that are squared off and serrated. **Heart-leaf arnica**, which grows in shady areas, is similar, though with wider, heart-shaped leaves.

Cinquefoils always have five-petaled yellow blossoms. **Fan-leaved cinquefoil** generates leaflets in threes. **Diverse-leaved cinquefoil** has five to seven leaflets. **Shrubby cinquefoil**, a woody plant with needlelike leaves, usually grows in rocky soil.

Along open slopes, you'll have excellent views northwest into the 530,000-acre Pasayten Wilderness, one of the state's largest wilderness areas. With a map

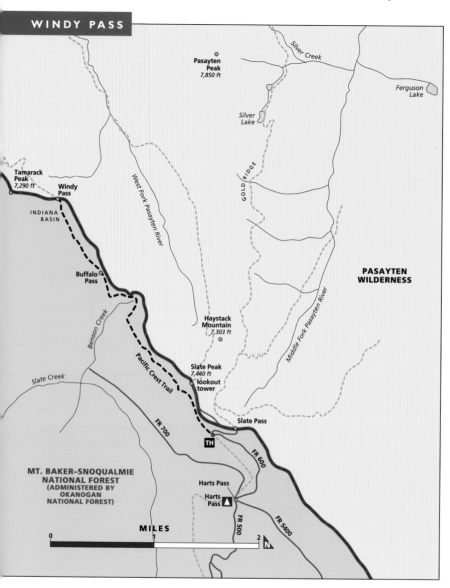

WINDY PASS

of the region, you can identify many prominent peaks. To the south, 8,301-foot Mt. Ballard and 8,420-foot Azurite Peak dominate the horizon. Far to the west lie Jack Mountain and Crater Mountain, two glaciated peaks that hold snowfields through the summer.

Asters and daisies, usually in shades of purple with a yellow center, grow along the trail. Found in open forest and along meadow edges, **showy aster** has large sawtoothed leaves. **Leafy bracted aster** dwells in open areas. Growing in rocky habitat at higher elevations, **alpine aster** matures 15 to 40 rays of a blue to purple color. Daisies, or fleabanes, are often confused with asters. **Longleaf fleabane** shows 40 to 60 narrow, pink to lavender rays with a yellow center. **Subalpine daisy**, commonly found in meadows here, has wider rays.

FALSE HELLEBORE OR CORN LILY
Veratrum californicum

HEIGHT: Up to 6'
BLOOMS: July to August

An extremely tall member of the lily family, false hellebore, also known as corn lily, has numerous green-tinged white clusters of flowers growing up a tall, single stem. Fine, woolly hairs cover its thick stem. Most noticeable, however, are its many large, flame-shaped, veined leaves, which sometimes reach 2 feet in length.

False hellebore grows mainly in wet meadows above 4,000 feet in elevation. This plant contains certain alkaloids that make it extremely poisonous to both livestock and humans. In small doses, however, these same alkaloids can lower blood pressure. Once the leaves dry up, these chemicals diminish, rendering the plant harmless.

Penstemons can be difficult to differentiate, as well, because they all have funnel-shaped flowers made of five lobes—two lobes tilting up and three curving slightly down, creating a landing pad for bees. Found in meadows and forest openings, **small-flowered penstemon** exhibits whorls of purple blossoms with white throats. While most penstemons prefer sunny sites, an exception is **woodland penstemon**, with clusters of flowers on leaning stems in shady areas. **Cliff, shrubby,** and **Davidson's penstemon** typically grow low to the ground on rocky slopes. These woody varieties vary in color from lavender to pink.

Early in the season, soon after snowmelt, look for fields of **glacier lily**, with elegant arching yellow petals. **Pasqueflower**, or **western anemone**, also blooms soon after snowmelt, showing five creamy white petals surrounding a cluster of stamens; by August, this plant has gone to seed with a tufted head atop a tall stem. **Alpine buttercup** presents varnished yellow bowls following the melt-off. Delicate **shooting star** displays upward-pointing fuchsia petals and a black anther tube.

In late summer, flashy **red columbine** produces a scarlet hanging head with long stamens of bright yellow. Spotted **Columbia** or **tiger lily** attracts the attention of hummingbirds with its yellow-orange arching petals and protruding stamens.

Chocolate lily is one of the only brownish flowers in the region. Often found in dry soil, **harebell** has light blue dangling bells.

At mile 1.7, the trail skirts the top of Benson Basin. Moisture-loving plants grow along Benson Creek. Early in the summer, **blue violet** displays blossoms much like the garden-variety violet. **False hellebore**, also called **corn lily**, unfurls large cabbagelike veined leaves that dwarf its greenish flowers. **Mountain bog gentian** is an elegant deep purple flower with five petals often wrapped like a large bud. In late summer, **pink** or **Lewis' monkey-flower** forms mats of fuchsia blossoms along the stream.

Members of the lousewort family also inhabit wet areas. The conspicuous **elephant's head**, a kind of lousewort, shows many tiny pink blossoms that look like the trunks and ears of elephants. The pink to white blossoms of **sickletop lousewort** are curved, resembling hand sickles. **Bracted lousewort** and **coiled-beak lousewort** also have curved flowers, pale yellow in color.

As you traverse to Buffalo Pass, look for flowers growing among the rocks. Low-growing **alpine golden daisy** has a number of yellow ray heads. Taller with wider rays, **Oregon sunshine** is another yellow inhabitant of rocky places. Stonecrops grow in dry, stony soil, putting forth five-petaled yellow flower heads and small fleshy leaves. **Lance-leaved stonecrop** and **spreading stonecrop** are found here.

The trail passes above several mine sites, pockets of desecrated landscape on private land. At mile 3.5, you reach Windy Pass, the turnaround spot for this hike. At Windy Pass, the Pacific Crest Trail crosses from the west side of the ridge to the east side for the first time on this hike. Views to the east offer the glaciated mountains of Ptarmigan Peak, Osceola Peak, Monument Peak, and many others. Hardy hikers might wish to continue on through to the flowery meadows of Pasayten Wilderness.

Wildflower Hike 13 # Gold Ridge

Meadows below Haystack Mountain, Pasayten Wilderness

Beginning at 6,870 feet in elevation, this is the highest trailhead in the state, so carry oxygen (just kidding). On its way to Silver Lake, the Buckskin Ridge Trail (Trail No. 498) travels along the flanks of Gold Ridge and passes through scenery as glorious as the Windy Pass portion of the Pacific Crest Trail (see Hike 12, p. 73). But because it is slightly more difficult—with a number of ascents and descents—it receives only a fraction of the hikers. You might consider setting up a base camp at Harts Pass Campground and doing both hikes. Beautiful Silver Lake is the turnaround point for a 10-mile round-trip hike. Carry water if you don't plan on going that far, and be prepared to filter water if you do.

Trail Rating	Moderate
Trail Length	10 miles round trip
Location	Pasayten Wilderness, northwest of Winthrop
Elevation	6,870 to 6,256 feet
Bloom Season	July to late September
Peak Bloom	Mid-July to early August
Contact	Okanogan National Forest, Methow Valley Ranger District Office, (509) 997-2131
Directions	From the small town of Winthrop, drive west on WA 20 (North Cascades Highway) for 13.0 miles and turn right (north) at the Mazama sign. Drive 0.4 mile to a T intersection and turn left onto Mazama Road, which parallels the Methow River. Follow this road for 9.0 miles to a signed junction. Stay right and follow Harts Pass Road (FR 5400) 10.0 miles to Harts Pass. (This steep, one-lane road is the highest in the state. Trailers are not allowed, but passenger vehicles can travel this road with care. Check with the Forest Service before starting out because, in some years, the road is not open all the way until August.) At Harts Pass, turn right onto Slate Peak Road (FR 600) toward Slate Peak. Proceed 1.6 miles to the second switchback and park at the Buckskin–Silver Lake Trailhead.

From the signed trailhead, you soon climb a rocky slope to a saddle that overlooks a basin below Slate Peak. Entering the Pasayten Wilderness, you then descend talus slopes where several kinds of flowers grow under rocky conditions. A member of the sunflower family, **Oregon sunshine**, or **woolly sunflower**, shows a bouquet of golden ray flowers above sage green leaves. **Dwarf mountain butterweed**, also a yellow composite, flourishes in the rocky rubble. **Alpine golden daisy** produces yellow ray heads on 1- to 6-inch stems.

Several members of the saxifrage family dwell in the rocks along the first 0.5 mile of trail. Low-growing **spotted saxifrage** generates small five-petaled blossoms, white with maroon and yellow dots. A close cousin, **tufted saxifrage** has five-petaled white flowers; it is found as far north as the arctic tundra. **Elmera**, another saxifrage, produces a stalk full of cream-colored, cup-shaped blossoms.

The trail levels out in the basin, which grows lush with flowers during the peak bloom times of July and August. The blue stalks of **broadleaf lupine** are a standard in most of Washington's subalpine meadows. **Sitka valerian** has fuzzy white heads consisting of many tiny blossoms. **Magenta paintbrush** displays colorful bracts. Also plentiful here, **Gray's lovage** has a white umbrella head made of a cluster of flowers. **American bistort** is another common white flower, with a cylinder-shaped head made of many small blossoms atop a stem standing 18 to 24 inches tall.

Composites, also called ray flowers, are a conspicuous group here. **Mountain arnica** is a common bright yellow sunflower, usually with just one blossom per stem. Also yellow, **arrowleaf butterweed** produces several clusters of many ¾-inch ray flowers. **Subalpine daisy** is prevalent in the basin, producing elegant blossoms with numerous lavender rays around a yellow center. **Leafy aster**, which grows 12 to 30 inches tall here, has thin lavender rays around a yellow center.

A number of water-seeking plants take root in the seeps and runoff from Slate Peak and Haystack Mountain. Found near running water, monkey-flowers display five-petaled, funnel-shaped blossoms. **Pink monkey-flower** generates paired fuchsia blossoms and opposing leaves. **Mountain monkey-flower** is a striking yellow flower with red dots, often carpeting small areas. Growing in moist soil, **mountain bog gentian** bears elegant deep purple blossoms. **False hellebore**, or **corn lily**, is easy to spot with its large, veined leaves, which sometimes grow up to 2 feet long.

At mile 0.6, you'll reach a trail junction; continue going straight. (The trail to the right drops down to the Middle Fork of the Pasayten River.) Climbing small side ridges and dropping into lush valleys, the trail traverses the east flank of Gold Ridge, passing an assortment of flowers.

DWARF MOUNTAIN BUTTERWEED

Senecio fremontii

HEIGHT: 3" to 5"

BLOOMS: July to mid-August

Dwarf mountain butterweed has a daisy-like appearance. It has a cluster of bright yellow flowers and a mat of large round leaves at the base of the stem, which is thick and deep red. Dwarf mountain butterweed grows in rocky areas at high elevations.

All senecio plants are poisonous. While cows and livestock might sometimes graze on the fairly unpalatable dwarf mountain butterweed, the animals rarely eat enough quantity to cause them harm. The name senecio comes from the Latin word *senex,* which means "old man." The plant is so named because its flower changes to a tuft of fuzz in autumn, and a light hair covers the entire plant.

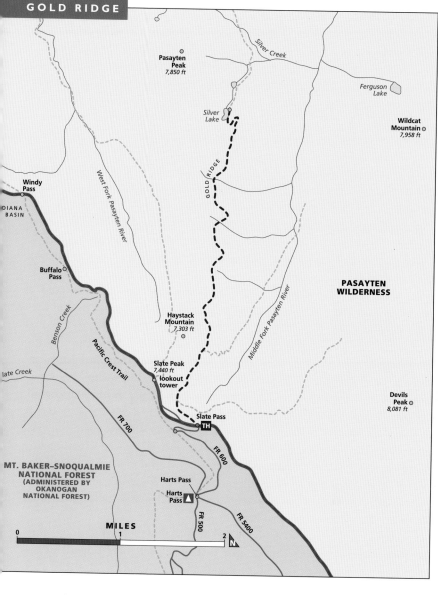

Members of the huge penstemon family occupy a wide variety of habitats—but with so many kinds, they can be difficult to differentiate. **Small-flowered penstemon** grows in meadows and bears whorled clusters of many trumpet-shaped purple blossoms. **Davidson's** and **shrubby penstemon** inhabit poor rocky soils along the ridge, growing low to the ground to stay out of the wind and to retain heat from the soil or rock. Their blossoms, which might be pink, lavender, or purple, sometimes form striking mats of flowers.

The lousewort family is another prevalent group here, usually preferring rich, moist soil. Abundant in open meadows, **elephant's head** has stalks with many pink blossoms, each resembling an elephant's trunk and ears. An odd-looking plant, **bracted lousewort** generates fernlike leaves and a cone-shaped flower head of many curved yellow or reddish purple blossoms. Also with fern-like leaves, **coiled-beak lousewort** displays pale yellow flowers curving downward. Preferring the shade along meadow edges, **sickletop lousewort** produces pink or white blossoms that fan out in clustered heads.

Look for a number of conspicuous flowers. Fanciful **red columbine** generates a scarlet hanging head with large, bright yellow stamens. **Columbia** or **tiger lily** attracts hummingbirds with its arching yellow-orange spotted petals and protruding stamens.

In early to mid-July, soon after snowmelt, the first wildflowers start blooming here. Yellow **glacier lily** and white **avalanche lily** at times carpet the glades in color. Another early bloomer, **pasqueflower**, or **western anemone**, has two distinct displays. It first puts forth a 6-inch-tall flower with five to eight white petals around a yellow center; later in the summer, the plant goes to seed, revealing hairy mop-head ovals on taller stalks—much showier than at the flowering stage.

On the flanks of Gold Ridge, you'll find a number of cinquefoils, all with five-petaled, bowl-shaped yellow blossoms. **Fan-leaved cinquefoil** generates three serrated strawberrylike leaves, while **diverse-leaved cinquefoil** bears five to seven deeply toothed leaves. Growing in rocky habitats, **shrubby cinquefoil** produces narrow spiky leaves on woody stems.

From the slopes of the ridge, views to the east are superb. Here you can gaze across the massive Pasayten Wilderness, with Wildcat Mountain and Mt. Rolo rising across the Pasayten River valley. To the southeast, Robinson Mountain usually holds snow all summer. Pasayten Wilderness and neighboring Glacier Peak Wilderness preserve more than 1.1 million acres, four times the size of Mt. Rainier National Park.

At mile 4.6, the trail drops steeply and reaches an unmarked junction. Turn left to continue 0.4 mile to Silver Lake, nestled below a rocky ridge. This is a great spot for an icy dip, a picnic, or to cast a line for trout.

Maple Pass

*Yellow fawn
lily at
Heather Pass*

The Maple Pass Loop offers great access to open mountain country. New scenery unfolds at seemingly every twist and turn, with impressive views down into the cirque basins that hold Rainy Lake and Lake Ann. The trail receives some hiker traffic but rarely is crowded. I've heard a few people rate this hike as one of their favorites in the state. Hiking poles are recommended, for the trail ascends first to Heather Pass and then to Maple Pass, logging a total elevation gain of 2,000 feet.

You'll find the trailhead at the south end of the Rainy Pass picnic area parking lot, where a sign provides trail information. Take the dirt Maple Pass Loop (Trail No. 740) toward Lake Ann and Maple Pass. (Another

Trail Rating	Moderate
Trail Length	7.1-mile loop
Location	Wenatchee National Forest, west of Winthrop
Elevation	4,850 to 6,850 feet
Bloom Season	July to mid-September
Peak Bloom	Mid-July to mid-August
Contact	Okanogan National Forest, Methow Valley Ranger District Office, (509) 997-2131
Directions	From the town of Winthrop, drive west on WA 20 (North Cascades Highway) for 35 miles to Rainy Pass. Or, from Newhalem, drive east on WA 20 for 37 miles to the pass. Park at the picnic area.

trail from the parking area, this one paved, leads to Rainy Lake. This paved trail will serve as your return route when you hike back to the parking area.)

Traveling through mature forest, the trail passes several white-flowering, shade-loving plants. **Hooker's fairybell**, which displays two or three hanging bells, grows up to 2½ feet tall. The fragrant **star-flowered false Solomon's seal** has a cluster of many tiny star-shaped white flowers and ribbed leaves.

As you pass avalanche chutes, look east for a view of 7,660-foot Stiletto Peak. These clearings host **fireweed**, tall stalks with pink spiky flower heads. Blooming late in summer, **yarrow** bears feathery leaves and lacy white blossoms. Another common white flower, **pearly everlasting** has paperlike round blossoms. **Thimbleberry**, a woody shrub with white blossoms and large maplelike leaves, produces edible thimble-shaped berries in late summer—but don't sample wild plants unless you're absolutely sure they're not poisonous.

As you ascend, look across the highway for views of Cutthroat Peak and Whistler Mountain. The trail then drops to parallel the outlet stream from Lake Ann, passing marshy areas. **Subalpine spirea**, similar to the garden variety, is a woody plant with fuzzy pink flower clusters.

At mile 1.3, you'll come to a signed junction. The loop trail heads right to Heather and Maple Passes. (If you want to visit Lake Ann, situated in a hanging valley with several cascades on the slopes above, take the left fork for a 1-mile round-trip detour.)

Continuing on the Maple Pass Loop, you'll see several kinds of penstemon, all of which have five-petaled pink to purple trumpet-shaped blossoms. In open forest, **woodland penstemon** shows clusters of flowers on leaning stems.

Cascade penstemon is common in meadows, with its whorl-like cluster of purple blossoms and sawtoothed triangular leaves. Higher up, on rocky ridges, **Davidson's** and **shrubby penstemon** bear pink to purple blossoms and small rounded leaves.

The trail climbs along the north side of Lake Ann, crossing several talus slopes. In stable rock, look for **stonecrop**, with star-shaped yellow blossoms and conspicuous stamens. **Black twinberry**, a shrub, bears yellow tubular flowers and pairs of black berries cupped by maroon bracts. **Shrubby cinquefoil** has five-petaled yellow blossoms growing on woody stems.

Lush meadows just below Heather Pass host many flowers. In June or early July, just after the snowmelt, yellow **glacier lily** covers slopes in a spectacular show. **Globeflower** also follows the snow, bearing five or six white sepals around a golden center. Globeflower is sometimes confused with **pasque-flower**, another early-blooming white flower that resides in these meadows.

From about mid-June to mid-August, the meadows are filled with standards of the subalpine environment. White **Sitka valerian** has fuzzy heads of many tiny blossoms. Somewhat similar at first glance, **Gray's lovage** displays a larger white umbellate head of many tiny blossoms. Growing 18 to 24 inches tall, **American bistort** also has a white head of many small flowers, but in a cylinder shape.

Broadleaf lupine is prevalent in subalpine meadows throughout Washington. Displaying stalks covered with purplish blue, podlike blossoms, this member of the pea family adds nitrogen to the soil. **Magenta paintbrush** has showy bracts that hide its tiny flowers. Its cousin, the red **small-flowered paintbrush**, is common to this area.

The sunflower family comprises many of the flowers along the trail, including asters, butterweeds, arnicas,

QUEEN'S CUP
Clintonia uniflora

HEIGHT: 4" to 8"
BLOOMS: May to July

Queen's cup, a kind of lily, displays a single, immaculately white flower made up of six petals and deep yellow stamens. Its two to three shiny leaves have hairy undersides. Queen's cup is found from low to middle elevations across much of the Cascade Range.

In the fall, the flower drops off to reveal a single blue edible berry. The bright blue berry has considerable value as a dye, which, when highly concentrated, provides an extremely unusual color.

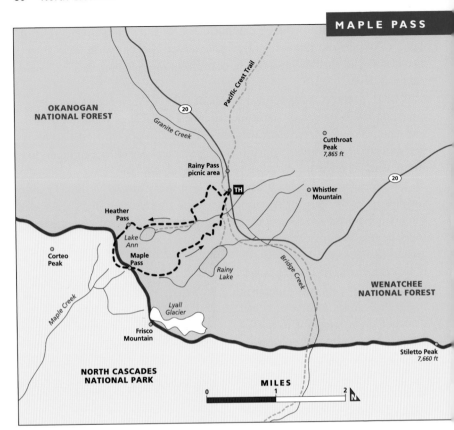

MAPLE PASS

and yarrow. With sparse, separated lavender rays around a yellow center, **Cascade aster** has several flower heads on each stem. **Leafy aster**, with a more organized arrangement of rays, often has only a single flower per stem. **Subalpine daisy**, a cousin to the aster, usually has as many as 40 white or lavender rays.

Yellow flowers are common here in late July and August. **Arrowleaf butterweed** grows 2 to 3 feet tall with a cluster of ray heads and sawtoothed triangular leaves. Shorter and with fewer blossoms, **mountain arnica** has squared-off yellow petals with jagged tips. Cinquefoils display five-petaled yellow blossoms. **Fan-leaved cinquefoil** has leaflets in threes. **Diverse-leaved cinquefoil** counts five to seven leaflets. Found farther up the trail growing in the rocky soil of higher elevations, **shrubby cinquefoil** is a woody plant with needlelike leaves.

At mile 2.3, you'll reach Heather Pass, named after **pink mountain heather**, a common subalpine shrub with evergreen needles and, in late summer, pretty hanging pink bells. From here you'll see grand views of prominent Black Peak and Fisher Peak, which often hold snowfields through the summer. At a junction with an unsigned, unmaintained trail that heads west to Lewis Lake, the loop trail stays left, heading south toward Maple Pass, 1,100 feet above Lake Ann.

Few species can survive the harsh conditions and poor soil of high elevations. Look for **spreading phlox**, which forms dense mats of spiky leaves and five-petaled, star-shaped lavender blossoms. Also in low-growing mats, **Tolmie's saxifrage** has five white petals and five petal-like stamens, making it look like a 10-petaled flower.

At mile 3.4, you reach 6,600-foot Maple Pass. Plan to spend some time here just taking in the fabulous views. To the west and south are a horde of peaks in North Cascades National Park and Glacier Peak Wilderness, where the snowcapped cone of Glacier Peak pokes into the sky. Glaciers also cloak distant McGregor Mountain and nearby Corteo Peak. Ptarmigan and marmots reside in the rocky habitat of the ridge.

The skyline trail heads south, then wraps east toward Frisco Mountain. Reaching 6,850 feet, the trail turns left (east) to descend the ridge separating Lake Ann and Rainy Lake. Steep switchbacks lead to views of Rainy Lake, 2,000 feet below. Partway down, the trail enters forest for the last section of the loop.

Queen's cup bears white flowers with six petals. **Twinflower** displays hanging pairs of pale pink trumpet-shaped blossoms; rounded evergreen leaves appear at the base of a leafless stem. Found in deep shade, the evergreen-leaved **prince's pine**, or **pipsissewa**, shows a cluster of three to eight pink flowers.

At mile 6.6, you reach a junction with the paved Rainy Lake Trail. Turn left to return to the trailhead, 0.5 mile farther, to complete the loop. Or, if you're still feeling energetic, take a right to detour to Rainy Lake, 0.4 mile away.

Wildflower
Hike 15 *Twisp Pass*

*Pink mountain
heather blooms
on Twisp Pass*

Expect an all-uphill hike on the trail to Twisp Pass (Trail No. 432). Although the trail is not overly steep, the 2,400-foot elevation gain surely will give you a good workout. In this part of the state, the high country is often rocky and brushy. You won't find enormous meadows here, but the pocket meadows and forest clearings are comparatively lush.

If you want to car camp, drive another 0.6 mile past the trailhead to the campground at the end of the road. Behind the campground outhouse, there is a boot track that climbs steeply for about 60 yards to meet up with the main trail, where you go left (west). Although the trail to Twisp Pass is commonly used, it would rarely be considered crowded, except on an occasional summer weekend.

Trail Rating	Difficult
Trail Length	9 miles round trip
Location	Lake Chelan–Sawtooth Wilderness, northwest of Twisp
Elevation	3,660 to 6,060 feet
Bloom Season	July to late September
Peak Bloom	July to early August
Contact	Okanogan National Forest, Methow Valley Ranger District Office, (509) 997-2131
Directions	From WA 20 in the Methow Valley town of Twisp, turn west onto the paved Twisp River Road (FR 44) at the Twisp River Recreation Area sign. Follow this riverside road for 25 miles, continuing on as it changes to gravel FR 4440. Park at the Gilbert Trailhead parking area on the right.

From the signed trailhead, you'll be hiking west, up the Twisp River valley. Bracken fern, white-flowering **thimbleberry**, and pink **wild rose** are thick in places. Black cottonwoods tower above the river as you hike west. Named for its lengthy bloom season, **pearly everlasting** has clustered flower heads of wrapped white bracts around small yellow centers. **Large-leaved avens** sprouts strawberrylike leaves and five round yellow petals with a greenish center.

In forest openings along the first mile, look for the lavender rays and yellow centers of **showy aster**, which has large, toothed leaves, and **leafy aster**, with smooth narrow leaves. Showing similar flower heads, **Cascade aster** and **Engelmann's aster** also reside in the area. In the upper meadows, you'll see **showy fleabane** and **subalpine daisy**, which are easily confused with asters.

You quickly enter the Lake Chelan–Sawtooth Wilderness. This 146,000-acre wilderness borders Lake Chelan and North Cascades National Park, preserving rocky peaks, mountain lakes, and subalpine meadows. The trail passes under a canopy of Douglas fir. Western yew, usually less than 20 feet tall, has flat evergreen needles and red berries instead of cones. The bark of this tree contains taxol, which has proven effective against certain types of cancer, though it takes 10 good-sized trees to provide enough taxol for one treatment. Other trees in the understory of the lower trail include Douglas maple and western mountain ash.

In the shade of the forest, you can spot two types of Solomon's seal. **Star-flowered false Solomon's seal** exhibits small six-pointed white flowers and slender, lance-shaped leaves. With a cone-shaped cluster of many tiny cream-colored blossoms, **false Solomon's seal** has broader leaves and longer stems. **Wild strawberry** bears small five-petaled white blossoms.

In forest clearings, and on up into the higher meadows, you can see several kinds of Indian paintbrush. **Scarlet** and **magenta paintbrush** are named for the brilliant color of their bracts. **Harsh paintbrush** exhibits red-orange bracts.

Showy flowers attract insects and hummingbirds to their flamboyant blossoms. **Tiger lily**, also known as **Columbia lily**, has spotted yellow-orange blooms. **Red columbine** generates hanging blossoms with spurs and long yellow stamens.

Look for several avalanche chutes where the snowslides have prevented trees from taking hold. Growing in these disturbed sites, **yarrow** sprouts lacy white flowers and feathery leaves. **Fireweed** grows up to 6 feet tall with purple to pink spiky flower heads. **Black twinberry** is a shrub bearing tubular yellow flowers and pairs of black berries cupped by maroon bracts. **Slender hawksbeard** presents small yellow ray flowers measuring up to ¾ inch across. Views open to the west, to pyramid-shaped Lincoln Butte.

At mile 1.7, you reach a junction. Stay left and cross the foot-log over the North Fork of the Twisp River, which, in dry years, might be the last reliable water source along the way. (The trail to the right goes to Copper Pass, another popular destination, 4.0 miles away.) **Wild ginger**, with brown flowers and large heart-shaped leaves, grows near the river, really just a stream here. White **Sitka valerian** and yellow **mountain arnica** also grow here.

OREGON SUNSHINE OR WOOLLY SUNFLOWER
Eriophyllum lanatum

HEIGHT: 6" to 16"

BLOOMS: April to August

A member of the sunflower family, Oregon sunshine bears inch-wide yellow flowers with 8 to 13 rays. Its fuzzy, dissected, olive green leaves give rise to its Latin name, *lanatum,* which refers to wool. They also explain the plant's other common name, woolly sunflower.

Oregon sunshine often grows on rocky slopes and in dry soils at various elevations across the state. Its bloom time depends on its elevation. Not surprisingly, it prefers sunny locations.

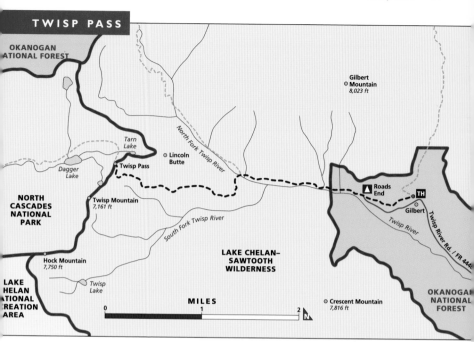

As you continue along the trail, the landscape opens up, with views now extending across the South Fork of the Twisp River. **Spreading stonecrop** resides along this rocky ridge, with five pointed yellow petals and egg-shaped leaves. Also flourishing in this rock garden, **Columbia Lewisia** displays basal, lance-like leaves and small white flowers with petals veined in pink. A fairly early bloomer, **Oregon sunshine**, or **woolly sunflower**, presents 8 to 13 yellow ray flowers on each plant. A common flower in dry, stony soils, **spreading phlox** generates spiky leaves and five-petaled blossoms in pink, white, or lavender. Sun-drenched slabs of rock make a fine rest spot.

The trail travels briefly through forest, then breaks out to cross talus slopes and avalanche chutes. Well-built rock walls help delineate the trail. Low-growing **arctic daisy** bears many white rays. **Edible thistle**, showing spiky purple flowers on tall stems, is named for its root, which can be boiled and eaten. An even larger plant, **cow parsnip** generates giant umbrella-shaped white flower heads and large, coarsely toothed leaves.

Around mile 3.7, you come upon meadow-covered slopes for the last part of the hike leading up to Twisp Pass. Along with many of the flowers already observed, stalks of **broadleaf lupine** add patches of purple-blue to the mix. In wet areas, **Lewis' monkey-flower** displays many trumpet-shaped fuchsia blossoms. **Thread-leaved sandwort** produces small star-shaped white flowers and grasslike leaves. **Larkspur**, a purple-blue delphinium, dwells along meadow edges.

Several yellow composites occupy the meadows. **Helianthella**, a yellow sun-flower, is widespread, sometimes covering entire slopes. **Arrowleaf butterweed** bears several small sparsely rayed flowers. **Northern goldenrod** has narrow rays on its many flower heads. Tiny toothed notches on the ends of its yellow petals distinguish **mountain arnica**.

After a winter of heavy snowfall, small streams course the upper section of the basin. Look for the large, veined leaves of **false hellebore**, also called **corn lily**. Named for its ladderlike leaves, **elegant Jacob's-ladder** displays five light blue petals around small yellow centers. **Blue stickseed** bears blue blossoms on tall dark stems.

Early in the summer, you'll see many small flowers in this vicinity. Fuchsia **shooting star** shines as one of the most exquisite flowers in the glades. **Yellow violet** appears similar to its purple garden-variety cousin. **Globeflower** and its look-alike, **pasqueflower**, both bear five white petals around stamen-fuzzy yellow centers. Blooming soon after snowmelt, **buttercup** exhibits yellow varnished disks. Yellow **glacier lily** and its cousin, white **avalanche lily**, can carpet entire patches of the meadow.

One last climb passes corn lily, mountain ash, and huckleberry. Exhibiting small bell-shaped blossoms, **pink mountain heather** has evergreen needles on its woody branches. Rock areas host spreading phlox, paintbrush, and sandwort. The saucer-shaped blossoms of **shrubby cinquefoil** bloom here on woody stems. **Alpine pussytoes** display white ball-shaped blossoms and spoon-shaped, sage-colored leaves. A treasure of the high country, **alpine forget-me-not** exhibits low mats of miniature blue blossoms with yellow centers.

At mile 4.5, you finally reach your turnaround point at 6,060-foot Twisp Pass, on the edge of North Cascades National Park. Scraggly trees partially obscure the view and flowers are somewhat sparse. Look for the pink to lavender tubular blossoms of **Davidson's penstemon**, as well as more pink mountain heather. The trail proceeds down the other side of the pass to Dagger Lake. Or you can explore to the northeast, where a boot track takes off up the ridge. Otherwise, return the way you came, with views down valley as you go.

Kraule-Sunnyside

Aspen trees and arrowleaf balsamroot-dotted meadow, Okanogan National Forest

This hike begins and ends at Sun Mountain Lodge, an amazing log structure built on a ridge with 360-degree views. Sun Mountain's 3,000 acres offer a multitude of outdoor activities. Numerous hiking trails lead from here into the nearby Okanogan National Forest. With the second-largest cross-country ski trail system in the United States, Nordic skiing at Sun Mountain ranks as some of the nation's best. Mountain biking is equally excellent, and the lodge has bikes for rent. From the pool, you can watch the sunset over Cascade peaks to the west. The lodge serves delicious food (the chicken curry soup comes highly recommended). And then there are the flower walks.

Trail Rating	Easy
Trail Length	3-mile loop
Location	West of Winthrop
Elevation	2,600 to 2,850 feet
Bloom Season	April to late July
Peak Bloom	Late April to late May
Contact	Sun Mountain Lodge Outdoor Center, (800) 572-0493, ext. 735
Directions	From Winthrop, head south on WA 20. Just after leaving the center of town, the highway crosses the Methow River. Immediately after the bridge, turn right on Twin Lakes Road. Drive 3.5 miles and turn right on Patterson Lake Road at the Sun Mountain sign. Follow the road 6.4 miles to Sun Mountain Lodge.

The wildflowers are extraordinary here in late April and May. Ponderosa pine and sagebrush ecosystems overlap, supporting flowers from both habitats. The folks in the lodge's outdoor center will give you a free map and help you plan any combination of hikes, as numerous options exist in the area's network of trails. Trail junctions are well marked and, with a map, you can easily find your way.

From the tennis courts just south of the lodge—not to be confused with the tennis courts near the stables—this easy loop hike begins on the Kraule Trail, which has some interpretive signs along the way. Right off, you enter meadows of showy flowers. In early May, the meadows explode with the large yellow sunflowers of **arrowleaf balsamroot**, plentiful along much of the trail. Blue stalks of **lupine**, also abundant, bloom from mid- to late May. Sprinkled throughout is **narrow-leaved desert-parsley**, with yellow sprays like fireworks.

The trail soon passes a thick grove of large **chokecherry** trees, with pale white blossoms hanging down like giant caterpillars. The stems of **Nuttall's larkspur**, growing 6 to 16 inches tall, look as if they are covered with small bluish purple butterflies. This perennial is common in the sage and ponderosa pine ecosystems of eastern Washington. With clusters of small yellow ray flowers on each stem, **western groundsel**, or **western butterweed**, stands 20 to 30 inches tall.

You'll need to search a little to see some of the less conspicuous flowers. Blooming in late April and early May, **long-flowered bluebell** grows close to the ground, with several tube-shaped, blue to pink flowers on each stem. Also low-growing, **prairie star** has five small white petals, each fringed with three lobes.

Among stony outcrops, look for the purple, tubular flowers of **rockcress** growing on 6- to 10-inch erect stems.

A number of edible flowering plants here were once harvested by American Indians. One of more than 30 types of parsleys that grow in Washington, **large-fruited desert-parsley**, or **biscuitroot**, has greenish or dirty-white sagging flowers. Its tuberous roots were pounded into a flour paste and steamed or roasted. A common woody shrub, **squaw currant** blooms in May with pale pink to white tube-shaped flowers. Its orange-red berries, rich in vitamin C, ripen in late summer. **Spreading stonecrop**, a short, five-petaled yellow flower with long stamens, was used medicinally.

From the meadows, you see clear views of 8,898-foot Gardner Mountain to the west and 8,726-foot Robinson Mountain to the northwest, up the Methow Valley. These peaks hold snow-fields through most of the summer. Wolf Creek noisily drains snowmelt from the high peaks in the Lake Chelan–Sawtooth Wilderness, a vast wilderness that stretches north to North Cascades National Park and south to Lake Chelan.

The trail briefly passes through forest again, where shade-tolerant, white-petaled **western spring beauty** begins to bloom in April. **Ballhead waterleaf** shows small bluish-purple flowers in clustered balls. As you leave the trees, look to the right, where neon green lichen covers an ancient ponderosa pine snag.

Passing through more fields of arrowleaf balsamroot, the trail drops to the wooded valley bottom. Low-growing **sagebrush buttercup** is common in early April, displaying yellow varnished petals. Another early bloomer, **grass widow** has six purple to pink petals forming a disk-shaped flower. **Yellow bell** looks just like its name.

BALLHEAD WATERLEAF
Hydrophyllum capitatum

HEIGHT: 4" to 9"
BLOOMS: April to June

A perennial herb, ballhead waterleaf bears tight round clusters of small bluish purple blossoms with long violet stamens. This short-stemmed plant grows low to the ground. Its alternating leaves, which are much larger in proportion to the flower head, have four to seven lobes.

Appearing east of the Cascades, ballhead waterleaf is often found in association with ponderosa pines. Translated directly from Greek, *hydrophyllum* means "waterleaf," a reference to its grooved leaf stem, which enables water to flow down the stem to the plant's fibrous roots. This variety is also known as dwarf waterleaf.

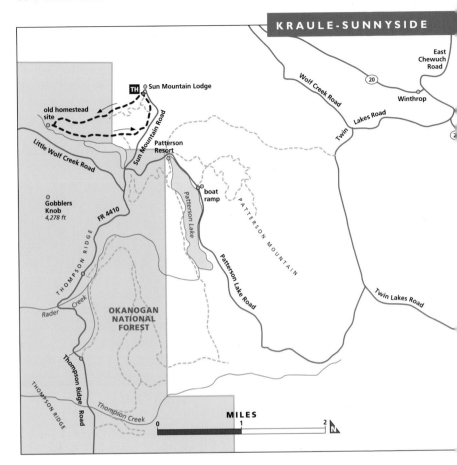

KRAULE-SUNNYSIDE

The trail crosses a wet area featuring **stream violet**, a yellow violet with heart-shaped leaves. **False hellebore** is better known for its beautiful mass of large, veined leaves than for its pale white flowers. Another water seeker, **Hooker's fairybell** reveals creamy white bells hanging in twos or threes from branching stem tips. Flaunting a hanging blossom with protruding stamens, **yellow columbine** is inconspicuous until it blooms in early summer. A shrub growing in open forest, **thimbleberry** puts forth five-petaled white flowers and, later in the summer, raspberrylike fruit.

The Kraule Trail ends at a T junction with the Sunnyside Trail. Taking a left continues this loop hike, heading back to the Sun Mountain Lodge. But before returning to the lodge, take a quick detour on the right fork. You'll travel a short distance to the old Hough homestead site, where a picnic area with tables and restrooms now joins the derelict cabin.

After this detour, return to the junction and take the Sunnyside Trail east, following a seasonal stream through open forest of alder, aspen, ponderosa pine, and Douglas fir. In May, the forest floor is speckled with the many tiny star-shaped white blooms of **false Solomon's seal**, which has broad, 3- to 8-inch lance-shaped leaves. By early June, the pink-flowering **wild rose** is seen throughout the forest. **Heart-leaf arnica**, with showy yellow ray flowers, also grows here.

The trail soon breaks out of the forest, into more hillsides of balsamroot, lupine, desert-parsley, and Nuttall's larkspur. In exposed, rocky soil, look for **bitterroot**, which opens its showy pink flowers in May. **Serviceberry**, a large common shrub that sometimes reaches more than 15 feet in height, is one of the first plants to bloom here, with clusters of five-petaled white flowers. **Lemonweed**, or **puccoon**, is a weedy-looking plant with spiky leaves and pale yellow flowers. Western butterweed's yellow clusters of ray flowers are abundant in these meadows.

On the right, a lake created by a beaver dam makes an excellent spot to view wildlife. At the next trail junction, the right fork leads to the beaver pond while the left fork heads uphill, back to Sun Mountain Lodge.

As the trail climbs and parallels the road, Gardner Mountain appears above the yellow-speckled meadows. To the right, rounded Patterson Mountain rises above Patterson Lake. Most of the meadow flowers observed so far continue along this last section of trail. Just before the end of the loop, you'll see a huge serviceberry, spectacular in bloom, set against an aspen grove like an exclamation point. The hike ends back at Sun Mountain Lodge. Now, for a bowl of that chicken curry soup.

*Wildflower
Hike 17* Patterson Mountain

*Arrowleaf
balsamroot
decks a meadow
on Patterson
Mountain,
Methow Valley*

V isible from the entire Winthrop area, Patterson Mountain looks like the
rounded back of a sleeping dinosaur. Patterson Mountain Trail circles
the mountain, passing mostly through open meadows with occasional stands
of aspen and evergreens. The route begins across the road from the boat-
ramp parking at Patterson Lake. About 30 yards up the trail stands a sign
for Patterson Mountain.

In late April and early May, the trail corridor grows thick with **arrowleaf
balsamroot**; the profusion of these yellow sunflowers makes it a challenge to
see beyond this great display to the less conspicuous flowers. **Prairie star** grows
6 to 10 inches tall and features small five-petaled white blossoms fringed with
three-lobed tips. **Lemonweed**, or **puccoon**, is an odd, spiky-leaved plant with

Trail Rating	Moderate
Trail Length	5-mile loop
Location	West of Winthrop
Elevation	2,400 to 3,511 feet
Bloom Season	April to late June
Peak Bloom	Late April to late May
Contact	Sun Mountain Lodge Outdoor Center, (800) 572-0493, ext. 735
Directions	From Winthrop, head south on WA 20. Just after leaving the center of town, the highway crosses the Methow River. Immediately after the bridge, turn right on Twin Lakes Road. Drive 3.5 miles and turn right on Patterson Lake Road at the Sun Mountain sign. Go 4.0 miles to Patterson Lake. Halfway along the lake, there is a large parking lot on the left. This parking area, which accesses a boat ramp, requires a prepaid pass from the Washington Department of Fish and Wildlife, available where fishing licenses are sold. However, a free pullout big enough for two cars is next to this pay parking area.

small pale yellow flowers. One of several buckwheats here, **thyme-leaved buckwheat** has a dense cluster of yellow, cream, or pinkish flowers on its many short branches.

Near the beginning of the trail, you'll find a spring-fed seep hosting low-growing, tubular **yellow monkey-flower**. A bush showing pale pink to cream cylinder-shaped flowers, **squaw currant** yields edible berries in late summer. **Gray's** and **narrow-leaved desert-parsley** are common along the trail, both with sprays of tiny yellow flowers. Several kinds of lupine grow here, including **prairie** and **silky lupine**, both with bright blue podlike flowers.

At mile 0.2, the trail splits. The right fork is your return route. Take the left fork and pass through the gate, heading in a clockwise loop along Patterson Mountain. A rock outcrop hosts **bitterroot**, an inconspicuous plant until its showy pink flowers bloom in mid-May. **Western groundsel**, or **western butter-weed**, has several small yellow ray flower heads on each 20- to 30-inch stem.

At a junction just after the gate, stay right (the trail to the left goes to the Patterson Lake cabins). As you enter an aspen-shaded area, look for **yellow bell**, a small lily. Pinkish purple **grass widow** blooms in early spring. Another early bloomer, **desert shooting star** has an upswept, bright pink flower with a yellow ring around the anther tube. Later in the spring, **ballhead waterleaf** displays tiny five-petaled flowers in clustered bluish purple balls.

As you ascend the hilltop, the exceptional views up Methow Valley include snow-covered 8,726-foot Robinson Mountain and other distant Cascade peaks. The open areas are dense with balsamroot, silky lupine, and western butterweed. In about a mile, steps climb over a fence and the trail enters a wooded area where ponderosa pine and Douglas fir shade white-flowering **western spring beauty**. **Long-flowered bluebell** shows clusters of hanging, tubular blossoms. A showy yellow composite with 10 to 15 ray petals, **heart-leaf arnica** grows in open forest. Adding their unique sounds to the sylvan symphony, beeping nuthatches and drumming grouse are two of the many bird species that live here.

The trail leaves the woods again. Look for the off-white flower of **large-fruited desert-parsley**, or **biscuitroot**, a type of desert-parsley that American Indians prized for its edible taproot. Large and woody, the roots were usually pounded into a flour paste, then boiled, steamed, or roasted. When dried, the flour cakes could be stored for many months.

DESERT SHOOTING STAR
Dodecatheon conjugens

HEIGHT: 2" to 8"
BLOOMS: April to late May
A yellow ring anchors the arching purplish pink petals of the desert shooting star flower. Stamens form a long, thin point, while petals fly backward in the opposite direction.

The shape of the shooting star is somewhat strange, requiring bees to hang upside down while pollinating, shaking the pollen out. Found across eastern Washington, this distinctive plant often grows near ponderosa pine.

Below and to your left (east) is the town of Winthrop. The trail traverses the flank of Patterson Mountain, crossing open meadows filled with many of the flowers already identified. **Nuttall's larkspur**, also called **common larkspur**, is a member of the delphinium family whose purple butterflylike blossoms are found across much of eastern Washington. A large dandelion-type flower with a single yellow head, **microseris** grows from here eastward to Wyoming.

At mile 2.0, a marked trail on the left will take you on a 1.0-mile round-trip hike to the summit of Patterson Mountain, where views of the surrounding area are superb. After you return from the summit, go left at this junction to complete the loop. The snow-covered peaks of the Lake Chelan–Sawtooth Wilderness line the southern horizon. As you round the mountain, Patterson Lake becomes visible

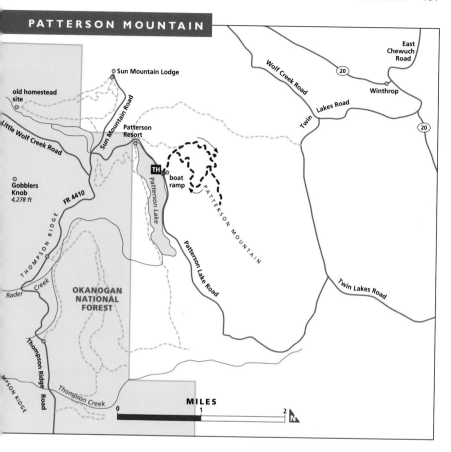

below. Consider a stop here, as this is a great picnic and photography spot, with yellow balsamroot meadows streaming down the hillside. Late April and early May are the best times to catch these immense fields of balsamroot in bloom.

Continuing downhill, you'll pass a gigantic ponderosa pine and a small grove of stunted, twisted aspen. **Serviceberry**, a large shrub with white blossoms, flowers in late April and early May. The open meadows continue with flowers already seen, but bloom time occurs a little earlier here on the warmer, south-facing slopes than elsewhere on the mountain.

Wildflower
Hike 18

Meadowlark–Blue Jay

Ponderosa pines shade arrowleaf balsamroot on Thompson Ridge

Trail Rating	Easy
Trail Length	4.6-mile loop
Location	Okanogan National Forest, west of Winthrop
Elevation	3,000 to 3,300 feet
Bloom Season	April to late July
Peak Bloom	Late April to late May
Contact	Sun Mountain Lodge Outdoor Center, (800) 572-0493, ext. 735
Directions	From Winthrop, head south on WA 20. Just after leaving the center of town, the highway crosses the Methow River. Immediately after the bridge, turn right on Twin Lakes Road. Drive 3.5 miles and turn right on Patterson Lake Road at the Sun Mountain sign. Travel 5.3 miles to FR 4410, also known as Thompson Ridge Road. Turn left here and follow the gravel road 1.5 miles. Look for a small pullout on the left and a sign for the Inside Passage Trail.

With a perfect mix of meadow and forest, much of this route is gentle and open enough for cross-country rambles—and what a great place for picnicking and bird watching! This easy loop starts out on the Inside Passage Trail, picks up the Meadowlark Trail, then loops on the Blue Jay Trail before hooking back up with Meadowlark and ending on the Inside Passage Trail. Mountain bikers also use these trails. Maps of this area are available at Sun Mountain Lodge or in town at Winthrop Mountain Sports.

From the trailhead, follow the Inside Passage Trail into the woods. In 100 yards, the Lower Inside Passage Trail takes off to the left, and in another 100 yards, Pete's Dragon Trail departs to the right. You, however, want to stay straight, keeping to the main Inside Passage Trail. You'll cross Rader Creek, a rich riparian habitat of aspen, river birch, alder, and pink-flowered **Nootka rose**. Listen for chickadees, nut-hatches, and song sparrows.

Just after the stream crossing, the Upper Inside Passage Trail goes right while the main trail curves left. Stay left, as this is the official beginning of the Meadowlark Trail. Traveling uphill along a cooler north-facing slope, you'll pass through mixed forest of Douglas fir and ponderosa pine. Look for **ballhead waterleaf** with tiny flowers forming bluish purple globes. **Long-flowered bluebell** has clusters of tube-shaped, blue to pink blossoms. **Prairie star** grows 8 to 10 inches tall and shows five small white petals, each tipped with three fingerlike lobes.

At mile 0.25, the trail begins to round a ridge and then breaks out into open slopes where you'll see showy yellow flowers. **Arrowleaf balsamroot**, king of the foothills with its giant sunflowers and leaves, is prevalent along much of the trail. **Gray's** and **narrow-leaved desert-parsley** both have umbellate flower heads made of tiny yellow blossoms. Another sun dweller, **western butterweed**, or **western groundsel**, displays

DOUGLAS' BRODIAEA
Brodiaea douglasii

HEIGHT: 16" to 28"

BLOOMS: Late April to early June

A member of the lily family, Douglas' brodiaea reveals a cluster of trumpetlike blue or lavender flowers that grow at the top of a thin stem. Dark lines extend down the middle of the petals. The plant bears only two slender leaves.

Brodiaea, also known as triteleia, has a lily bulb with excellent nutritional value, which American Indians ate raw or boiled. Douglas' brodiaea grows in dry, open areas alongside sagebrush and ponderosa pine.

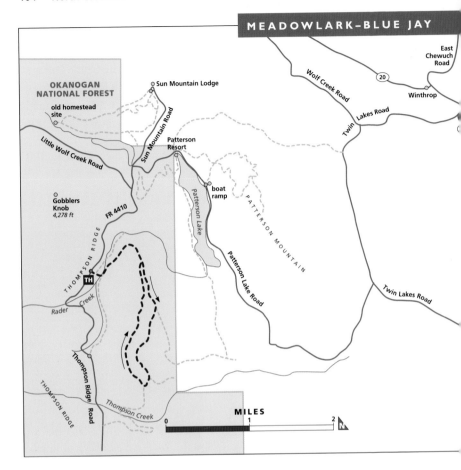

clusters of yellow ray flowers on 20- to 30-inch stems. Views open to distant snow-covered mountains, including 8,470-foot Big Craggy Peak to the north and 8,242-foot Tiffany Mountain to the northeast.

Serviceberry, a shrub common in open areas, can reach 20 feet tall. It blooms early, showing clusters of five-petaled white blossoms. Another white-flowering shrub, **syringa**, blooms later, usually in early summer, when it puts forth wonderfully fragrant blossoms. **Chokecherry**, a small tree, has fuzzy white caterpillarlike blossoms.

At mile 0.6, you'll reach a junction with the Blue Jay Trail. Go left, following the Blue Jay Trail on a 3.4-mile loop that ends back at this junction. **Western spring beauty** is common in the open forest, growing low to the ground with five white petals. An early bloomer, **desert shooting star** displays upward arching pink petals and a yellow ring around its protruding anther tube.

You'll soon come to large meadows with many of the flowers already noted. Blue to purple **silky** and **prairie lupine**, members of the pea family, bloom here in mid- to late May. Found throughout eastern Washington, **Nuttall's** or **common larkspur** has five showy purple petals. Look east for excellent views across the valley to the rounded hump of Patterson Mountain.

At a marked junction, follow the Blue Jay Trail to the right. The trail soon enters the largest meadow yet, thick with arrowleaf balsamroot and lupine. Large ponderosa pines provide a bit of shade for ballhead waterleaf and **Douglas' brodiaea**, whose blue or lavender trumpets point horizontally from stem tops.

Grass widow has delicate pink to purple disks and often blooms in April, along with **yellow bell**, which looks like its name.

Entering woods once more, the trail soon passes a small pond on the right. Look for wildlife tracks around this shallow body of water, which is filling in with water grasses. Cream-colored **death camas** grows here; its leaves and bulbs are very poisonous.

Arrowleaf balsamroot, Sun Mountain Lodge area

The trail climbs a small hill and enters a burn area where the yellow ray flowers of **heart-leaf arnica** brighten the landscape. Arnica, and lupine too, thrive in areas where fire has opened up the forest floor. The Forest Service conducts controlled burns to reduce the buildup of material that fuels forest fires, like the huge fires that have burned in the Chelan area. The area along this part of the trail is now recovering with lush forest vegetation.

Back into open meadows, the trail gently climbs to meet with the Meadowlark Trail. Turn right here. It is a little more than a mile of gradual downhill to reach the junction where the loop began. Most flowers observed along the Blue Jay Trail also reside along the Meadowlark Trail. Back at the loop junction, stay left. You'll soon reach Rader Creek and the parking area on Thompson Ridge Road. Just up the road is the Sun Mountain Lodge, a wonderful log lodge with great food and plenty of recreation options.

*Wildflower
Hike 19* # Freezeout Ridge

Freezeout Ridge, Okanogan National Forest

Trail Rating	Moderate
Trail Length	6 miles round trip
Location	Okanogan National Forest, northeast of Winthrop
Elevation	6,580 to 8,242 feet
Bloom Season	July to late August
Peak Bloom	Mid-July to early August
Contact	Okanogan National Forest, Tonasket Ranger District Office, (509) 486-2186
Directions	From Winthrop, drive north on East Chewuch Road, following the signs to Pearrygin Lake State Park. Pass the state park turnoff at Bear Creek Road. At 6.6 miles past Winthrop, just before the Chewuch River bridge, turn right on FR 37. Set your odometer. From here, it is 16.2 miles to the trailhead, with a number of junctions along the way.
	At mile 1.2, stay on FR 37, which branches right. At mile 7.5, keep right again, continuing east on FR 37. At mile 13.0, go left (north) onto FR 39, toward Tiffany Spring Campground. After passing Roger Lake on the right at mile 14.5, continue another 1.7 miles to a parking area at Freezeout Pass, 6,580 feet. The trailhead is across the road to the west.

The trail to Freezeout Ridge provides quick and relatively easy access to expansive views and broad subalpine meadows. A half-mile climb to the top of Tiffany Mountain makes this hike a 6.0-mile round trip. Freezeout Ridge is dry and receives lots of sun, so blooms are best following a wet winter. Most years, the early flowers begin blooming in early July and continue through August until the first hard freeze, which can come early at this elevation.

While not steep like many hikes in Washington's mountains, Freezeout Ridge has the wonderful open feel of a peak ascent. The oft-deserted trail ascends gradually most of the way, with a few short, steeper pitches, making it an excellent hike for children.

Beginning at a saddle at 6,580 feet, the Freezeout Ridge Trail (Trail No. 345) climbs gently through a forest of lodgepole pine and Douglas fir. Several types of yellow ray flowers dwell along the trail in the first 2.0 miles. Preferring partial shade, **heart-leaf arnica** grows 10 to 16 inches tall. Standing 6 to 8 inches high, **alpine golden daisy** has 30 to 70 yellow rays. Also look for **Elmer's butterweed**, 6 to 20 inches tall with up to 10 yellow ray flowers per plant. **Lyall's goldenweed** is a low-growing dandelion-type flower. Another flower found on this dry, rocky ridge, **lance-leaved stonecrop** has small yellow petals and fuzzy, projecting stamens.

There are about two dozen kinds of **lupine** in Washington, and their blue spiky blossoms are often the most noticeable in subalpine meadows. **Small-flowered penstemon** has whorls of purple flowers, usually on 16- to 24-inch stems, although it does not grow that tall in this harsh environment. Similar looking but with wider leaves, **Ryberg's penstemon** grows here, at the northwest edge of its Rocky Mountain range. With blue to lavender

THREAD-LEAVED SANDWORT
Arenaria capillaris

HEIGHT: 3" to 6"

BLOOMS: June to August

Thread-leaved sandwort's slender stem bears tiny, delicate white flowers with five petals and 10 stamens. One striking characteristic is its three purplish sepals. Long needlelike leaves form a dense mat. From the Cascades to the Rockies, thread-leaved sandwort grows abundantly in arid areas at higher elevations.

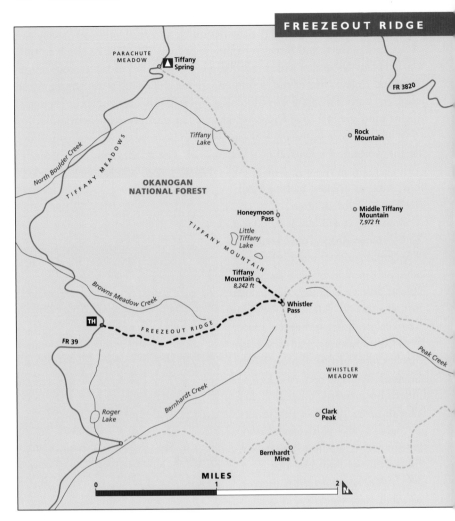

FREEZEOUT RIDGE

PARACHUTE MEADOW
Tiffany Spring

FR 3820

Tiffany Lake

North Boulder Creek

TIFFANY MEADOWS

Rock Mountain

OKANOGAN NATIONAL FOREST

Honeymoon Pass

Middle Tiffany Mountain 7,972 ft

TIFFANY MOUNTAIN

Little Tiffany Lake

Tiffany Mountain 8,242 ft

Browns Meadow Creek

Whistler Pass

TH

FREEZEOUT RIDGE

Peak Creek

FR 39

WHISTLER MEADOW

Bernhardt Creek

Roger Lake

Clark Peak

Bernhardt Mine

MILES

0   1   2

trumpet-shaped flowers, **elegant Jacob's-ladder** grows 6 inches tall and has compound leaves resembling ferns.

Around mile 1.0, the forest begins to open up. A common flower, **thread-leaved sandwort** generates a small white five-petaled blossom and grasslike leaves. **Wild strawberry** is also common, a miniature of the garden variety. Also found at elevations lower than this, **old-man's whiskers** has unusual-looking pink globes that are enclosed by several arching sepals. **Diverse-leaved cinque-foil** displays bright yellow disklike flowers made up of five petals; it also has five to seven deeply toothed leaves and averages 10 to 12 inches in height.

At mile 1.5, you'll reach the open meadows of Freezeout Ridge, with pockets of subalpine fir. The trail travels through flowered and grassy meadows with a scattering of granite boulders. Roger Lake lies to the south, in the forest below, where there is a primitive campground. Buckwheats are prevalent in this dry, rocky ridge habitat. **Umbrella buckwheat** shows cream-colored flowers in a ball-shaped umbel, along with a low mat of bright green leaves. **Oval-leaf buckwheat** has a similar flower head, usually cream-colored but occasionally yellow or reddish, but distinctly different light green leaves.

Tiffany Mountain rises ahead to the left. Although it looks like a large rounded hill, at 8,242 feet it is one of the highest peaks in the area. Lying in the rain shadow of the Cascades, it receives an average of only 15 inches of precipitation annually. Some of the plants that dwell in the dry soils here are also found in the low-elevation desert areas of eastern Washington. With bright red bracts and alternating narrow leaves on a stem an average of 20 inches tall, **scarlet paintbrush** is abundant along the ridge. **Harebell** also thrives in this dry environment, showing a delicate hanging blue flower. Look for lacy white **yarrow**, which has soft, fringed leaves. **Cushion fleabane**, often found with sagebrush in eastern Washington, grows about 6 inches tall and has purple rays, yellow disks, and tufts of narrow paddle-shaped leaves.

At mile 2.5, the trail divides. For a 5.0-mile round-trip hike, turn around here. Otherwise, continue left along a more obvious path, which heads toward the summit of Tiffany Mountain on a steeper 0.5-mile uphill climb. (The faint track to the right heads to the saddle at Whistler Pass.) Fewer flowers reside in the rocky soil and harsh conditions of this lofty elevation, where grasses now begin to dominate. **Pink mountain heather**, an evergreen with pink hanging bells and needlelike leaves, grows at the base of the mountain. Able to tolerate the extreme environment along the ridge, **rock** or **cliff penstemon** splashes the landscape with bright pink tubular flowers. Also a survivor on this stony, windswept ridge, **spreading phlox** grows low to the ground, revealing pink, lavender, or white blossoms.

A fire lookout once perched on the summit, and the views here are indeed expansive. To the east are the foothills and farmland of the Okanogan River valley. Look west to see the snowfields on Gardner Mountain, Mt. Ballard, Robinson Mountain, and many others. To the north, 530,000-acre Pasayten Wilderness is one of the state's largest, stretching west to North Cascades National Park and north to Canada. You are now standing at 8,242 feet. If this peak were located farther west in the Cascade Range, it would be covered with glaciers.

*Wildflower
Hike 20*

Iron Goat

*Alders along the
Iron Goat Trail,
Mt. Baker–
Snoqualmie
National Forest*

The Iron Goat Trail (Trail No. 1074) differs from other trails in this book. Because it remains in a forest setting the entire route, you will not find the showy floral displays typical of the high meadows. Instead, you'll enjoy an array of subtle forest flowers. If you choose to hike farther east toward the Wellington Trailhead, you'll discover some more conspicuous blossoms in the open habitat of avalanche chutes.

The route follows an old railroad grade, making this gradual hike a good choice for both young and old. Free of snow long before the high country opens up, the lower trail (near the Martin Creek Trailhead) is usually accessible in May; the upper trail (near the Wellington Trailhead) opens around June.

Trail Rating	Easy
Trail Length	2.6 miles round trip
Location	Mt. Baker–Snoqualmie National Forest, east of Skykomish
Elevation	2,400 to 2,600 feet
Bloom Season	April to late August
Peak Bloom	May to early July
Contact	Mt. Baker–Snoqualmie National Forest, Skykomish Ranger District Office, (360) 677-2414
Directions	After stopping at the Skykomish Ranger District Office to pick up a map, drive east from Skykomish on US 2 for 6.0 miles. At milepost 55, go east on the Old Cascade Highway (FR 67), which parallels US 2. At 2.3 miles, turn left on FR 6710 and proceed 1.4 miles to the Martin Creek Trailhead.

Available at the Skykomish ranger station, a brochure for the hike gives a brief history and a map of the area. In the late 1800s, the Great Northern Railway was completed over Stevens Pass, marking the first crossing of the Cascades and connecting St. Paul, Minnesota, with Seattle. This amazing engineering feat opened areas of the Pacific Northwest to settlement and trade.

Winter was a difficult time to travel by rail. Deep snow sometimes delayed trains for days. In 1910, one of the worst railroad disasters in history took place when two trains, stopped by weather, were swept away by an avalanche on Windy Mountain. Nearly 100 lives were lost. To bypass this dangerous section of track, the Cascade Tunnel, the longest railroad tunnel in the United States, was built in 1929. The abandoned railroad right-of-way is now the Iron Goat Trail. Pieces of metal and glass are scattered along the route, but please leave them where they are so that other hikers can view these artifacts.

The Iron Goat Trail is accessible from several trailheads, but this hike starts from the Martin Creek Trailhead. Near this trailhead is a spring. Look here for **large-leaved avens**, with five separated yellow petals surrounding a greenish center and strawberrylike leaves on stems 1 to 3 feet tall. Tall stems of pink to purple **fireweed** bloom here, too. The showy **red columbine** displays upward-arching scarlet petals and long yellow stamens.

The Iron Goat Trail quickly enters a mature alder forest where several flowering shrubs dwell. **Thimbleberry** presents papery five-petaled white blossoms and large maplelike leaves; in late summer it bears edible thimble-shaped red berries. **Salmonberry** has toothed leaves and reddish pink blossoms about 1 inch wide.

An encounter with the thorny branches of **devils club** is one you won't soon forget. This armored plant reveals huge 14-inch leaves and small, barely noticeable whitish green flowers; in late summer, look for a cone of bright red berries.

STAR-FLOWERED FALSE SOLOMON'S SEAL
Smilacina stellata

HEIGHT: 1' to 2'

BLOOMS: April to June

Star-flowered false Solomon's seal, a delicate perennial, boasts tiny star-shaped white flowers. Like all members of the lily family, its thin, flat leaves are alternating and bear noticeable veins. The plant produces greenish yellow berries that change to a dark blue or reddish black at maturity.

Solomon's seal flourishes in nitrogenous soils and can be found throughout the state in moist forest clearings, valley bottoms, and among low shrubs. It was once believed that nosebleeds could be cured through contact with Solomon's seal. A cough syrup was made from the roots, which were collected in the fall.

Oregon grape, another shrub, has clusters of yellow flowers, hollylike leaves, and, later in the season, it produces small grapelike berries that are deep blue in color. Ferns are prevalent along this section of trail.

Forest flowers are often small and white—very different from many of the showy subalpine species. **False lily-of-the-valley** matures a spike of white clustered blossoms above glossy, heart-shaped leaves. Abundant in forest openings, **queen's cup** reveals a single six-petaled, star-shaped flower and tonguelike basal leaves. **Star-flowered false Solomon's seal**, also with six petals, develops an elegant mat of long, slender leaves. **Trillium**, another common plant here, has three pointed white petals that turn purplish with age. The forest canopy includes hemlock, bigleaf maple, red alder, and Douglas fir.

At mile 0.2 there is a junction; go straight. (The path to the left leads to the upper section of the Iron Goat Trail.) For the next 0.25 mile you'll come upon a number of edible plants, but remember never to sample any without positive identification. **Wild ginger** has a brownish flower with three pointed petals ending in long, slender tails. American Indians used its roots and the round evergreen leaves for medicinal purposes. **Miner's lettuce**, which early prospectors discovered

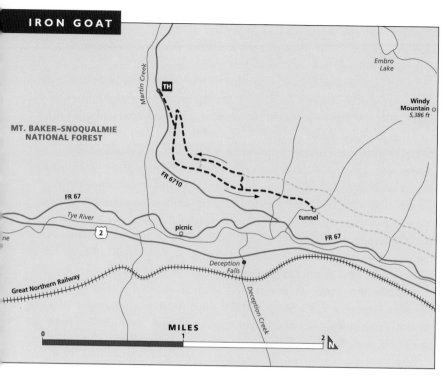

IRON GOAT

made a good salad, displays small five-petaled white blossoms; its two opposing leaves form a saucer around the stem. **Wild strawberry**, a miniature of the garden variety, sprouts small white flowers and pea-sized berries. Sometimes used to make jam, **elderberry** grows about 10 feet tall with clusters of white flowers.

Generally, the Iron Goat Trail follows the direction of the Tye River, passing areas where immigrants from Japan, Scandinavia, Ireland, Germany, and the Philippines once camped. In the 1890s, nearly 6,000 men immigrated to the Pacific Northwest, many of them working for the Great Northern Railway, building the railroad or, later, maintaining the tracks.

At 0.6 mile from the trailhead, you'll come to another junction, this one with a connector trail that switchbacks up a hill to reach the upper section of the Iron Goat Trail. Continue straight on the lower Iron Goat Trail route, which will lead you 0.7 mile from this junction to a dead end at mile 1.3, your turn-around point for this 2.6-mile round-trip hike. As you proceed along the lower Iron Goat Trail from the junction with the connector trail, you can hear the Tye River as it rushes below on the right.

At mile 1.3, the trail reaches an old tunnel. As of this printing, this is as far as you can hike on the Iron Goat Trail's lower section. (Construction to extend the trail is planned; check at the Skykomish ranger station for current trail status.) Return the way you came, or turn right at the last junction and head uphill on the connector trail. When you reach the upper Iron Goat Trail, a left returns you to the Martin Creek Trailhead; this option adds an extra 0.2 to the total mileage.

For yet another option, a right turn on the upper Iron Goat Trail takes you east to the Wellington Trailhead, 6.0 miles away. Along this portion of the upper trail, you'll see where several avalanche chutes have created openings in the forest. In these sunlit clearings you'll find fireweed, lacy **yarrow**, and white-flowering **pearly everlasting**. Yellow-orange **tiger lily**, or **Columbia lily**, grows in open areas. Lavender, pink, or purple **foxglove** displays many funnel-shaped flowers on 2- to 6-foot-tall stems. The red bracts of **Indian paintbrush** brighten the avalanche chutes. **Showy** and **leafy aster** both have lavender rays around yellow centers; showy aster has toothed leaves, whereas those of leafy aster are smooth. **Slender hawksbeard** presents small yellow ray flowers. Thimbleberry and **mountain ash**, the latter with rounded clusters of off-white blossoms, often join bracken fern to form dense undergrowth.

In shady forest areas, **clasping twistedstalk** bears distinctive white bell-shaped blossoms. **Foamflower, fringecup,** and **one-sided wintergreen** display small white flowers. **Youth-on-age** derives its name from small new leaves growing from the base of old ones. Its flower is brownish and tube-shaped.

The trail passes around several tunnels along the way to Wellington Trailhead. These are unsafe to enter, so please curb your curiosity. Going all the way to the Wellington Trailhead and back to the Martin Creek Trailhead is 14.0 miles round trip. With a little advance planning, you can do a 7.0-mile shuttle hike by dropping a car off at the Wellington Trailhead beforehand. The trailhead is accessible via the Old Cascade Highway (FR 67); inquire at the Skykomish ranger station for directions, a map, and further information.

Leavenworth Ski Hill

CENTRAL CASCADES
AND MT. RAINIER
NATIONAL PARK

*Wildflower
Hike 21*

*Desert parsley and lupine at Leavenworth Ski Hill,
Wenatchee National Forest*

Easy	**Trail Rating**
0.6-mile loop	**Trail Length**
Wenatchee National Forest, north of Leavenworth	**Location**
1,440 to 1,500 feet	**Elevation**
April to late July	**Bloom Season**
Late April to early June	**Peak Bloom**
Wenatchee National Forest, Leavenworth Ranger District Office, (509) 548-6977	**Contact**
After stopping at the ranger station in Leavenworth for a map and flower list, turn north on Ski Hill Drive at the west end of town. Drive 1.5 miles. As the road makes a sharp curve east, the Leavenworth Ski Hill lot is on the left.	**Directions**

Cross-country ski trails by winter, flower trails by spring and summer. Near the unique Bavarian-style town of Leavenworth, the network of trails at Leavenworth Ski Hill displays impressive floral shows in April, May, and June. Although you might feel lost at times with the numerous junctions, the area's cross-country trails eventually lead back to the trailhead at the parking lot near the ski lodge. Most of the way is fairly gradual, through open ponderosa pine forest. Mountain bikers also use these trails, so you might want to hike here on a weekday when use is minimal.

Near the trailhead, yellow **arrowleaf balsamroot** blooms conspicuously in May. The big sunflower heads and large, pale green, flame-shaped leaves are a common sight across much of eastern Washington and the Cascade foothills. **Mule's ear** has a very similar flower, but its leaves are a darker shade of green. Several kinds of desert-parsley grow here, also near the trailhead. All with sprays of tiny flowers arranged in umbellate heads, **fern-leaved**, **narrow-leaved**, and **barestem desert-parsley** have distinctly different leaves. **Lupine** blossoms in May. This flower, a member of the pea family, adds nitrogen to the soil, and varieties are found from the Washington desert all the way up to 7,000 feet in the Cascade Range. Two other pea family members reside in the area. **Purple peavine** sprouts blossoms that are almost lost in its numerous leaflets. Purple flowers lined in a row mature on the trailing vines of **woolly vetch**.

From the trailhead, take the trail to the right and hike east, paralleling Ski Hill Drive to the right. Ponderosa pine mixes with Douglas fir; bigleaf maple and Douglas maple grow in the

LONG-FLOWERED BLUEBELL
Mertensia longiflora

HEIGHT: 2" to 6"
BLOOMS: Late April to early May

Named after F. C. Mertens, a German botanist, *Mertensia longiflora*, or long-flowered bluebell, resides in dry places. Found predominantly east of the Cascades, this common flower often grows alongside sagebrush and ponderosa pine, under the shelter of trees or bushes.

The tubular blossoms of the long-flowered bluebell resemble the garden-variety forget-me-not, only with longer flowers of a light purple to blue hue. Heavy blossoms often bend the stems, making the flowers look like elongated bells. The plant has broad, alternate leaves.

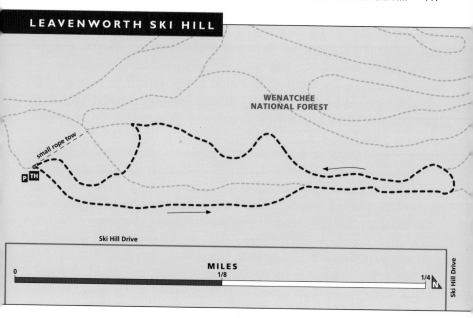

understory. Several flowering trees and shrubs extend along much of the trail. **Serviceberry** is technically a shrub, but the large 15-footers are quite treelike. Its clusters of white blossoms coincide with the bloom time of balsamroot. American Indians mixed the edible berries with meat to make pemmican, a staple food. You will also see **thimbleberry** along much of the trail, with five tissuelike white petals and large maplelike leaves. In late summer, the bush produces an edible thimble-shaped berry, but remember not to eat trailside plants without absolute identification. Another plentiful shrub, **wild rose** produces pink blossoms with yellow stamens and, later in the season, a vitamin C–rich rosehip.

At mile 0.2, a trail comes in from the left, but continue straight. The trail leads east, then curves 180 degrees to head west toward the downhill area. (As the trail begins to curve, you'll reach a junction with another trail leading to the right, the beginning of a 0.2-mile loop. Stay left at this junction to remain on the route described here.)

Several types of yellow flowers are common in the open forest. Cinquefoils have five pale to deep yellow petals around a mass of stamens. **Sticky cinquefoil**, **graceful cinquefoil**, and **silverweed** are three varieties along the trail. **Silvercrown** grows to 4 feet tall with bristly yellow ray heads. Presenting many flowers with 5 to 12 rays each, **western butterweed**, or **western groundsel**, is another common yellow blossom in late May or early June. **Yellow salsify** displays a yellow ray flower and a large dandelionlike seed head. **Heart-leaf arnica**, another composite, has 10 to 15 rays and heart-shaped leaves.

The path cuts through forest, passing several smallish white flowers. **Woodland star**, also known as **prairie star**, bears several white blossoms with five-fingered petals. **Miner's lettuce**, also with five white petals, has edible, saucer-shaped leaves. Growing around 6 inches tall, **western spring beauty** is yet another small white, five-petaled flower found along the trail. Sprouting veined, lance-shaped leaves, **star-flowered false Solomon's seal** bears six-petaled blossoms. **Wild strawberry** has flowers and fruit that are miniatures of the garden variety. **Long-flowered bluebell** sports clusters of tubular blossoms, blue to pinkish in color.

Quite a few members of the lily family dwell along the trail, many with edible bulbs. Blooming early, **glacier lily** displays arching yellow petals and exposed stamens and anthers. **Yellow bell** is another early-blooming yellow lily, with hanging bell-shaped blossoms. An unusual flower, **chocolate** or **checker lily** reveals a large, brownish bell-shaped flower with green and yellow mottling. The **mariposa lily** has an elegant white flower.

At mile 0.4, **orange honeysuckle** bears clusters of skinny tubular blossoms. Round purple flower heads mature on **ballhead waterleaf**. Growing hollylike leaves, **Oregon grape** sprouts fragrant yellow blossoms in June. This evergreen is common along the route. Averaging 10 to 20 feet tall in this vicinity, two small white-flowering trees, **chokecherry** and **bitter cherry**, bloom in late May or June.

At mile 0.5, you'll come to a junction with a trail leading left; turn left here. The trail drops into the ski area meadows, where sun-loving plants thrive. **Sticky geranium** hosts a lovely pink blossom. **Harsh paintbrush** displays brilliant red-orange bracts. **Showy phlox** produces bouquets of fragrant five-petaled pink flowers. Cinquefoil and western butterweed add yellow to the meadow. **Corn lily**, or **false hellebore**, displays large, veined leaves and off-white blossoms on spreading branches. You will also see the purple-blue blossoms of **Nuttall's larkspur**.

In addition to hiking the cross-country ski trails, you can also make several loops on the downhill slopes, where you'll see many of the same flowering plants and get more of a workout. A trail toward the top of the small rope tow leads to some nice displays of balsamroot, lupine, larkspur, and desert-parsley.

Esmerelda Basin

Paintbrush dots a meadow in Esmerelda Basin, Wenatchee National Forest

Except for the steep first quarter mile, the trail through Esmerelda Basin (Trail No. 1394) is fairly level, making it a fine walk for children. There are plenty of streams along the way if you want to filter drinking water. This hike reaches Fortune Cookie Pass in 3.0 miles, then returns to the trailhead on the same trail. The trailhead is also the departure point for the trail to Ingalls Pass, which enters the Alpine Lakes Wilderness on its way to Lake Ingalls and on to Stuart Pass—another fantastic hike.

The signed trail begins on the east side of the parking area. **Yarrow** is common here, bearing lacy white blossoms and feathery leaves. Another common trailside plant, **pearly everlasting** has paperlike white ball-shaped

Trail Rating	Moderate
Trail Length	6 miles round trip
Location	Wenatchee National Forest, north of Cle Elum
Elevation	4,270 to 5,900 feet
Bloom Season	June to late September
Peak Bloom	July
Contact	Wenatchee National Forest, Cle Elum Ranger District Office, (509) 674-4411
Directions	From the town of Cle Elum, exit I-90 just east of town (Exit 85). Take WA 970 east for 2.0 miles. At a junction, stay left on WA 970. Proceed 4.0 miles to another junction and turn left (north) on Teanaway Road. Drive 7.0 miles and go right onto North Fork Teanaway Road. This road becomes FR 9737 when it enters Wenatchee National Forest. Follow the signs for Esmerelda Basin Trail, which is at the end of the road, 22.0 miles from WA 970.

flowers growing in clumps of many stems. **Cascade penstemon**, an icon of these mountainous areas, displays clusters of deep bluish purple, tube-shaped flowers.

The trail follows the upper North Fork of the Teanaway River, small but lively as it cascades over a series of falls. Near the top of the cascade, look for **heart-leaf arnica** sprouting a beautiful yellow sunflower head and wide, rounded leaves. Another yellow composite, **Elmer's butterweed** exhibits a cluster of up to 10 flower heads on each 8- to 20-inch stem. In nearby rocky areas, **spreading phlox** shows a thick bouquet of pink to lavender blossoms early in the season.

At mile 0.5, you'll reach a junction with the trail to Ingalls Pass, Lake Ingalls, and Stuart Pass. (This trail leads steeply up a long rocky slope to Ingalls Pass, which offers incredible views of 9,415-foot Mt. Stuart and Alpine Lakes Wilderness, a 393,000-acre preserve with more than 700 lakes and tarns and 450 miles of trails.) Stay left at this signed junction to enter the more mild-mannered Esmerelda Basin.

Look for **Queen Anne's lace**, a relative of the common carrot, which has flat to slightly rounded white flower heads that contain 20 or more small blossoms. **Thimbleberry** is prevalent here, sprouting large maplelike leaves and papery five-petaled white blossoms. **Showy aster** blooms along much of the trail, showing many flower heads, each with about 20 rays and a yellow center.

Several brilliant red flowers will attract your attention. **Red columbine**, which has five scarlet petals arching back from a cluster of protruding yellow stamens, also attracts the attention of hummingbirds. A delicate flower, **scarlet gilia**, or **skyrocket**, shows a cluster of trumpet-shaped flowers that often keep blooming well into fall. The bright red bracts of **Indian paintbrush** are also noticeable along much of the route.

The trail crosses many small streams in early summer. I lost track after counting 10 or 11 crossings. Each rivulet waters its own mini-habitat of flowers. Look for the white, cylinder-shaped flower heads of **American bistort** near these streams. **Yellow monkey-flower** also dwells in extremely moist areas, blanketing the ground with low-growing yellow trumpets. Another water-seeker, **elephant's head** looks quite odd, revealing stalks covered with tiny blossoms shaped like the great animal's ears and trunk. Horsetail, an ancient plant, resembles miniature bamboo with segmented, erect stems.

Flowers, many of which you've already encountered on this hike, continue along the trail as it ascends a gradual slope. Low-growing **shrubby penstemon** is a woody-stemmed plant that shows pairs of pink to lavender, trumpet-shaped flowers and small oval leaves. Commonly used in garden landscaping, **shrubby cinquefoil** grows 1 to 4 feet tall and has five-petaled, disk-shaped yellow blossoms. In dry, rocky areas, look for **stonecrop**, with 5 pointed petals and 10 protruding stamens; its small leaves are fleshy and brownish in color. Seven or eight species of stonecrop exist in Washington. American Indians used the edible leaves of stonecrop medicinally.

In areas of open forest, look for elegant **Queen's cup**, with one six-petaled white flower above shiny, tonguelike leaves. White-flowering **wild strawberry** and yellow heart-leaf arnica also grow in the open forest.

Just a little past mile 1.0, the trail passes a football field–sized meadow

SCARLET GILIA OR SKYROCKET
Gilia aggregata

HEIGHT: 8" to 18"
BLOOMS: May to July

A member of the phlox family, scarlet gilia bears vibrant trumpet-shaped flowers, with many blossoms on a single stem. Hummingbirds seek out these tubular flowers. Also known as skyrocket, scarlet gilia has lobed, thin leaves near its base.

American Indians used an infusion of scarlet gilia as a laxative and a fever medication. Scarlet gilia resides in many habitats, from the dry ponderosa pine zone to open sites at fairly high elevations in the Cascades. The flower might be blooming into late September or early October.

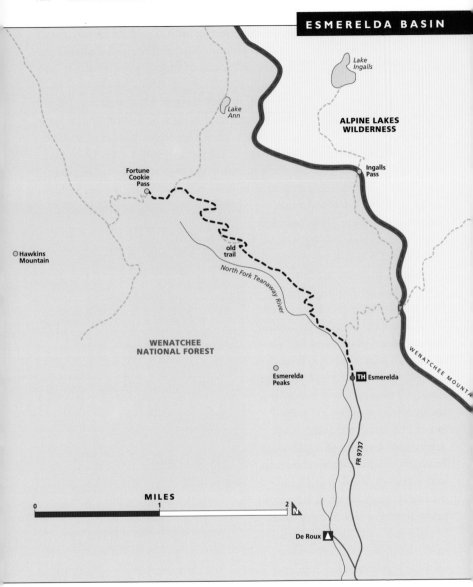

ESMERELDA BASIN

on the left, the first true meadow you come upon. Look for the lavender ray flowers of **Cascade aster** and the vivid bracts of **magenta paintbrush**. With clusters of yellow ray flowers and sawtoothed, arrow-shaped leaves, **Canadian butterweed** is one of several butterweeds in the area. **Cottongrass**, plentiful in the meadow, has fluffy seed heads resembling cotton. The exotic **white bog-orchid** displays fragrant, wing-tipped white blossoms on thick stalks. Purple **subalpine thistle** can grow to 6 feet tall. Yellow **mountain arnica**, a kind of sunflower, also brightens the meadow.

Glacier lily blooms early in the summer, after the snowmelt, displaying hanging blossoms with arching yellow petals and protruding stamens. **Shooting star**, another elegant inhabitant of moist areas, shows fuchsia blossoms around an anther tube. Also maturing early, **spring beauty** displays low-growing, five-petaled white flowers. **Pasqueflower**, or **western anemone**, usually pushes up through the snow, producing star-shaped white blossoms followed later in the summer by shaggy seed heads.

At mile 1.4, the main trail leads right. (An old trail on the left is blocked.) The trail switchbacks through forest and then opens onto a dry hillside where the creamy white, fuzzy-looking blossoms of **buckwheat** are abundant. The trail crosses several more streams. Look for **mountain blue-eyed grass**, with six small lavender petals around yellow centers. Leafless with lavender penstemon-like blossoms, the parasitic **naked broomrape** attaches to plants such as stonecrop and saxifrage.

Between miles 1.6 and 2.0, several small openings host many of the meadow flowers previously noted, along with some new ones. **False hellebore** has green-tinted white blossoms and large, beautiful veined leaves. The delicate blue hanging bells of **harebell** decorate the forest's edge. Lovely but poisonous, **monkshood** displays lobed purple blossoms. **Diverse-leaved cinquefoil** is striking, with disk-shaped yellow blossoms and serrated, strawberrylike leaves.

The trail climbs now, mainly through forest, for 0.8 mile on its way to Fortune Cookie Pass. At a signed junction just before the pass, continue straight another 0.2 mile to the pass. (A right at the junction leads north 1.2 miles to Lake Ann.) The meadows around the pass feature many of the flowers you have already seen along the way. In midsummer, you'll see especially good displays of **Sitka valerian**—with its rounded, dense cluster of small white to pink blossoms—as well as Indian paintbrush, bistort, yarrow, and arnica. These open areas make a great place for a picnic or even a nap. And the way home is all downhill.

Wildflower
Hike 23

Noble Knob

Noble Knob, Norse Peak Wilderness

Trail Rating	Moderate
Trail Length	7 miles round trip
Location	Mt. Baker–Snoqualmie National Forest, southeast of Enumclaw
Elevation	5,700 to 6,011 feet
Bloom Season	June to late September
Peak Bloom	July to late August
Contact	Mt. Baker–Snoqualmie National Forest, Snoqualmie Ranger District Office, (360) 825-6585
Directions	From Enumclaw, drive east on WA 410 for 18.0 miles to the tiny town of Greenwater. Continue on WA 410 for 13.3 miles and look for a small sign for Corral Pass on the left. Turn left here and climb FR 7174 for 6.0 steep, bumpy miles to a T junction at Corral Pass (passenger vehicles should have no problem on this road). The right fork leads to a campground, but take the left fork to the end of the road and park at the Noble Knob trailhead.

Hopefully you can hike this trail on a clear day, when views of Mt. Rainier are superb. The Noble Knob Trail (Trail No. 1184) starts from Corral Pass. A spur trail ascends to Noble Knob. You won't find water along the way, although snowfields usually linger well into July. Come supplied with water, food, bug repellant, and a map.

From the signed trailhead, you'll start hiking north into a ridge-top forest. Along the start of the trail, look for huckleberries, which ripen in late August and September. Found in many habitats throughout Washington, **yarrow** sprouts lacy white blossoms and feathery leaves. **Pearly everlasting**, also white, resides in forest clearings and along meadow edges.

By mile 0.6, the trail slips in and out of small meadows, and at mile 1.3 the landscape opens for a long expanse. If you're here in late July or August, you'll find **broadleaf lupine** blooming abundantly, adding blue to the floral mix. This sweet-smelling flower may be the showiest plant in the state's subalpine meadows. In mid- to late summer, look for several kinds of paintbrush in forest clearings and open meadows. The colored bracts of **scarlet** and **magenta paintbrush** add brilliant reds to the scenery; **harsh paintbrush** displays red-orange bracts.

The white cylinder-shaped blooms of **American bistort** appear fuzzy at a distance. Often found growing with bistort and lupine, white **Sitka valerian** bears stamen-fuzzy blossoms on 2-foot-tall stems. The common **thread-leaved sandwort** exhibits small five-petaled, star-shaped white flowers and grasslike leaves. In forest clearings, **beargrass** generates rounded, cone-shaped white flower heads and long grassy leaves.

Yellow blossoms also speckle the landscape. **Arrowleaf butterweed** is the tallest yellow flower, showing a cluster of ray heads and sawtoothed, triangular leaves. Shorter and with fewer blossoms than butterweed, **mountain arnica** has

FAN-LEAVED CINQUEFOIL
Potentilla flabellifolia

HEIGHT: 4" to 12"
BLOOMS: May to August
A member of the rose family, fan-leaved cinquefoil is a spindly plant with deep yellow, buttercup-shaped flowers. Its notched leaves, in groups of three leaflets, grow close to the ground and often form small mats.

A regular of moist subalpine meadows, cinquefoil thrives throughout the Cascades and Olympics. Much like a strawberry plant, it sends out runners in many directions, dominating small patches.

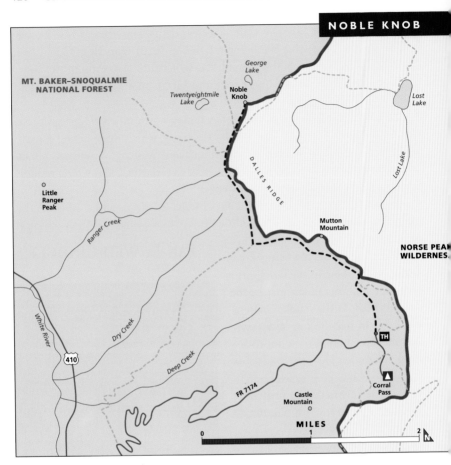

NOBLE KNOB

MT. BAKER–SNOQUALMIE
NATIONAL FOREST

George
Lake

Twentyeightmile
Lake

Noble
Knob

Lost
Lake

DALLES RIDGE

Lost Lake

Little
Ranger
Peak

Ranger Creek

Mutton
Mountain

NORSE PEAK
WILDERNESS

Dry Creek

White River

410

Deep Creek

FR 7174

Castle
Mountain

TH

Corral
Pass

MILES

0   1   2

squared-off petals with toothed tips. Dwelling in shady areas, yellow **heartleaf arnica** has wide, heart-shaped leaves.

Along the ridge, look for cinquefoils with their five-petaled yellow blossoms. **Fan-leaved cinquefoil** generates leaflets in threes, similar to strawberry leaves. **Diverse-leaved cinquefoil** has five to seven leaflets. **Shrubby cinquefoil**, a woody plant with yellow disks and needlelike leaves, often prefers rocky soil.

Several types of asters grow here. With purple ray flowers, a yellow center, and large sawtoothed leaves, **showy aster** prefers open forest and meadow edges. **Leafy bracted aster**, also purple, dwells in open meadows. Growing in open meadows and on rocky slopes, **Cascade aster** presents 6 to 15 widely separated lavender rays. **Alpine aster**, with 15 to 40 blue-purple rays, likes rocky habitats.

Because they are similar to asters, daisies and fleabanes can be tricky to identify. **Cut-leaved fleabane** shows 40 to 60 thin, pink to lavender rays with a yellow center. Look for wider rays on the deep pink to purple **subalpine daisy**. A tiny plant, **dwarf mountain fleabane** displays white or pink rays and resides in dry soils.

A large family, penstemons are common here. The flowers are funnel-shaped and five-lobed, with two of the lobes tilting up and three curving slightly down—creating a landing pad for bees. **Small-flowered penstemon**, which grows in meadows and forest openings, exhibits whorls of purple blossoms with white throats. Penstemons found on rocky slopes are generally woody, grow low to the ground, and often have mats of tiny leaves, helping the plant to preserve heat and block the wind. Rock-dwelling **cliff** and **shrubby penstemon** vary in color from lavender to pink. While most penstemons prefer sunny sites, an exception is **woodland penstemon**, found in the forest with pinkish purple to bluish purple flowers in clusters on leaning stems.

Early in the season, look for the graceful **glacier lily**, which blooms in June with yellow arching petals. **Pasqueflower**, or **western anemone**, also begins blooming soon after snowmelt, opening five creamy white petals around a cluster of yellow stamens. **Snow** or **mountain buttercup** follows the melting snow with glossy yellow saucer-shaped flowers. **Shooting star**, another early bloomer, displays upward pointing fuchsia petals and a black anther tube.

Some distinctive and ostentatious flowers bloom in late summer. **Red columbine** shows off an ornate, scarlet hanging head with large yellow stamens. **Columbia** or **tiger lily** dazzles with spotted yellow-orange arching petals and protruding stamens. **Chocolate lily** is one of the only brownish flowers in the region. **Harebell**, with light blue hanging bells, often grows in dry soil. Look for harebell flowering abundantly near the base of Noble Knob.

Between miles 1.4 and 1.7, the rocky soil hosts a different mix of subalpine flowers that usually bloom late and grow low to the ground. **Pink** and **white mountain heather** bear numerous hanging, bell-shaped flowers and evergreen needles. In shades of pink, lavender, or white, **spreading phlox** is a mass of star-shaped flowers with spiky leaves. **Woolly sunflower**, or **Oregon sunshine**, has 8 to 13 yellow rays.

At mile 1.8, you'll come to a junction with the Deep Creek Trail (Trail No. 1196). Stay to the right, following the Noble Knob Trail along the west side of the ridge and into forest. At mile 2.9, you'll reach the junction with the Dalles Ridge Trail (Trail No. 1173), which branches off to the left. Continue straight here, toward Noble Knob. The trail then drops 0.1 mile to a saddle with a three-way junction. Trail No. 1184 continues at the left fork, while the Lost Lake Trail (Trail No. 1185) branches to the right. Follow the middle fork for the last 0.5 mile as you ascend to Noble Knob. This perch offers views east into the 51,000-acre Norse Peak Wilderness and west to stately Mt. Rainier.

*Wildflower
Hike 24* Berkeley Park

*Meadows above
Berkeley Park,
Mt. Rainier
National Park*

Berkeley Park is one of many classic subalpine hikes in Mt. Rainier
National Park. Berkeley Park itself is smaller than many of Rainier's parks,
but the hike there showcases the wildflowers and the amazing views. Mt.
Rainier's northeastern flank dominates the view, with the immense Emmons
Glacier the premier attraction. Because this area is drier than the high country in the Paradise area, the flowers are less prolific. Still, you'll see a large
variety, including many interesting alpine flowers.

A large network of trails laces this area, so groups should stick together. On
one outing, our group found two lost children just before dark. Fortunately,
we were able to reunite them with their concerned mother and escort them
all to the parking area with our flashlights. Expect summertime crowds at

Trail Rating	Moderate
Trail Length	6 miles round trip
Location	Mt. Rainier National Park, south of Enumclaw
Elevation	5,800 to 6,800 feet
Bloom Season	July to late September
Peak Bloom	Mid-July to mid-August
Contact	Mt. Rainier National Park, (360) 569-2211
Directions	From Enumclaw, drive east on WA 410 toward Crystal Mountain. Turn right at the White River entrance to Mt. Rainier National Park (there is an admission fee) and continue 13.5 miles to the road's end at Sunrise. (The road to Sunrise is open only from late June or early July to September or early October, so contact the park before you set out.) The Sunrise area has a visitor center, cafeteria, and restrooms. Check in with a ranger for current trail conditions.

the Sunrise parking lot. Hike in the early morning or early evening for more solitude. If you do arrive midday, however, you'll generally leave the crowds behind after the first mile or so.

At the northwest corner of the parking lot, just to the right of the restrooms, you'll see a wide paved trail. Start hiking here. Almost immediately, a trail branches left to a picnic area. Stay right on the paved trail, and in about 100 yards you'll come to a trail board. Follow signs to Berkeley Park, Mt. Fremont, Burroughs Mountain, and Grand Park; they are all in the same direction.

Lying in a rain shadow of Mt. Rainier, the area is dry and dominated by grasses. Some 2,000 years ago, the mountain spewed pumice, which settled on the surrounding slopes. The loose, rocky soil drains quickly, holding little moisture from rain or snowmelt. This environment creates challenges for the local flowers, which have had to adapt to survive here.

With purplish blue podlike blossoms covering its stems, **subalpine lupine** might be the showiest flower here in late summer, although the displays are nothing like those at Paradise. **Magenta paintbrush** also blooms late in the season, exhibiting spiky maroon bracts. **American bistort** dots the landscape with fuzzy white cylinder-shaped flowers. A dandelionlike flower, **short-beaked agoseris** has hairy leaves and numerous floppy yellow rays.

At mile 0.1, the trail divides. Stay left, heading northwest toward the ridge top. Several kinds of purple ray flowers with yellow centers grow here. **Alpine aster** is the smallest, often only 4 to 8 inches tall. A cousin, **Cascade aster** generally grows taller but with scraggly, separated rays. A more distant relative, subalpine daisy is a common composite, usually with lavender rays, but occasionally white or pinkish.

Earlier in the summer, you'll see different groupings of flowers. **Western anemone**, or **pasqueflower**, begins its cycle as a small flower with five to eight petals forming a cream-colored bowl around a cluster of stamens. Later in the summer, it goes to seed, exhibiting hairy tufts on tall stems. The classic **glacier lily** follows the snowmelt, sprouting a hanging yellow head with arching petals and jutting stamens. **Snow buttercup**, with five-petaled shiny yellow disks, also blooms soon after melt-off.

SPREADING PHLOX
Phlox diffusa

HEIGHT: 1" to 3"
BLOOMS: June to August
Spreading phlox covers the ground in a dense mass. A profusion of showy blossoms—pink, purple, or occasionally white—often hides the leaves, which are spiky and joined in pairs at the base. Phlox means "flame" in Greek, a reference to the vibrant colors that are characteristic of the phlox family.

Phlox grows, in some form, in every region of the state. From low to high elevations, it colors open fields and high meadows, rocky slopes and dry soils. Hummingbirds are attracted to this lovely little flower, and humans find its appeal just as irresistible.

Scattered across the meadows, islands of trees have taken hold, although stunted by the harsh environment. Some of these small trees are hundreds of years old. In these protected habitats grow flowers such as **small-flowered penstemon**, which shows rounded clusters of many trumpet-shaped purple blossoms. **Elegant Jacob's-ladder**, named for its ladderlike leaves, has five small blue petals around a tiny yellow center. A lovely yellow composite, **broadleaf** or **mountain arnica** is found in these sheltered areas, especially along the ridge. **Corn lily**, or **false hellebore**, dwells along the tree borders, generating six-petaled greenish flowers and large, veined leaves.

At mile 0.4, the trail arrives at a junction with the Sourdough Ridge Trail. Stay left, heading west toward Frozen Lake. In rocky areas along the trail, you'll see low mats of **spreading phlox**, with striking five-petaled pink or lavender blossoms and spiny leaves. **Cliff penstemon** often dwells in rock crevices, its five pink, scarlet, or rose-purple petals uniting to form a tube-shaped blossom. Also adapted to stony soil, **northern goldenrod** bears tight clusters of small yellow ray heads.

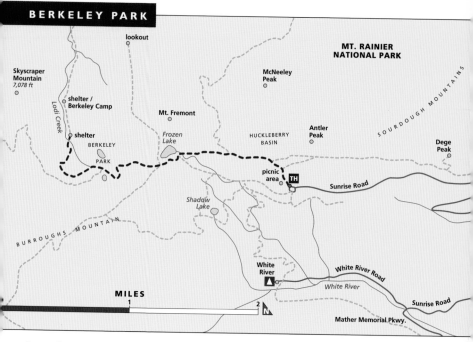

BERKELEY PARK

Several points along the trail offer wide-open gazing to the north, where you can see ridge after ridge of the distant Cascades. Craggy Mt. Stewart lies toward the eastern end; farther to the west is the snowcapped cone of Glacier Peak.

As you continue heading west, you'll pass lavender Cascade aster, yellow arnica, and **sickletop lousewort**, with fanned-out white to pink blossoms. Several white flowers are common along the ridge. **Yarrow** has lacy cream-colored flowers and feathery leaves. **Sitka valerian** presents tall stalks of stamen-fuzzy blossoms. **Pearly everlasting** is notable for its clusters of white paperlike balls.

Look for the delicate blue hanging bells of **common harebell** on narrow, sparse stems. **Cliff paintbrush**, common in rocky places, has brilliant red bracts. Woody-stemmed **pink mountain heather** produces bright pink bells and evergreen needles. From places along the ridge, you can look down into Huckleberry Basin. Use your binoculars to scan for bears in the valley below or mountain goats on the far cliffs.

At mile 1.4, Frozen Lake appears like a mirage in the desolate landscape. It's sometimes covered with ice until late July. Snowfields usually border the lake most of the summer. Near the outlet stream, a trail drops down to the left, leading back to the parking lot through the Shadow Lake valley. Note this spot, for it is an alternate return route. But for now, continue on the main trail, following it up and around the south side of the lake.

At almost 6,800 feet, this environment is home to a number of alpine flowers. These plants are usually low growing, an adaptation that helps them avoid the wind and gain solar heat from the ground. **Dwarf mountain** or **alpine lupine** is a miniature version of its tall subalpine cousin. **Tolmie's saxifrage** produces low dense mats showing five white petals with five petal-like stamens. Five-petaled **shrubby cinquefoil** adds yellow to the austere landscape.

At mile 1.6, there is a signed three-way junction. Continue straight (west) across a flat basin. (A left leads to the ethereal world of Burroughs Mountain; the right fork goes north, climbing toward Mt. Fremont.)

Bracted lousewort displays creamy beaked blossoms. **Alpine pussytoes** produces clusters of white budlike blossoms on soft woolly mats of basal leaves. Paintbrush, cinquefoil, and alpine aster add splashes of color. Listen for the shrill whistles of marmots, plump rodents that live among the rocks.

As you drop down on the far side of the basin, the stems of **elephant's head** display pink blossoms in the shape of elephant trunks and ears. Dainty white **arctic sandwort** dwells in high rocky areas. The dense cushion of **moss campion** is speckled with tiny pink blossoms.

The trail passes across a wide flat shelf with flower-rich meadows to the right. These meadows grow thick with subalpine lupine, American bistort, and magenta paintbrush, mixed with harebell, northern goldenrod, yarrow, shrubby cinquefoil, and alpine aster. You can see a tarn to the north surrounded by flower-filled meadows.

At mile 2.4, there is another junction. Take the right fork to Berkeley Park. (The left fork is the Wonderland Trail, which goes 1.2 miles up to terrific views at Skyscraper Pass.) Following the trail to Berkeley Park, you descend a wide talus slope before arriving in the green valley.

In the basin of Berkeley Park, the soils are richer and the area is more protected, enabling a variety of flowering plants to flourish. You'll see many of the flowers already noted. Found in damp areas, **mountain bog gentian** bears elegant deep purple blossoms. A blooming shrub, **rosy spirea** has fuzzy pink flowers, similar to the garden variety. Early in the summer, look for **Jeffrey's shooting star**, with delicate hanging fuchsia blossoms.

The trail soon enters forested areas with small pocket meadows. You'll likely see **early blue violet** and **Cusick's speedwell**, another purple blossom with protruding stamens. Where the trail reaches Lodi Creek, a short creekside stroll reveals **Lewis' monkey-flower**, with gorgeous pink trumpets. At mile 3.0, Lodi Creek is your turnaround point.

Retrace your route back to Frozen Lake. Follow the same trail back the way you came or, to return to the parking area via the Shadow Lake valley, take a right at the junction near the east end of the lake. This alternate return route adds 0.2 mile to the total distance. The Shadow Lake area harbors many of the same flowers as Berkeley Park. Once you reach the Shadow Lake valley, it's a short, steep climb to the parking area.

Spray Park

Wildflower Hike 25

Mt. Rainier looms above Spray Park, Mt. Rainier National Park

Difficult	*Trail Rating*
8 miles round trip	*Trail Length*
Mt. Rainier National Park, south of Buckley	*Location*
4,570 to 6,370 feet	*Elevation*
July to late September	*Bloom Season*
Late July to late August	*Peak Bloom*
Mt. Rainier National Park, (360) 569-2211	*Contact*

From the town of Buckley, with your tank full of gas, drive south on WA 165 to Wilkeson. Continue south on WA 165 for another 9.0 miles to a junction with the Carbon River Road. Stay right on WA 165 and continue 17.0 miles up to Mowich Lake. Proceed to the south end of the lake, where you'll find a large parking lot and an unmanned fee station near a small campground with walk-in sites. *Directions*

Spray Park's bountiful meadows and superb views of Mt. Rainier are among the finest in the park. The great variety of flowers found along this trail reflects forest, subalpine, and alpine habitats. Several tarns near tree line make for great reflection photos. Spray Park might be busy at times, especially during peak bloom in late July and August, but you will never experience the hordes that congregate at Paradise. On weekdays here, you'll find plenty of solitude.

The trail begins at the south end of Mowich Lake, the park's largest and deepest lake, at the south side of the walk-in campground. From the trailhead and the sign for the Wonderland Trail, hike south on a connector trail that drops down to a junction with the Wonderland Trail within 0.25 mile. Go left on the Wonderland Trail, which leads to Spray Park and beyond.

You'll first enter deep forest. Look for **queen's cup**, with white six-petaled flowers and elegant tonguelike leaves. A common forest inhabitant, **false Solomon's seal** has clusters of star-shaped, cream-colored flowers and lance-shaped leaves. Three large leaves—like giant shamrocks—identify **vanilla leaf**, with a single spike of tiny white flowers. Frontier women used it to scent their clothes and cabins.

Pinesap has pink to yellowish flowers but no green leaves. It is a saprophyte, a type of plant that obtains nutrients from decayed organic matter in the soil rather than from photosynthesis. Another saprophyte, **western coralroot** is an orchid with narrow, leaflike pink flowers that open on stems up to 20 inches tall.

The trail winds gently up and down through tall Douglas fir, grand fir, hemlock, and silver fir. At about mile 1.0, the trail crosses Lee Creek. The crown-shaped pink flowers of **pipsissewa** dangle from wiry stems. **Woodnymph** displays a single star-shaped white flower that hangs above evergreen leaves. The white bell-shaped flowers of **Hooker's fairybell** also droop downward, on stems that grow up to 3 feet tall.

At mile 1.7, you'll come to a spur trail that leads 0.1 mile to an overlook on Eagle Cliff. (Take this optional diversion for views of the Spray Creek valley and North Mowich Glacier; otherwise, continue on.) The main trail soon turns east and passes Eagle Roost Camp, the only backcountry camp in the area.

At mile 2.0, a signed spur trail leads to Spray Falls, 160 feet high and one of the most scenic cascades in the park. Take this 0.25-mile detour to view the falls. Near Spray Creek, you'll find **foamflower**, with tiny white petals and pro-truding stamens above broad, maplelike leaves. Nearby, look for **twinflower**, with pairs of pale pink bells. Along the creek, pink **Lewis' monkey-flower** and **yellow monkey-flower** open trumpetlike blossoms in August. The tube-shaped flowers of **tall bluebell** dwell along the stream banks. So does **cow parsnip**, which can tower up to 9 feet tall, sprouting creamy white flower clusters and three-bladed leaves measuring up to 1 foot across.

After this detour to Spray Falls, return to the main trail, which soon begins a steep series of switchbacks as it climbs to Spray Park. Along the trail, look for **one-sided wintergreen**, a small evergreen with a cluster of greenish white, bell-shaped flowers and shiny oval leaves. You'll also see the blinding glaciers of Mt. Rainier peeking through the trees as the forest begins to open up. Here the flower show really begins.

A bright yellow ray flower, **mountain arnica** thrives in partial shade. **Yarrow** displays lacy white flower heads and aromatic, featherlike leaves. A common flower here, **harebell** grows 8 to 16 inches tall with bell-shaped blue flowers. **Pearly everlasting** is notable for its clusters of pearl-like white flowers on 1- to 3-foot stems.

The trail departs from the scattered clumps of trees and enters the expansive meadows of Spray Park. The alpine habitat is very fragile, so be sure to stay on established trails, on rock surfaces, or on the snowfields that can linger all summer in the higher elevations. Hessong Rock and Mt. Pleasant appear to the north. Mt. Rainier, always awesome, shows off the Carbon, Russell, and Mowich Glaciers, which creep down its northwest flank. White **avalanche lily** and yellow **glacier lily** thrive here in early summer, opening soon after snowmelt. **Western anemone**, or **pasqueflower**, is another early bloomer, transforming itself over the summer from a low-growing white blossom to a tall, dirty-white, tufted seed head. **Snow** or **mountain buttercup** also blossoms soon after melt-off, with low-growing varnished yellow blossoms.

In late July, there is an incredible abundance of flowering plants. The blue stalks of **subalpine lupine** cover large areas. Mixed in are **American bistort**, a tube-shaped white flower, and **Sitka valerian**, which has clusters of white flowers. The bracts of **Indian paintbrush**

SITKA VALERIAN
Valeriana sitchensis

HEIGHT: 16" to 36"

BLOOMS: July

Sitka valerian has white to pale pink flowers that form a cluster. The tiny blossoms are approximately ¼ inch long. The plant's spiky, toothed leaves grow from the ground and also up the middle of the stalk. This perennial, known for its strong, sour odor, was dubbed "the medicine that stinks" by Alaskan Tlingits.

Although the flowers and fibrous roots of Sitka valerian smell unpleasant, the roots actually taste sweet, and tribes east of the mountains traditionally steamed and ate them. Valerian grows in moist meadows, in thickets, along stream banks, and in open subalpine forests and meadows throughout the Cascades.

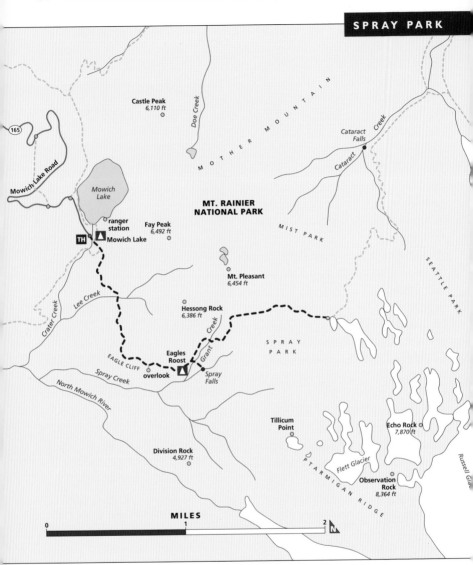

add brilliant shades of orange, red, and magenta to the meadows. **Columbia** or **tiger lily** is a beautiful plant whose yellow-orange hanging blossoms have tiny spots and protruding stamens with large anthers.

Using a topographic map, you can locate a couple of small tarns just off the trail. These are good spots to find **elephant's head**, with stalks of pink flowers that resemble the trunk and ears of the pachyderm. Also found in moist areas, **bracted lousewort** displays pale yellow beaked flowers. One of the most elegant wildflowers of late summer, **mountain bog gentian** shows deep blue trumpets that face skyward.

Several cinquefoils reside here, all with five-petaled, disk-shaped yellow flowers. Low-growing **fan-leaved cinquefoil** has three toothed leaflets, like a strawberry leaf. **Diverse-leaved cinquefoil** sprouts five to seven larger, deeply serrated leaves. Found higher up the trail, in the harsher alpine environment, **shrubby cinquefoil's** needlelike leaves grow on woody stems.

Penstemons are common here. You can recognize them by their tubular-shaped flowers, with two upper lobes and three lobes below. Look for bluish purple **Cascade penstemon**, with sawtoothed leaves. **Small-flowered penstemon**, also with bluish purple whorls of flowers, has narrower, smooth-edged leaves. Found on rocky slopes, **Davidson's penstemon** displays swarms of pink to lavender flowers growing in a low mat.

The rocky soil toward the far end of Spray Park hosts a diverse mix of alpine flowers, which generally bloom late in the season and grow low to the ground. **Pink** and **white mountain heather** are woody evergreens with numerous hanging bell-shaped flowers. **Spreading phlox** has needlelike leaves and masses of pink, lavender, or white star-shaped flowers. **Alpine** or **dwarf mountain lupine** grows only 2 to 5 inches tall and often forms large mats. Both sunflowers, **alpine aster** has 15 to 40 blue-purple rays, while **alpine golden daisy** has as many as 70 yellow rays.

At mile 4.0, you reach a ridge—your turnaround point for an 8-mile roundtrip hike. (The Wonderland Trail continues on, dropping down to the Carbon River.) But before you turn back, take time to enjoy the incredible views. Prominent above on Mt. Rainier is Willis Wall, a sheer 2,000-foot cliff that rises above Carbon Glacier. Visible to the north are the crags of the Alpine Lakes Wilderness, Glacier Peak, and, if it's very clear, distant Mt. Baker. Sunset bring a headlamp for the twilight return trip.

Wildflower
Hike 26

Van Trump Park

Comet Falls, Mt. Rainier National Park

Trail Rating	Difficult
Trail Length	7 miles round trip
Location	Mt. Rainier National Park, southeast of Tacoma
Elevation	3,600 to 5,800 feet
Bloom Season	July to late September
Peak Bloom	Late July to late August
Contact	Mt. Rainier National Park, (360) 569-2211
Directions	From the Tacoma area, drive south on WA 7, then east on WA 706 to the Nisqually entrance to Mt. Rainier National Park. Pay up and continue east toward Paradise for 10.7 miles. The parking area is on the north side of the road, 0.3 mile west of the Christine Falls bridge.

This popular hike offers a little bit of everything: glacier views, deep forest, alpine meadows, wildlife, and waterfalls. Passing through a variety habitats—forest, meadows, creek banks, and talus slopes—you'll see an assortment of plants and flowers. Get an early start so you can appreciate all this hike has to offer, and so you can find a spot in the parking area, which can fill up on nice weekend afternoons in the summer.

The Van Trump Park Trail (also called the Comet Falls Trail) is steep for much of the way, making this a tough haul for children and for hikers in less than peak form. Actually, it's pretty strenuous for anybody, so take your time and use trekking poles. Water is available in several places, so you won't need to carry much if you take a purifier. Because of steep, potentially dangerous snowfields, this is not an early season hike.

In the summer of 2001, a minor geologic event took place here (a major event if you happened to be in the area at the time). A melting section of the Kautz Glacier on Mt. Rainier created a torrent of mud and debris that cascaded over Comet Falls and down Van Trump Creek to the Nisqually River. Fortunately, no one was hurt. Piles of mud and debris still linger from the massive mudflow.

Hike north from the parking lot, climbing immediately through stately forest. A bridge crosses to the east side of Van Trump Creek. **False lily-of-the-valley** grows in wet areas, displaying a sprig of stamen-clustered white blossoms. **Slender bog orchid** produces a spike of greenish wing-tipped blossoms. **False bugbane** has fuzzy balls of white flowers and large, toothed leaves. **Dwarf dogwood**, or **bunchberry**, bears a blossom with four white sepals from May on into July.

BUNCHBERRY OR DWARF DOGWOOD
Cornus canadensis

HEIGHT: 3" to 5"
BLOOMS: June to July

Bunchberry blossoms look very similar to those of the dogwood, although bunchberry is much smaller. Its flowers consist of four white, veined, petal-like bracts around tiny greenish flowers; its leaves are also heavily veined. Bunchberry grows in low- to mid-elevation mountain forests.

In fall, a cluster of red berries appears at the center of each blossom. Although the berries are mealy and rather unpleasant tasting to humans, they provide food for animals and birds such as ruffed grouse. Grouse also consume the leaves, as do white-tailed deer.

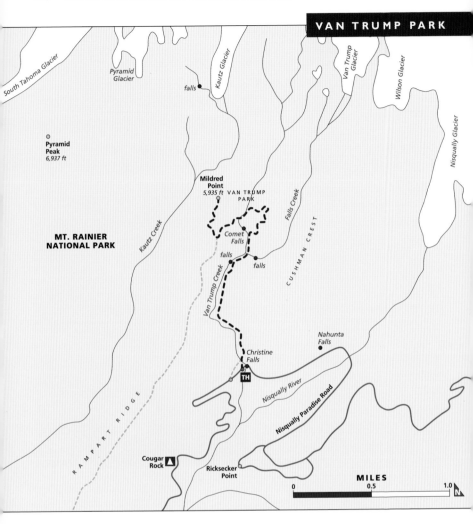

The trail continues uphill through shady woods. Early in the summer, the forest hosts a number of white-flowering blossoms, such as **trillium**, **queen's cup**, **wild strawberry**, **vanilla leaf**, and **salal**. Salal is a shrubby plant with shiny leaves and white bell-shaped blossoms. Forest flowers are mostly finished by late July and August, when the flowers in Van Trump Park are in bloom.

In the forest shade, look for several saprophytes, which take their nutrients from dead organic matter rather than from chlorophyll. Lacking green leaves, these plants are mostly pinkish, cream, or white. The ghostly **Indian pipe** has a single, white to translucent hanging flower head. **Pinesap** looks similar to Indian pipe but with a pale coral hue. **Western coralroot**, an orchid with narrow leaflike pink flowers, is another saprophyte found here, growing on stems up to 20 inches tall.

Switchbacks and more switchbacks finally reach a bridge over Falls Creek at mile 1.5. At mile 1.7, you'll catch your first glimpse of Comet Falls, whose waters plunge straight down to resemble the tail of a comet. Other views of the 320-foot waterfall soon follow. Look for **fringecup** with a spike of cup-shaped cream flowers. Also along seeps are **Brewer's mitrewort**, with geranium-type leaves and a stalk of pale green spidery blossoms, and **brook saxifrage**, which sprouts heart-shaped leaves and ¼-inch white five-petaled flowers.

At mile 1.9, a spur trail leads left for 0.1 mile toward the base of the falls, offering a chance to soak in the mist. Here you'll find **tall bluebell**, as well as **butterwort**, with sawtooth-edged leaves and five-petaled violet-blue blossoms. Watch your step on the slick rocks.

Back on the main trail, continue up and out of the creek basin along another set of switchbacks. The forest opens to an abundance of blossoms. White-flowering shrubs include **thimbleberry** and **western mountain ash**. A pink-flowering shrub, **salmonberry** yields edible raspberrylike fruit in late summer. Just make sure not to consume any type of wild plant without positive identification.

The purple-pink stalks of **fireweed** and the white ball-shaped flowers of **pearly everlasting** adorn the open slopes as the trail climbs up into Van Trump Park. You'll also find the familiar blooms of **magenta paintbrush**, lavender **leafy aster**, blue **broadleaf lupine**, and creamy **beargrass**. **Corn lily** and **cow parsnip** sprout giant leaves. **Tiger lily** adds splashes of orange. **Red columbine** is conspicuous with its spurs and projecting yellow stamens.

Earlier in the summer, smaller flowers are found here, such as **blue violet** and **pasqueflower**, or **western anemone**, creamy white with a yellow center. Yellow **glacier lily** and white **avalanche lily** bloom early, taking advantage of the moist soil soon after snowmelt.

The trail turns left and briefly levels out. Three members of the figwort family dwell here. **Bracted lousewort** displays flowers varying in color from white to yellow to maroon. Near pockets of trees, look for **sickletop lousewort**, with curled popcornlike white blossoms. **Bird's-beak lousewort** also has curled blossoms, in shades of pink to white.

At mile 2.6, a spur trail forks to the right. The main trail continues straight ahead, crossing Van Trump Creek. During high water, however, this creek crossing can be dangerous. If you get to the creek and it looks unsafe, return to this spur trail and take it 0.3 mile to where it dead-ends at a superb viewpoint. This will cut some mileage off the total hike, but you will still see many of the same flowers.

If the creek looks safe to cross, continue on. You will pass through meadows of lupine, paintbrush, and **mountain arnica**, a yellow ray flower. White-blooming **Sitka valerian**, **American bistort**, and pasqueflower grow here as well. **Cusick's** veronica, or **Cusick's speedwell**, shows a four-petaled, deep purple-blue blossom with protruding stamens and pistil.

About 0.5 mile beyond the stream crossing, a small trail departs to the right, leading to Mildred Point. Take this right turn. An evergreen shrub, **pink mountain heather** displays delicate hanging pink bells and needlelike leaves. **White mountain heather**, a less common relative, also is found here. **Shrubby cinquefoil** generates five-petaled yellow disks.

At the end of the steep trail, at mile 3.5, you'll reach 5,935-foot Mildred Point in Van Trump Park. This is a fine place to rest and take in the view before heading back to your starting point. Mountain goats live on the cliffs above. Kautz Glacier and the knife-shaped ridge of Success Cleaver extend from Mt. Rainier's summit. To the south, you can see the peaks of the Tatoosh Range across the Nisqually River valley. To the southwest stands the flattened top of Mount St. Helens.

Pink mountain heather, Mt. Rainier National Park

Paradise Meadows

*Wildflower
Hike 27*

*The summer
show at Paradise
Meadows,
Mt. Rainier
National Park*

Perhaps this is it: *the* premier wildflower hike in Washington. It is easily the best known. John Muir described Paradise Meadows as "the most extravagantly beautiful of all the alpine gardens I ever beheld in all my mountaintop wanderings." After searching the state for 15 years for wildflowers to photograph, I cannot dispute this claim.

During some winters, more than 70 feet of snow fall here. Its melt-off spawns summer's luxuriant blossoms, with particularly impressive displays in wet years. In 1983, there was a total precipitation (rain and snow) of 130 inches, equal to 81 gallons per square foot. Be advised that snow often covers the trails in this area until mid- to late July.

Trail Rating	Moderate
Trail Length	4.7-mile loop
Location	Mt. Rainier National Park, southeast of Tacoma
Elevation	5,400 to 7,050 feet
Bloom Season	July to late September
Peak Bloom	Late July to late August
Contact	Mt. Rainier National Park, (360) 569-2211
Directions	From the Tacoma area, drive south on WA 7, then east on WA 706 to the Nisqually entrance to Mt. Rainier National Park (there is an admission fee). Continue 16.0 miles on the main road to a junction. Go left, following the signs to Paradise. Continue 2.1 miles to the Henry M. Jackson Memorial Visitor Center and stop for a map and to check trail conditions. The trailhead parking area and the Paradise Inn are another 0.1 mile farther.

Paradise is definitely the park's most crowded area. The Paradise parking lot holds at least 200 vehicles, and many other hikers park at the visitor center and walk the short distance to the trailhead. If the lots are full, you might consider hiking nearby Mazama Ridge (see Hike 28), returning to Paradise another day. If you wish to avoid crowds, start your hike before 9 a.m., or, better yet, around 7 a.m. Evening is also a good time: There will still be plenty of people, but it won't be group after group, as you'll often encounter on a beautiful summer afternoon.

The free Paradise trails map available at the visitor center gives trail names and distances. It will help keep you on track, as there are 13 miles of trails in the Paradise area. Many options for hiking in the meadows on different trails exist, and all provide wonderful wildflower-viewing opportunities. The route described here is a loop hike. It starts on the Skyline Trail, follows the Glacier Vista Trail for 0.2 mile, rejoins the Skyline Trail, takes the Golden Gate Trail on the way back, then ends on Skyline to return to the parking lot.

Be aware that subalpine plants are fragile and easily damaged by off-trail hiking, which is prohibited in this area. It is crucial that hikers stay on the trails, especially with such a heavy concentration of people here.

The trailhead is at the northwest edge of the Paradise parking lot. The Skyline Trail begins by climbing wide stone steps. Follow this paved path into "flowerland." There is a maze of trails in lower Paradise. If Mt. Rainier is visible, you can use it for orientation; on a late summer day, the chances of it being shrouded in clouds are fifty-fifty, as the mountain creates its own weather. Look toward Mt. Rainier and you'll see a prominent hill with an island of trees about 0.5 mile away. This is Alta Vista. The Skyline Trail leads you up the left (west) side of this knoll.

A botanist could probably find more than a hundred species of flowers in just the first 0.5 mile of this trail. Some flowers are very conspicuous. Easily noticeable are the blue-flowering stalks of **subalpine lupine**, a perfumed member of the pea family. Often found near lupine, **Sitka valerian** sprouts white stamen-fuzzy blossoms on lanky stems. **American bistort** produces cylinder-shaped heads of many tiny white flowers. The fuzzy pink blossoms of **rosy spirea** grow on woody stems and have a roselike scent. Another woody plant, **pink mountain heather** has graceful hanging pink bells and a tight web of evergreen needles.

Continue on the steep, paved trail to the west side of Alta Vista. Along the way, several trails join or depart. Follow the signs for Skyline Trail. The trail levels out a bit at about mile 0.4. In a good year, the meadows here display just about every color in the rainbow. The yellow disk heads of **fan-leaved cinquefoil** and the bracts of **magenta paintbrush** are abundant. **Mountain** or **broadleaf arnica**, a yellow composite, is also prevalent. By late summer, the early blooming **pasque-flower** has already gone to seed, displaying hairy oval heads.

Often difficult to differentiate, asters and daisies display many ray flowers ranging in color from white to pink to purple. The common **subalpine daisy** may be pink, white, or lavender. **Leafy** and **Cascade aster** both show purple rays around yellow

PINK OR LEWIS' MONKEY-FLOWER
Mimulus lewisii

HEIGHT: 1' to 2'

BLOOMS: July to August

The casual observer might find pink monkey-flower similar to a garden-variety snapdragon. It has several showy, tubular flowers on a single stem and pink to purplish red blossoms that grow 1 to 2 inches long. The plant's conspicuously veined leaves are large, toothed, and sticky, forming pairs all the way up the stem.

Pink monkey-flower grows at middle to high elevations in the mountains and is commonly found along streams (especially icy ones) on both sides of the Cascades. Some tribes used this plant as a charm.

disks. **Alpine aster**, also with lavender and yellow heads, is found at higher elevations along the trail.

Keep an eye out for smaller, less conspicuous flowers. Found in damp meadows, **smoothstem willowherb** bears small four-petaled, pink to lavender blossoms. Blue-violet **Cusick's veronica**, or **Cusick's speedwell**, has four petals, two long stamens, and one longer pistil. Usually less than 5 inches tall, **partridgefoot** hosts a cluster of fuzzy creamy white blossoms.

In about a mile, the wildflowers—and the concentration of people—begin to thin as the trail climbs higher. Flowers here have adapted to the rocky soil and the short growing season of the harsh subalpine environment. They generally grow low to the ground, spreading wide instead of growing tall. Nevertheless, some are very showy, especially in this stark setting. Ground-hugging penstemons exhibit pink to lavender, five-lobed trumpets. **Davidson's** and **rock penstemon** sometimes form extensive mats.

Elegant Jacob's-ladder, a cousin of the lower-elevation showy Jacob's-ladder, presents five blue to purple petals around a small yellow center. **Alpine golden daisy** and **Lyall's lupine**, miniatures of their larger relatives, usually grow in gravelly or rocky areas. **Alpine paintbrush** adds scarlet patches to the landscape.

At mile 1.0, you have the choice of staying right on the Skyline Trail, or taking a left to Glacier Vista. Take the trail to Glacier Vista (which reconnects with the Skyline Trail in 0.2 mile) for exceptional views of the Nisqually Glacier. This massive sheet of ice drops nearly 10,000 vertical feet and is almost 5 miles long. In 1857, the ice sheet extended about 6 or 7 miles to below the present-day Nisqually River bridge, but over the years the glacier has slowly retreated. Smooth and white at its top, the glacier becomes dirty, crevassed, and rock-strewn toward its base. On warm summer afternoons, you can often hear the powerful crash of huge boulders falling from the glacier-carved cliffs.

Continue north on Glacier Vista Trail to rejoin the Skyline Trail. Continue north on the Skyline Trail toward Rainier's summit. At the next junction, in another 0.4 mile, a signed trail branches off to the left toward Camp Muir, a climber's camp. Stay right here, continuing on the Skyline Trail. A 0.3-mile stroll from this junction takes you to 6,800-foot Panorama Point, perched above the surrounding landscape. From here, you can see the entire Paradise River valley and the Tatoosh Range, as well as the snow-covered cone of Mt. Adams and flat-topped Mount St. Helens, both nearly 50 miles distant. On very clear days, you can see Mt. Hood in Oregon, nearly 100 miles away.

Immediately past Panorama Point, the trail divides. The right fork, the Low Skyline Trail, is often roped off, as it crosses a steep and dangerous snowfield. Stay to the left, keeping to the High Skyline Trail. This route climbs through a rocky moonscape to bypass the snowfield and continues to the high point of the hike at 7,050 feet. Just think, you're only 7,360 feet from the summit of Mt. Rainier!

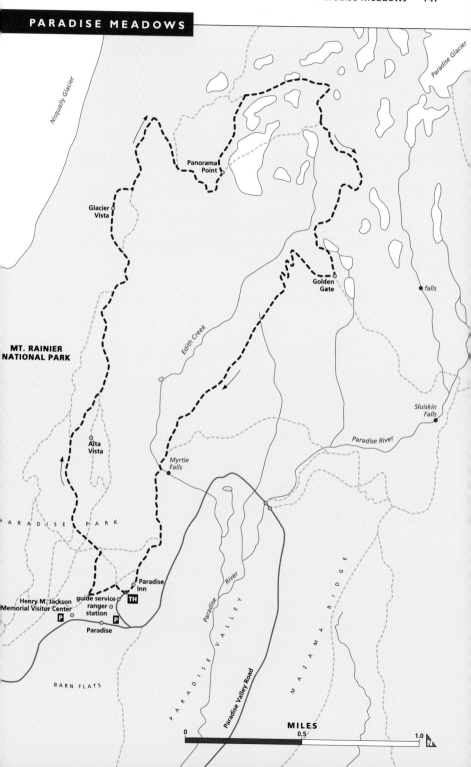

Paradise Glacier

Nisqually Glacier

Panorama
Point

Glacier
Vista

Golden
Gate

• falls

Edith Creek

MT. RAINIER
NATIONAL PARK

Sluiskin
Falls

Paradise River

Alta
Vista

Myrtle
Falls

P A R A D I S E   P A R K

Paradise River

Paradise
Inn

guide service
ranger
station

TH

Henry M. Jackson
Memorial Visitor Center

P

P

Paradise

P A R A D I S E   V A L L E Y

M A Z A M A   R I D G E

BARN FLATS

Paradise Valley Road

MILES

0   0.5   1.0

N

From here, you traverse rocky, snowy slopes, then begin descending. When you reach the junction with the Golden Gate Trail, turn left, following the Golden Gate Trail as it drops steeply into lush meadowlands. Near a stream crossing, look for the golden blossoms of **yellow monkey-flower**.

As you descend into the Edith Creek valley, the meadows become larger and more lush. You'll find bistort, valerian, arnica, pasqueflower, cinquefoil, aster, penstemon, and paintbrush, along with blue **harebell**, pink **elephant's head**, yellow to pink **lousewort**, and **corn lily**, with large leaves and tassels of pale green blossoms. In some years, the lupine grows so thick that the meadows appear carpeted in blue and the air fills with a wonderful fragrance. There are excellent photo opportunities here, with flower foregrounds and either Mt. Rainier or the Tatoosh Range as background.

The Golden Gate Trail rejoins the Skyline Trail just above Myrtle Falls. Edith Creek above the falls is home to the five-petaled **pink** or **Lewis' monkey-flower**. From Myrtle Falls, it's only 0.5 mile to the parking area and an ice-cream cone at the historic Paradise Inn, a log inn that opened in July 1917.

Flowering meadow with view of the Tatoosh Range, Mt. Rainier National Park

Mazama Ridge

*Wildflower
Hike 28*

*Paintbrush,
subalpine daisy,
and lupine,
Mt. Rainier
National Park*

When the crowds are just too much at Paradise (see Hike 27),
Mazama Ridge makes a great alternative. Relatively few people
hike in this area, the broad flower-filled meadows are similar to those of
Paradise, and the views are exceptional. You can see the Tatoosh Range
to the south and Nisqually, Paradise-Stevens, and Ingraham Glaciers to
the north. The route travels through subalpine and alpine zones its
entire length. In late September and early October, the huckleberries
ripen and the fall colors become brilliant.

With only 800 feet in elevation gain, this is a good hike for children.
The trail is nearly level much of the way, except for a short, steep switchback to the ridge. Several other trails lead to additional wonders along

Trail Rating	Moderate
Trail Length	6 miles round trip
Location	Mt. Rainier National Park, southeast of Tacoma
Elevation	5,250 to 6,050 feet
Bloom Season	July to late September
Peak Bloom	Late July to mid-August
Contact	Mt. Rainier National Park, (360) 569-2211
Directions	From the Tacoma area, drive south on WA 7, then east on WA 706 to the Nisqually entrance to Mt. Rainier National Park (there is an admission fee). Continue 16.0 miles on the main road to a junction. Go left, following the signs to Paradise. Continue 2.1 miles to the Henry M. Jackson Memorial Visitor Center and stop for a map and to check trail conditions. The Paradise parking lot and the Paradise Inn are another 0.1 mile farther. As you enter the parking lot, stay to the right. At the end of the parking lot, you'll see a road. Take this one-way road 0.7 mile and, just after a stone bridge, park in the parking area on the right. The trailhead is across the street from the parking area.

the way; sections of them are included in this hike's overall mileage, but you can forgo them for a shorter hike.

Across the road from the parking area, look for a sign for the 4th Crossing Trail. The trail follows the rushing Paradise River. Several small meadows display a variety of colors. An icon of the Cascades, **subalpine lupine** grows abundantly, blanketing some areas in blue. A member of the pea family, this sweet-smelling beauty enriches the soil with nitrogen.

Often accompanying lupine, **American bistort** exhibits cylinder-shaped flower heads composed of many tiny white flowers. The red bracts of **small-flowered** and **magenta paintbrush** are common here. Also prevalent, **Sitka valerian** has clusters of white flowers with protruding stamens, giving them a fuzzy appearance. In late summer, **yellow monkey-flower** blooms among the wet rocks near the river.

At mile 0.3, you'll come to a junction with the Skyline Trail. Take a right onto the Skyline Trail, following the river valley briefly before climbing steep switchbacks for 0.4 mile to Mazama Ridge. The nearby Paradise River is abundant with the late-blooming fuchsia trumpets of **Lewis' monkey-flower**, which seem to grow as closely to the water as they possibly can.

At about 0.7 mile from the trailhead, you'll reach Mazama Ridge at the end of the climb. Here you can look west across the Paradise Valley to the historic Paradise Inn. At the T junction on the ridge, stay to the left and hike 0.5 mile north, continuing on the Skyline Trail to Sluiskin Falls. Look for the showy, bell-shaped flowers of **pink mountain heather**, a needle-leaved evergreen shrub. **Spreading phlox** decorates dry slopes with five-petaled pink to lavender blossoms. As the trail ascends into a harsher alpine environment, look for several low-growing plants. **Lyall's** or **alpine lupine** is a dwarf lupine that grows in rocky areas; it is often joined by **Davidson's penstemon**, with masses of pink to lavender trumpets. Bright red **cliff paintbrush** also dwells in these high rocky areas. Two types of sunflower—**alpine aster**, with 15 to 40 blue-purple rays, and **alpine golden daisy**, with as many as 70 yellow rays—add style to this harsh environment.

Continue past Sluiskin Falls for 0.1 mile to the Stevens–Van Trump Historical Monument, a stone bench built to honor the first recorded ascent of Mt. Rainier. From the monument, the views south are outstanding. From left to right are the Goat Rocks peaks (8,000 feet), Mt. Adams (12,276 feet), and Mount St. Helens (8,363 feet, which is 1,300 feet shorter than before the 1980 blast).

Turn around at the monument and go back down the Skyline Trail to the T junction at the top of the switchbacks. Go left (south) on the Lakes Trail, which eventually leads to the Reflection Lakes. The trail

TIGER OR COLUMBIA LILY
Lilium columbianum

HEIGHT: 10" to 30"
BLOOMS: June to August

Wild tiger lilies look similar to their cultivated counterparts. With showy blossoms exploding from slender stems, they stand out in meadow areas. Nodding yellow-orange flowers with purple spots near the center and long purple stamens grace the stems.

Tiger lily bulbs are edible, but they taste bitter and peppery unless boiled. The Lakes and Okanogan peoples dug the roots as a food source. The bulbs could be boiled, steamed, or mashed into a paste, which was dried into small cakes. The bulbs were more often used as a flavoring or condiment than as a main dish. Often, controlled burns were used to ensure good tiger lily crops two years into the future. Bulbs were also mixed with stink bugs to provide protection against witchcraft. With a wide ecological tolerance, the plant grows throughout Washington.

gradually descends through beautiful flower-filled meadows, both large and small. In late summer, they are dominated by lupine, bistort, paintbrush, and Sitka valerian.

Several plants from the sunflower family reside in the meadows. With toothed leaves, **mountain arnica** speckles the landscape in yellow. Growing taller and with more flower heads on each stem, **arrowleaf butterweed** is another common yellow ray flower. Several purple asters are regulars in the area, including **leafy aster** and **Cascade aster**. Similar-looking but with more rays, usually 30 to 60, **subalpine daisy** also inhabits the neighborhood.

In early summer, soon after snowmelt, the first wildflowers make their move in this terrain. At times, yellow **glacier lily** and white **avalanche lily** grow so thickly that they carpet the fields in color. Another early bloomer is **pasqueflower**, or **western anemone**, which has two distinct displays. First, the flower grows about 6 inches tall with five to eight white petals around yellow, stamen-crowded centers. Later in the summer, the plant goes to seed on taller stalks, revealing hairy mop-heads, showier than the flowering stage.

The trail gently descends around patches of subalpine fir. Views extend south to the Tatoosh Range, featuring Pinnacle, Plummer, and Unicorn Peaks. The path passes pocket meadows exhibiting **harebell**, with delicate blue hanging bells. Arnica, paintbrush, bistort, and lupine flourish in the glades. **Gray's lovage** generates lacy leaves and white balls of many tiny flowers. Bearing whorls of purple tubular flowers, **small-flowered penstemon** is one of several penstemons in this landscape. **Coiled-beak lousewort** boasts spiky leaves and creamy white, beak-shaped flowers. Five small blue to lavender petals around a yellow center decorate **elegant Jacob's-ladder**.

After you've hiked 1.2 miles past the T junction at the top of the switchbacks, you'll arrive at a junction where the High Lakes Trail (not to be confused with the Lakes Trail) leads right (west). Stay straight here on the Lakes Trail toward Reflection Lakes. In 0.2 mile, a view opens from Faraway Rock. The Reflection Lakes lie below with a backdrop of the Tatoosh Range. A small tarn in this area offers water for filtering and photographing. If you've arranged a shuttle, you could drop down 0.6 mile to Reflection Lakes. Otherwise, turn around here.

Hike back to the High Lakes Trail junction, and, if your energy is holding out, turn left (west). Just past this junction, the glades yield many of the flowers mentioned previously, including small-flowered penstemon, bistort, arnica, and elegant Jacob's-ladder, which flourishes near meadow edges. Wet areas near a small stream harbor **elephant's head**, showing many tiny pink blossoms. Look carefully and you'll see the flowers' elephantlike trunks and ears. Also in moist places, **false hellebore**, or **corn lily**, sprouts large, veined cabbagelike leaves that dwarf its greenish flowers.

MAZAMA RIDGE

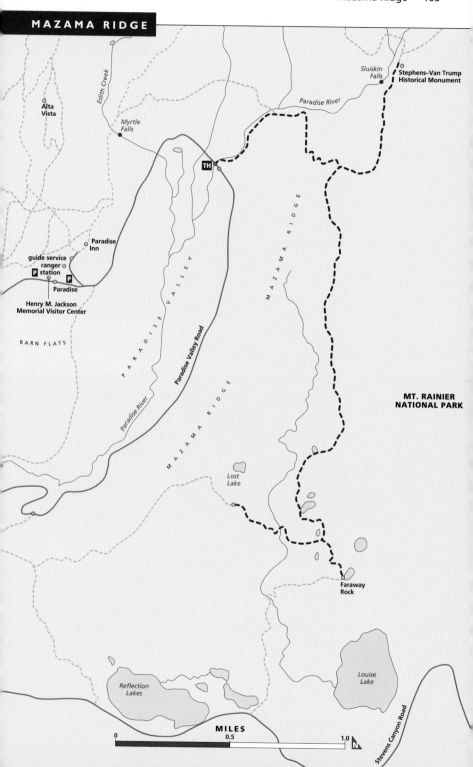

Alta Vista

Edith Creek

Myrtle Falls

Sluiskin Falls

Paradise River

Stephens–Van Trump Historical Monument

TH

Paradise Inn

guide service
ranger
station
P
P
Paradise

Henry M. Jackson
Memorial Visitor Center

BARN FLATS

PARADISE VALLEY

Paradise Valley Road

Paradise River

MAZAMA RIDGE

MAZAMA RIDGE

MAZAMA RIDGE

Lost Lake

MT. RAINIER
NATIONAL PARK

Faraway Rock

Reflection Lakes

Louise Lake

Stevens Canyon Road

MILES

0   0.5   1.0

N

After 0.3 mile on the High Lakes Trail, where the flowers taper off as the trail enters forest, return to the last junction. Take your time and you might find some of the less conspicuous flowers of the region. Early in the summer, **early blue violet** displays blossoms much like the garden variety. Two types of louse-wort inhabit meadow edges. **Sickletop lousewort** has white to pale pink curved blossoms, whereas **bird's-beak lousewort** shows deeper pink, curved blossoms.

On the more conspicuous side, **red columbine** produces a bold scarlet hanging head with large bright yellow stamens. **Columbia** or **tiger lily's** dotted blossom has yellow-orange arching petals and protruding stamens. Boasting bright yellow five-petaled disks, cinquefoils are also easily spotted. **Fan-leaved** and **shrubby cinquefoil** both flourish in the vicinity.

The hike back north faces Mt. Rainier, looking immense from here, tempting photographers. Find a flower foreground for some spectacular alpine photographs, or stop for a snack and take in the beauty of this stunning area.

Alpine meadows, Mt. Rainier National Park

Naches Peak

*Pasqueflower
and lupine
meadow on
Naches Peak,
Mt. Rainier
National Park*

The trail encircling Naches Peak definitely ranks near the top of my
list of favorites: It's nearly level, it's open, it's a loop trail, and it offers
great flowers and berries in season—plus, on weekdays, I've encountered
few other hikers here. With two tarns and fine views of Mt. Rainier and
the surrounding mountain scenery, this subalpine hike could easily be
nominated as one of the best wildflower hikes in the state.

Travel this route clockwise for incredible views of Mt. Rainier along
the last half of the hike. The route starts off following the Pacific Crest
Trail (Trail No. 2000). From the large parking area just east of Chinook
Pass, walk the Pacific Crest Trail uphill toward a log pedestrian bridge
that spans the highway.

Trail Rating	Easy
Trail Length	4.5-mile loop
Location	Eastern edge of Mt. Rainier National Park, north of Packwood
Elevation	5,350 to 5,900 feet
Bloom Season	July to late September
Peak Bloom	Late July to mid-August
Contact	Mt. Rainier National Park, (360) 569-2211, and Wenatchee National Forest, Naches Ranger District Office, (509) 653-2205
Directions	From Packwood, drive east on US 12 to WA 123 and go left (north). At Cayuse Pass, turn right (east) onto WA 410 and continue to Chinook Pass, a total of 31.0 miles from Packwood. (Chinook Pass is 46.0 miles southeast of Enumclaw via WA 410 and 49.0 miles west of Naches via US 12 and then WA 410.) About 0.1 mile east of Chinook Pass, park in the large parking area, which has restrooms, and find the trailhead. This hike begins just outside the eastern boundary of Mt. Rainier National Park.

This first section of trail immediately enters small meadows of lacy white **yarrow** and the brilliant red bracts of **Indian paintbrush**. The blue podlike blossoms of **subalpine lupine** are trademarks of this habitat; these flowers are widespread in mountain meadows throughout Washington. **Pink mountain heather**, a shrub that blooms in late summer, displays bright pink bell-shaped flowers, needlelike leaves, and woody branches. **Sitka valerian** might resemble yarrow at a distance, but a closer look reveals many protruding stamens, giving it a fuzzy appearance.

Cross the highway over the log pedestrian bridge and keep following the Pacific Crest Trail, now heading southeast. (If you continued all the way on the PCT, you would end up at the Mexican border.) The trail soon enters the William O. Douglas Wilderness, a 166,000-acre unit with numerous alpine lakes. Appointed to the U.S. Supreme Court by President Franklin D. Roosevelt, Douglas was raised in Yakima and knew this area well.

At about mile 1.0, you'll come upon a beautiful tarn surrounded by flower meadows, with lupine, paintbrush, Sitka valerian, and **American bistort**, a cylinder-shaped bundle of tiny white blossoms. In late summer, the seed heads of **western anemone**, also known as **pasqueflower**, appear as tall, furry mops. Blooming in late July and August, **Cascade aster**, a member of the sunflower family, has widely separated lavender rays surrounding yellow centers. An early bloomer, **glacier lily** follows the snowmelt, often coloring the meadows with carpets of yellow.

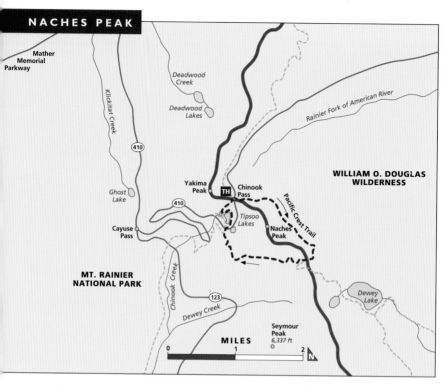

NACHES PEAK

Follow the trail through a rocky bowl. **Mountain sorrel** inhabits this rough terrain, with a spike of off-white, scaly flowers and blue-green kidney-shaped leaves. Several penstemons grow on rocky slopes and cliff faces, including **Davidson's**, **shrubby**, and **cliff** or **rock penstemon**, all with bright purple to pink tubular flowers.

At mile 2.2, the trail reaches a ridge with extensive views to the south: Snow-covered Mt. Adams and the Goat Rocks crags rise on the far horizon. Dewey Lake lies nestled in the forest, 700 feet below. Here is where you depart the Pacific Crest Trail, which continues to the left (south), dropping to Dewey Lake and beyond. (A detour to the lake adds an extra 2.2 miles to this hike.) Go right (west) onto the Naches Peak Trail, on which you'll round a ridge and enter Mt. Rainier National Park, where impressive views of Mt. Rainier await.

You'll descend through vibrant flowers to another tarn, this one beneath Naches Peak. **Leafy aster** bears purple ray flowers with golden centers. With the same coloring, **showy aster** has large, toothed leaves and often many flower heads per stem. Frequently confused with asters, **subalpine daisy** has many narrow, deep pink to purple rays around a slightly larger golden center.

Several yellow ray flowers brighten these meadows. **Mountain arnica** has 10 to 15 rays and sawtoothed, lance-shaped leaves. Another yellow mainstay of subalpine meadows, **arrowleaf butterweed** displays smaller and more numerous flower heads. Several cinquefoils reside here, all with five-petaled yellow disk-shaped flowers nearly an inch wide. Low-growing **fan-leaved cinquefoil** has three toothed leaflets similar to strawberry leaves. **Diverse-leaved cinquefoil** has five to seven leaves, larger and deeply serrated.

Beyond the tarn, huckleberry bushes yield a prolific crop in the fall. Come in September and you'll be treated to a berry feast, but remember to make sure you know what you're eating before devouring any wild plant. To the west, the Tatoosh Range rises above the deep valley of the Ohanapecosh River.

At mile 3.8, the trail drops down a series of switchbacks through open forest to Tipsoo Lakes. **Heart-leaf arnica**, one of a dozen arnicas native to the Northwest, opens its yellow rays early in the season.

SUBALPINE DAISY
Erigeron peregrinus

HEIGHT: 6" to 24"
BLOOMS: Early August

The subalpine daisy, a member of the sunflower family, appears in shades of pink, lavender, reddish purple, and sometimes white. The 2-inch ray flower's 30 to 60 petals reach out from a yellow disk. Each plant sprouts many stems, with one flower per stem. Its alternating leaves are large, deep green, and grow in clusters near the ground.

Subalpine daisy is common in Washington's mountains, growing in moist meadows and open forests. Some American Indian tribes used a pattern inspired by the flower's beautiful rays in basketry.

The trail arrives at Upper Tipsoo Lake. These meadows are very fragile, so please stay on the trail. Binoculars might be your best bet for viewing the flowers here. Look for moisture-loving plants above the lake, including early bloomers such as glacier lily, western anemone, and **mountain buttercup**, with five shiny yellow petals forming a cup-shaped blossom. Later in the season, members of the figwort family begin to bloom. **Sickletop lousewort** displays white popcornlike flowers. The pink blossoms of **elephant's head** appear to have trunks and ears. **Yellow monkey-flower** carpets small areas with golden trumpets.

Return to the parking area at Chinook Pass by crossing WA 410 and following a trail to Lower Tipsoo Lake, which is 0.1 mile away and visible from the highway. Follow the trail around to the far end of the lake, then make the final climb on the trail 0.2 mile up to Chinook Pass.

Tatoosh Ridge

*Meadows,
Tatoosh
Wilderness*

The Tatoosh Trail (Trail No. 161) is a steep but rewarding trail into the subalpine country of the Tatoosh Wilderness. The views from Tatoosh Ridge are expansive, often with Mt. Rainier or Mt. Adams on the horizon. Depending on how far you want to hike along the ridge, you can make this a 6- to 10-mile round trip. This well-maintained trail is not usually crowded, although weekdays are the best bet if you want solitude.

From the signed trailhead, you'll begin climbing through forest—which seems endless, thanks to the arduous ascent. Beneath the fir, cedar, and hemlock, blooming plants are generally small and sparse. Along the first mile, **twinflower** sprouts pairs of hanging blossoms in shades of

Trail Rating	Difficult
Trail Length	6 to 10 miles round trip
Location	Tatoosh Wilderness, north of Packwood
Elevation	2,900 to 5,600 or 6,310 feet
Bloom Season	July to late September
Peak Bloom	July to mid-August
Contact	Gifford Pinchot National Forest, Cowlitz Valley Ranger District Office, (360) 497-1100
Directions	On US 12 in Packwood, drive to the north end of town and stop at the Packwood USFS Information Center for details on road and trail conditions. Across from this ranger station, drive northwest on Skate Creek Road (FR 52). Go 4.0 miles and turn right onto FR 5270. Continue for 7.5 miles to the trailhead and parking area. This road is well graded and passenger cars with normal clearance can manage it.

white to pale pink above rounded evergreen leaves. Also common in the forest, **bunchberry**, or **dwarf dogwood**, produces four-petaled, star-shaped white blossoms framed by distinct flame-shaped leaves. **Vanilla leaf** has small, fuzzy, tube-shaped white flowers and three large shamrock-shaped leaves.

Climb and climb some more. At mile 1.8, the forest begins to open, giving way to small, steep meadows. **Fireweed**, with large purple-pink pointed flower heads and spiky leaves, often grows to 4 feet tall. **Tall bluebell** has blue to pinkish bell-shaped blossoms. The yellow ray flower of **mountain** or **broadleaf arnica** is common in meadows and forest openings. With large maplelike leaves, **thimbleberry** has five-petaled white blossoms in early summer and edible red berries in late summer. Huckleberry, its fruit ripening in late August and September, also grows here. Never consume any wild plant without absolute certainty as to its identity.

At mile 2.0, the clearings become larger and the flowering plants thicken. **American sawwort** bears deep purple, budlike flowers and sawtoothed triangular leaves. **False hellebore**, or **corn lily**, is notable for its large, flame-shaped veined leaves. Fuzzy white blossoms on tall bare stems belong to **Sitka valerian**, common in these meadows. Delicate **harebell** matures hanging blue bells. Named for its ladderlike leaves, **Jacob's-ladder** displays sky blue, five-petaled blossoms. **Gray's lovage** has large, dirty-white compound heads and carroty leaves.

Along the trail, you'll see a number of penstemons, all pink to purple in color with five-petaled, trumpet-shaped blossoms. In open forest, **woodland**

penstemon shows clusters of flowers on leaning stems. Common in open meadows, **Cascade penstemon** produces a whorl-like group of blossoms and sawtoothed, triangle-shaped leaves. With small rounded leaves, **Davidson's** and **shrubby penstemon** are found along the high rocky ridge.

At mile 2.3, you'll reach a small stream, which in dry years might disappear in late summer. Moisture-loving plants such as tall bluebell and the large-leaved false hellebore dwell in the area. Giant **cow parsnip** can top 6 feet tall, with huge maplelike leaves and white compound flower heads up to 10 inches across. Where the trail cuts back to cross the stream a second time, look for the elegant, snapdragonlike fuchsia blossoms of **Lewis' monkey-flower**.

In rocky areas above the stream, **stonecrop** grows stamen-fuzzy yellow blossoms on fleshy stems. Also in these rocks, **Oregon sunshine** bears yellow ray flowers and olive green leaves. **Pearly everlasting**, a common trailside flower, has small clustered flowers resembling lacy white pearls.

At about mile 2.5, a series of junctions makes things a little confusing. Stay left at the first junction. (The trail going right has a sign saying "abandoned.") In 150 to 200 yards, you'll come to an unmarked junction; here you want to stay right. In less than 0.25 mile, you'll reach yet another junction. Keep right to stay on the Tatoosh Trail, heading southeast across expansive meadows. (The signed trail for Tatoosh Lakes goes left. This 0.5-mile detour leads up and over the ridge and down into the Tatoosh Lakes cirque.)

During the next 0.5 mile, you'll pass a wonderful array of wildflowers. Mountain arnica, Sitka valerian, American sawwort, and Jacob's-ladder bloom alongside **magenta paintbrush** and orange-red **harsh paintbrush**. White tube-shaped blossoms of **American bistort** wave in the breeze. Flamboyant **red columbine** and orange **tiger lily** attract hummingbirds

BEARGRASS
Xerophyllum tenax

HEIGHT: Up to 5'
BLOOMS: July to September
The small flowers of beargrass bloom in a single white mass perched upon a tall, thick stalk. Its grasslike leaves are evergreen. A member of the lily family, beargrass grows at high elevations in eastern Washington and occasionally in the Cascades.

Many animals eat beargrass seedpods, especially elk. Mice, and sometimes bears, eat the roots, which often destroys the plant. American Indians wove beargrass with cedar bark to create watertight containers.

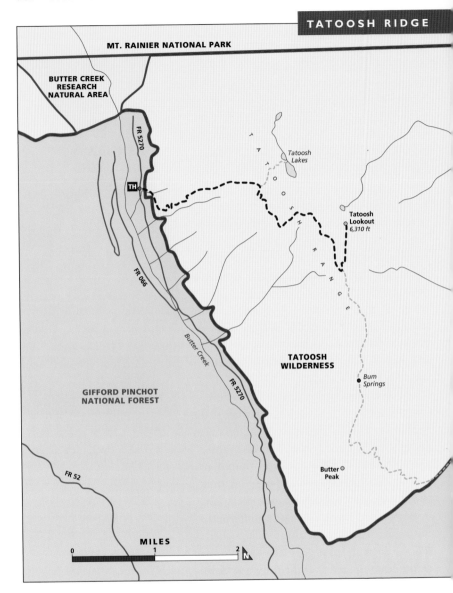

and photographers. Growing up to 5 feet, **thistle** produces hairy purple flowers and spiky leaves. **Fan-leaved cinquefoil** displays yellow disk-shaped flowers. **Broadleaf lupine** adds spires of blue to the landscape.

In the aster family, **Cascade aster** displays several lavender heads on each stem, with sparse, separated rays around a yellow center. **Leafy aster** often presents a single flower per stem, with a more organized display of rays. **Subalpine daisy,** a cousin to the aster, has many rays, usually around 40. This daisy can be white or lavender.

Yellow composites are prevalent on the slopes, especially sunflowers. **Arrowleaf butterweed** has several small ray flower heads and toothed, triangular leaves on each 20- to 40-inch stem. **Northern goldenrod** has several small ray flowers on each stem. Mountain arnica also grows abundantly here.

The first flowers of summer mature in late June or early July. **Pasqueflower**, or **western anemone**, blooms soon after snowmelt. Its flower has creamy white petals surrounding a cluster of stamens. In August, during its more conspicuous seed stage, it develops a hairy, oval-shaped tuft. Found near the ridge top, **glacier lily** sprouts drooped yellow heads with petals arching skyward. Small and white, **spring beauty** is another early bloomer.

At mile 3.0, you reach the ridge top, with views across a basin to the former site of the Tatoosh Lookout. Grand peaks loom into sight: Mt. Adams to the south and Mt. Rainier to the north. For a 6-mile round-trip hike, this is your turnaround point. It's another 2.0 miles to the lookout site. Growing in partial shade, **beargrass** exhibits clumps of coarse grasslike leaves and rounded clusters of tiny cream-colored blossoms.

To continue farther, follow the trail as it crosses the ridge, dropping slightly to circle the head of the basin. **Spreading phlox** blooms along the ridge, with low-growing, five-petaled pink to lavender blossoms. Evergreen shrubs with needle-like leaves, **pink** and **white mountain heather** decorate the crest with small, hanging bell-shaped flowers.

At mile 4.3, you'll find a junction with a side trail leading to the former lookout site. Turn left here and climb 500 feet in 0.6 mile to the site. The rocky ascent offers fewer flowers, hardy survivors in a harsh landscape. As the trail ascends, look for other low-growing plants. **Lyall's** or **alpine lupine** is a dwarf plant found in rocky areas. Bright red **cliff paintbrush** also dwells in high rocky locales. Two sunflowers that bloom here in late summer are **alpine aster**, with 15 to 40 blue-purple rays, and **alpine golden daisy**, with as many as 70 yellow rays.

From the ridge's high point at mile 5.0, the vista is expansive. Look far to the south and, if it's a particularly clear day, you might even see the snowy summit of Mt. Hood in Oregon. Enjoy the view—and the fact that it's all downhill from here.

Wildflower
Hike 31 **Bear Creek Mountain**

*Bear Creek
below Bear
Creek Mountain*

Bear Creek Mountain stands at 7,336 feet on the east side of the Goat Rocks Wilderness. From the mountaintop, you can easily see the glaciers of Old Snowy Mountain, Ives Peak, and Gilbert Peak. Bear Creek Mountain Trail goes to the summit of the same name, traversing meadows with excellent displays of wildflowers in late July and early August. This remote area sees little traffic. Before starting out, check with the Forest Service office for current road and trail conditions. Two miles from the trailhead runs a creek where you can filter water.

The trail to the top of Bear Creek Mountain (Trail No. 1130) begins at the end of FR 1204 near Section 3 Lake—really just a shallow pond. As it approaches the mountain, the route quickly enters the 105,600-acre Goat Rocks

Trail Rating	Moderate
Trail Length	7 miles round trip
Location	Goat Rocks Wilderness, east of Naches
Elevation	6,000 to 7,336 feet
Bloom Season	July to early September
Peak Bloom	Late July to late August
Contact	Wenatchee National Forest, Naches Ranger District Office, (509) 653-2205
Directions	From Naches, drive west on US 12 to the Rimrock Lake area (from Packwood, drive east). Two and a half miles east of the lake, turn south on Tieton Road (FR 1200). Follow this road for about 7 miles and turn left on FR 1204. Drive about 12 miles to the end of FR 1204, where you'll find the trailhead.

Wilderness, named for the mountain goats that live here. You'll go through thin forest, and at mile 0.5 you'll come to a junction. Stay left. (The right fork leads west, dropping down to Tieton Meadows.)

Soon the trail opens into small, flowery meadows. You'll easily spot the creamy white tops of **beargrass**, with flower heads consisting of numerous tiny blossoms. Beargrass usually takes five or six years to produce blooms; after it flowers and fruits, the flowering stalk dies.

Slightly resembling a clover head, **self heal** grows 4 to 20 inches tall and produces a purple flower. Both American Indians and Europeans have used the plant for medicinal purposes. The exotic **red columbine** displays five large crimson sepals, yellow tipped petals, and a spray of long yellow stamens. **Pearly everlasting** has clusters of rounded white disks that last well into late summer. Found in forest openings, **orange agoseris** resembles an orange dandelion.

Farther along the trail you'll come upon larger meadows, predominantly grass with flowers mixed in. Common flowers here include **Sitka valerian, yarrow,** and **American bistort**, each with a differently shaped, clustered white flower head. Blue **broadleaf lupine** is a subalpine standard. Indian paintbrush generates colorful bracts. **Small-flowered paintbrush** and **magenta paintbrush** add dashes of red to the high meadows.

At mile 1.3, the trail crosses a meadow several acres in size. You'll see most of the flowers already mentioned, along with some yellow composites. **Mountain arnica**, a sunflower, has a toothed edge at the end of its squared petals. **Arrowleaf butterweed** produces a cluster of yellow ray heads and triangular leaves. **Elmer's butterweed** displays wider yellow petals.

The lousewort family is also prevalent, usually preferring fairly rich soil. Growing in meadows, **elephant's head** reveals stalks with many pink blossoms, each with a "trunk" and "ears." **Bracted lousewort** has fernlike leaves and a cone-shaped flower head of many curved yellow or reddish purple blossoms. Also with fernlike foliage, **coiled-beak lousewort** produces pale yellow flowers that curve downward. Preferring partial shade, **sickletop lousewort** displays pink or white blossoms that fan out in clustered heads.

In early summer, right after snowmelt, the first wildflowers are small, but profuse. Yellow **glacier lily** and white **avalanche lily** sometimes grow so thickly

SPREADING STONECROP
Sedum divergens

HEIGHT: 2" to 6"
BLOOMS: May to July
One of several stonecrops found in Washington, spreading stonecrop has a small yellow ball-head of five-petaled, rosettelike flowers growing on a single stem. Its strong roots can reach down into cracks, taking hold in barren, rocky areas. This stonecrop can be distinguished from its close relative, lance-leaved stonecrop, by its leaves. Spreading stonecrop has alternating oval leaves that grow relatively sparsely upon the stem, whereas the white lance-leaved stonecrop has many long, thin, pointed leaves.

that they carpet the glades. Another early bloomer, **pasqueflower**, or **western anemone**, grows about 6 inches tall and has five to eight white petals around a yellow center. As the plant goes to seed later in the summer, it has a distinctly different look, with hairy mop tops on taller stalks—a display that is even showier than its flowering stage. **White mountain avens** has a similar-looking blossom.

Between mile 1.0 and 2.0 of this trail, you'll see several purple flowers in late summer. **Leafy aster**, which grows 12 to 30 inches tall, has thin lavender rays around yellow centers. A deeper shade of purple, **small-flowered penstemon** bears whorled clusters of many trumpet-shaped blossoms. Look for purple-blue **Cusick's speedwell**, or **Cusick's veronica**, in moist soil. Also growing in wet areas, **mountain bog gentian** sprouts a violet-blue blossom that is often tightly coiled, like a bud. **Harebell** displays hanging, bell-shaped blue flowers.

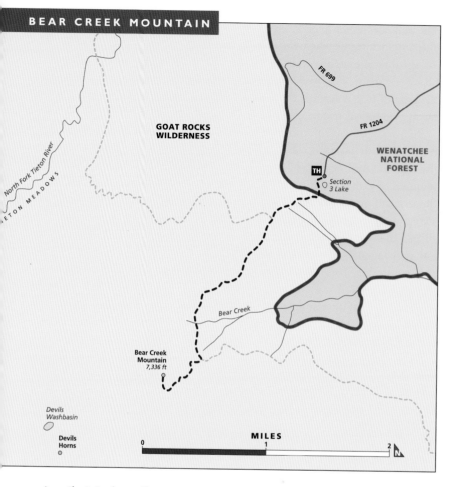

At mile 2.0, the trail crosses a stream, its banks lined with broadleaf lupine and **subalpine daisy**. With 30 to 100 rays, this daisy's flowers are usually lavender but can also be white or pink. **Corn lily**, or **false hellebore**, sprouts large, veined leaves in the shape of flames. Growing near water, **Lewis' monkey-flower**, also called **pink monkey-flower**, generates a vivid clump of funnel-shaped fuchsia blossoms. Pinkish purple **bog laurel** also resides here. Its blossom has 10 anthers that spring up with pollen when triggered by an insect.

This area offers the last good chance for camping, as the mountaintop is rocky and exposed to the wind. If you are planning to camp in the meadows, please be careful where you set up your tent so as not to damage the fragile environment.

At mile 2.5, you'll come to a junction. Continue on the right fork. (The left fork goes east to Conrad Meadows, along the South Fork Tieton River.)

The trail now begins to get steeper as it starts its climb up Bear Creek Mountain, entering rocky areas where the flowers are more sparse.

Shrubby cinquefoil produces buttercuplike flowers with narrow spiky leaves on woody stems. Also woody, blue to purple **shrubby penstemon** grows low to the ground to stay out of the wind and retain heat from soil or rock. **Elegant Jacob's-ladder** has five-petaled purple blossoms with yellow throats.

Snow might cover portions of the trail until late summer. In some years, a large, icy patch lingers all summer long. The rocky landscape continues. Toward the top, the trail begins to level, passing **pink mountain heather** and **white mountain heather**, both evergreen shrubs. These hardy plants bear bell-shaped flowers and needlelike leaves. **Spreading stonecrop**, with golden petals and stamens, grows among the rocks. **Spreading phlox**, revealing five-petaled, star-shaped blossoms in pink, lavender, or white, survives this harsh habitat with low-growing mats of spiny leaves.

At mile 3.5, you reach the summit. Watch your step, as the cliff drops hundreds of feet. The views here are unrestricted. The Goat Rocks—remnants of a volcano that once stood at more than 12,000 feet—provide a foreground for the distant Mt. Rainier and Mt. Adams. With a little luck, you might even spy mountain goats from your own rocky perch.

Boulders amid the wildflowers

Snowgrass Flat

Wildflower Hike 32

Goat Rocks Wilderness with Mt. Adams in the distance

Hiking through four miles of forest leads to some wonderful wildflower meadows beneath the snowfields of Goat Rocks. When Mount St. Helens erupted in May 1980, it sent tons of ash over this area and the meadows initially suffered. Since that time, however, the flowers have returned, benefiting from the rich nutrients deposited by the ash. With the right timing, you'll find pockets of solid wildflowers beneath Ives Peak and Old Snowy Mountain.

Bring binoculars to scan for mountain goats. Better yet, bring a sleeping bag and tent and plan on spending a day or two in this magnificent area. You can carry your own water or filter it from streams, as there are

Trail Rating	Difficult
Trail Length	10.2 miles round trip
Location	Goat Rocks Wilderness, near Packwood
Elevation	4,600 to 6,400 feet
Bloom Season	July to late September
Peak Bloom	Late July to late August
Contact	Gifford Pinchot National Forest, Cowlitz Valley Ranger District Office, (360) 497-1100
Directions	From Packwood, drive south on US 12 for 2.4 miles. Turn left (east) on Johnson Creek Road (FR 21). At 15.3 miles, look for two small lakes on the left. Just after the second lake, bear left on FR 2150, following the sign to Chambers Lake. Drive 0.9 mile to another junction and stay left again, continuing on FR 2150. Go 2.7 miles to the next junction and turn right on FR 040 (the road to Chambers Lake goes left). Proceed 0.1 mile and turn right on FR 405. Drive 0.2 mile to the Snowgrass Flat trailhead.

several along the way. Biting bugs can be a nuisance along lower Goat Creek, but you can usually hike this area quickly. Still, repellant is a good idea. These meadows often hold snow until late July, so August is the best time to witness Snowgrass Flat's floral show.

From the trailhead, take the Snowgrass Flat Trail (Trail No. 96). The first two miles of trail pass forest flowers, often inconspicuous white blossoms. The single white star-shaped flower of **woodnymph** hangs above evergreen leaves. **Twinflower**, another evergreen, reveals pairs of white to pale pink, funnel-shaped hanging blossoms. **Hooker's fairybell** also has hanging white flowers, bell-shaped with protruding stamens. **Pipsissewa** displays pink to white, crown-shaped flowers dangling from wiry stems. Other small white flowers along this section include **false lily-of-the-valley**, **foamflower**, and **clasping twistedstalk**. Many of these lower-elevation plants bloom in June, before hikers pass through in late July and August.

Western trillium is striking and instantly recognizable. Look for three large, white, pointed petals, which turn purplish with age. **Queen's cup** displays a white six-petaled flower and elegant tonguelike leaves. A common forest inhabitant, **false Solomon's seal** has clusters of tiny, cream-colored flowers and lance-shaped leaves. Three large leaves, like giant shamrocks, and a single spike of tiny white flowers identify **vanilla leaf**, a common plant that frontier women used to scent their clothes and cabins. In forest clearings, look for the yellow sunflowers of **heart-leaf arnica**.

Pinesap has pink to yellowish flowers but no leaves. A saprophyte, it relies on decayed organic matter in the soil for its nutrients. Another saprophyte, **western coralroot** is a pink orchid with narrow, leaf-like flowers on stems up to 20 inches tall.

At mile 1.8, the trail crosses Goat Creek, where, unless you're lucky, a horde of mosquitoes will greet you. At nearly a trot, I could outpace the mob. At mile 2.3, you begin climbing steeply, gaining nearly 1,000 feet in a little over a mile. At mile 3.7, you'll reach the junction with Trail No. 97, which branches to the right. Stay left. Soon, the forest begins to open.

With fernlike leaves, **elegant Jacob's-ladder** shows simple blue blossoms. **Old-man's whiskers**, or **long-plumed avens**, has purple-rose globes with arching sepals. In openings look for **yarrow's** lacy white flower and the white rounded heads of **beargrass**. A common flower, **thread-leaved sandwort** produces small white five-petaled flowers and grasslike leaves.

At mile 4.1, meadows begin to dominate and flowers take over as the trail enters Snowgrass Flat. In late July or August, **broadleaf lupine** blooms in abundance. This sweet-smelling flower might be the showiest plant in Washington's subalpine meadows. **Scarlet**, **magenta**, and **harsh paintbrush** also brighten the meadows in late July or August. Dwelling in meadows and forest openings, **small-flowered penstemon** is another common plant, exhibiting whorls of purple blossoms with white throats.

OLD-MAN'S WHISKERS OR LONG-PLUMED AVENS
Geum triflorum

HEIGHT: 6" to 20"
BLOOMS: May to June

Old-man's whiskers, or long-plumed avens, produces hanging rose-purple globes and bright green, feathery leaves. With small flowers that mature into silky, cottony, silver seedpods, it is also known as prairie smoke. Found in both eastern and western Washington, this delicate wildflower resides in a wide range of habitats, from dry, low elevations to lush meadows over 6,000 feet.

American Indians traditionally used the plant to make a tea similar to sassafras tea. They also used it as a body wash in sweat lodges, a bath soak for purification purposes, and as a cold or flu remedy.

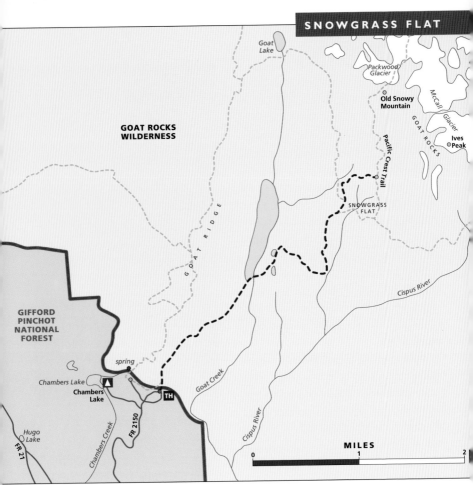

At mile 4.4, you'll come to another junction. Take a right here to stay on the Snowgrass Flat Trail (a left goes north to Goat Lake, 2.5 miles away). For the next half mile you'll pass through huge meadows as you continue through Snowgrass Flat. The white, soft cylinders of **American bistort** are downy at a distance. **Sitka valerian**, also white, bears stamen-fuzzy blossoms on 2-foot-tall stems.

Several composites speckle the meadows with yellow. The tallest is **arrowleaf butterweed**, showing a cluster of ray heads and sawtooth-edged triangular leaves. With fewer blossoms than butterweeds, **mountain arnica's** yellow petals are squared off with teeth at their tips. **Northern goldenrod** presents densely clustered yellow ray heads on 8- to 14-inch stems.

Cinquefoils, also yellow, display five-petaled, bowl-shaped blossoms. **Fan-leaved cinquefoil** bears leaflets in threes. **Diverse-leaved cinquefoil**, with similar disk flowers, has five to seven leaflets. Found in the upper meadows and often preferring rocky soil, **shrubby cinquefoil** is a woody-stemmed plant with needle-like leaves and yellow disks.

With large, sawtoothed leaves, **showy aster** prefers meadow edges. **Leafy bracted aster**, also purple with a yellow center, dwells in open areas. Growing in both open meadows and on rocky slopes, **Cascade aster** presents 6 to 15 widely separated lavender rays. Similar in look, daisy and fleabane are often confused with asters. **Cut-leaved fleabane** shows 40 to 60 thin, pink to lavender rays and a yellow center. **Subalpine daisy** has wider rays.

Early blooming flowers prevail just after snowmelt. **Glacier lily** makes its debut with elegantly arching yellow petals. **Pasqueflower**, or **western anemone**, joins in with five creamy white petals surrounding a cluster of stamens. This plant is more conspicuous during its seed stage in August, boasting a hairy oval head. Small and white, **spring beauty** is another early bloomer. **Snow or mountain buttercup** follows the melting snow with varnished yellow bowls. The flamboyant **shooting star** displays upswept fuchsia petals and a black anther tube.

In late summer, **red columbine** produces an ornate, hanging head of scarlet with large bright yellow stamens. **Columbia** or **tiger lily**, also blooming in late summer, boasts arching, yellow-orange, spotted petals and protruding stamens. **Chocolate** or **checker lily** is one of the only rusty-brownish flowers in the region. **Harebell**, with light blue hanging bells, often grows in dry soil.

The Snowgrass Flat Trail ends where it meets the Pacific Crest Trail at 5.1 miles. This is the turnaround point, though hardy hikers might wish to continue on this national scenic trail. (Traveling the PCT north from here takes you across the snowfields of Old Snowy Mountain. The PCT to the south wraps around the upper end of the Cispus River basin to Cispus Pass, with grand views of 8,184-foot Gilbert Peak.)

This wonderful high country definitely deserves a couple days of exploration, and the area's campsites provide many prime opportunities for an overnight stay. Be sure to bring warm clothing. Don't miss watching the fading light of sunset as it colors the Goat Rocks with a pink glow.

Wildflower Hike 33 **Pumice Plain**

Lupine above Spirit Lake, Mount St. Helens National Volcanic Monument

The word "surreal" comes up when people describe the blast zone of Mount St. Helens. After 123 years of silence, Mount St. Helens reawakened in the spring of 1980. With warning bulges, earthquakes, and emissions, the mountain at last exploded. A cloud of ash, rock, and gas—estimated at 650° F —shot northward as fast as 600 miles per hour, flattening 230 square miles of forest within minutes and sending 490 tons of ash over 22,008 square miles of the western United States. When the dust settled, Mount St. Helens was 1,300 feet shorter. Today, Mount St. Helens National Volcanic Monument preserves 110,000 acres around the mountain.

Trail Rating	Moderate
Trail Length	8.6 miles round trip
Location	Mount St. Helens National Volcanic Monument, south of Randle
Elevation	4,000 to 4,700 feet
Bloom Season	June to late August
Peak Bloom	Mid-July to early August
Contact	Gifford Pinchot National Forest, Mount St. Helens National Volcanic Monument, (360) 247-3900
Directions	Stop in Randle at the Cowlitz Valley Ranger District Office for current road and trail conditions, make sure your gas tank is full, and take plenty of water. From US 12 in Randle, drive south on FR 25 for 22.0 miles. Turn right (west) on FR 99, signed "Mount St. Helens—Windy Ridge Viewpoint." Follow this road 17.0 miles to its end, where there is a parking area.

This hike, different from any other in this book, illustrates an amazing ecological story of renewal. Plant recovery here is still in a very early stage. Every year adds new varieties of vegetation and a greater abundance of existing species. You will see firsthand the processes of plant dispersal, succession, and survival.

The hike begins as you pass through the gate at the south end of the parking area. Follow the Truman Trail (Trail No. 207) along the east side of Windy Ridge on a nearly level course. Along this gravel road, which you follow for the first 1.7 miles of this hike, you'll spot many disturbance species, the first plants to revegetate an altered landscape. Look for fuchsia-pink patches of **fireweed**, with clusters of four-petaled flowers on tall, erect, leafy stems. **Pearly everlasting** grows in clumps of many stems, each with a cluster of white blossoms. **Yarrow**, with white, lacy flower heads, has adapted to a wide variety of habitats in Washington.

A number of plants you see along the way actually survived the eruption. Their roots endured and, if in an area where the deposited rock and ash eroded quickly, they were able to send up new shoots. A few woody plants, such as **goatsbeard** and **elderberry**, were able survive this way. Goatsbeard, with clumps of stringy white flowers, grows up to 7 feet tall. Elderberry, which grows up to 10 feet, has clusters of creamy white flowers along with leaves grouped in five to seven leaflets.

On the right side of the road near a seep, look for **mountain monkey-flower**, sporting large, yellow, snapdragonlike flowers with small maroon dots. Also found in moist areas, **corn lily**, or **false hellebore**, has a spray of flower tassels and large, veined, flame-shaped leaves.

At mile 1.7, the trail rounds the ridge, offering great views across the vast Pumice Plain and Spirit Lake. At a junction with Trail No. 216D, stay right to keep on the Truman Trail, which traverses down a slope.

Cascade aster, a lavender composite with widely separated rays around a yellow disk, is making a comeback here. Able to survive in varied habitats, **scarlet paintbrush** produces bright red bracts. Another of the first group of recovery flowers, **Cascade penstemon** bears clustered purple whorls of trumpet-shaped blossoms. Blue **broadleaf lupine** is prevalent here and in many places along the trail. This fragrant flower adds nitrogen to the soil, supplying an important nutrient for other returning plants.

MOUNTAIN MONKEY-FLOWER
Mimulus tilingii

HEIGHT: 2" to 12"
BLOOMS: May to August
A subalpine plant, mountain monkey-flower grows along cold streams and in other wet places, forming dense green mats. These yellow flowers are slightly shorter than their monkey-flower cousins, but have the same large, two-lipped, tubular flowers. The paired leaves bear a distinct rounded shape.

At mile 2.0, there is a junction with Trail No. 216E. Take the right fork to stay on the Truman Trail, which gradually descends across the Pumice Plain. The lightweight gray pumice rock was deposited during the eruption; the air pockets in the rocks allow some of them to float on water. Often growing in mats among rocky rubble, **Cardwell's penstemon** displays purple to violet-blue, funnel-shaped blossoms on 4- to 12-inch stems. The low-growing **alpine lupine**, sometimes called **dwarf mountain lupine** or **Lyall's lupine**, also makes its home in these rocky areas.

At about mile 3.0, you'll see several plots that botanists laid out while conducting extensive research on habitat recovery. The trail continues downward, passing near the south end of Spirit Lake. The lake once nestled in a serene, wooded valley. Today the surrounding area is denuded and a mass of blasted timber floats on the lake's surface. At mile 4.3, this is a good turnaround spot.

PUMICE PLAIN

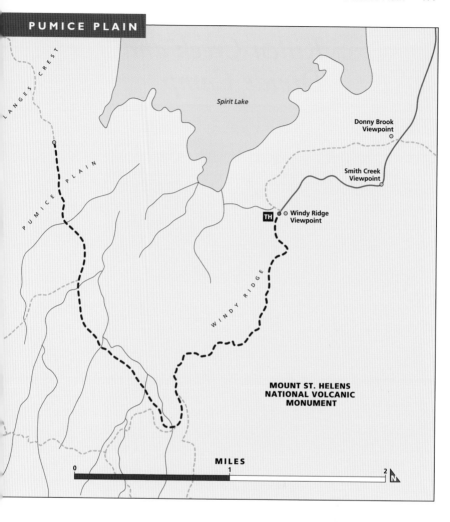

Spirit Lake

Donny Brook
Viewpoint

Smith Creek
Viewpoint

LANGES CREST

PUMICE PLAIN

TH ○ Windy Ridge
      Viewpoint

WINDY RIDGE

MOUNT ST. HELENS
NATIONAL VOLCANIC
MONUMENT

MILES

0   1   2 N

Wildflower
Hike 34
Killen Creek and Divide Camp

Mt. Adams rises above a lupine meadow, Mt. Adams Wilderness

The north side of Mt. Adams provides a spectacular landscape. Here, within the 42,280-acre Mt. Adams Wilderness, glaciers reach down to moraines, which empty into flower-filled meadows noisy with rushing streams. It's a fine place to pitch a tent, especially under a full moon, with moonlight glinting off the glaciers.

You can turn this hike into a loop by hiking up Killen Creek Trail (Trail No. 113), along the Pacific Crest Trail to Divide Camp Trail (Trail No. 112), and then down to FR 2329. Even if the day looks fair, bring warm clothing, as mountain weather is fickle.

Trail Rating	Difficult
Trail Length	8.6 miles round trip, or 9.5-mile loop
Location	Mt. Adams Wilderness, southeast of Randle
Elevation	4,600 to 6,160 feet
Bloom Season	July to late September
Peak Bloom	Late July to late August
Contact	Gifford Pinchot National Forest, Mt. Adams Ranger District Office, (509) 395-3400
Directions	This trailhead is way off the beaten track, so set out well-supplied with food, water, and gas. Visit the Cowlitz Valley Ranger District Office in Randle for current road conditions and to pick up a map of the area.
	From Randle, drive south on FR 25, soon crossing the Cowlitz River. In 1.0 mile, turn left on FR 23 and set your odometer. Stay on FR 23 for 32 miles, following signs to Takhlakh Lake. Turn left on FR 2329 and reset your odometer. At 0.8 mile, stay right at the junction with FR 5601 (Olallie Lake Road). Continue 1.6 miles and stay left at the junction with FR 026 (Takhlakh Lake Road), which puts you back on FR 2329. The parking area and trailhead are 6 miles farther.

From the Killen Creek trailhead, the route wastes no time in climbing uphill, straight toward the Mt. Adams summit. If you're carrying a heavy pack, this can be a tough few miles. This trail sees quite a bit of traffic—hikers and horseback riders, as well as climbers who use the trail to access higher elevations.

The first two miles of trail climb steadily through forest. In forest clearings, **beargrass** and **yarrow** show clumps of white. Huckleberries ripen in August, providing for a tasty treat during rest stops. Many forest dwellers bloom in June, before most hikers arrive. **Woodnymph** has a single, white, star-shaped flower hanging above evergreen leaves. **Twinflower**, another evergreen, reveals pairs of white to pale pink, funnel-shaped blossoms. The crown-shaped flowers of **pipsissewa**, generally pink to white, dangle from wiry stems. Other small white flowers along this section include **false lily-of-the-valley**, with spikes of tiny clustered flowers; **foamflower**, distinguished by its small star-shaped cups with 10 protruding stamens; and **clasping twistedstalk**, bearing bell-shaped blossoms with arching petals accompanied by lancelike veined leaves. **Western trillium** is clearly identifiable by its three large, white, pointed petals, which turn purplish with age.

Between miles 2.2 and 2.6, several open areas reveal **thread-leaved sandwort**, exhibiting small white five-petaled flowers and grasslike leaves. With fernlike leaves, **elegant Jacob's-ladder** shows blue blossoms. Look for the yellow sunflower of **heart-leaf arnica** in the forest clearings. **Wild strawberry** resembles the garden variety, only smaller.

DWARF MOUNTAIN, ALPINE, OR LYALL'S LUPINE
Lupinus lyallii

HEIGHT: 2" to 6"
BLOOMS: July to September
Found in high elevations of the Cascades on rocky, often volcanic slopes, dwarf mountain lupine is less common than other lupines. This lovely flower has stems tipped with pea-shaped, bright blue blossoms showing tears of white on the inner surface. Silky hairs cover the stems as well as the leaves, which are made up of five to nine leaflets.

If you have ever been fortunate enough to come across a field of lupine just after a rainfall or heavy dew, you will recognize the magic within the shape of the lupine's leaves. The leaflets catch a single drop of rain or dew and hold it in their center like a tiny, glistening jewel in the palm of a light green hand.

At mile 2.6, the trees give way to meadows, offering the first glimpses of Mt. Adams' summit. Soon after the snow melts, early flowers mature quickly, taking advantage of the wet ground. Several small flower types look stylish along the trail: fuchsia **shooting star**, yellow **glacier lily**, white **avalanche lily**, and **marsh marigold**, also white. **Western anemone**, or **pasqueflower**, produces six rounded white petals around yellow stamens. **Globeflower** looks similar but only has five petals.

At peak season in late July or early August, the meadows display many common subalpine flowers. **American sawwort** grows 3 to 4 feet high with violet blossoms and sawtooth-edged leaves. **Broadleaf lupine** boasts clumps of purple-blue flowers. Often growing near lupine, **American bistort** bears a single white cylindrical head made of many tiny blossoms. **Sitka valerian** also has a mass of tiny white blossoms.

Small-flowered penstemon reveal balled heads of many purple, trumpet-shaped blossoms. In varying shades of red, **harsh**, **scarlet**, and **magenta**

KILLEN CREEK AND DIVIDE CAMP

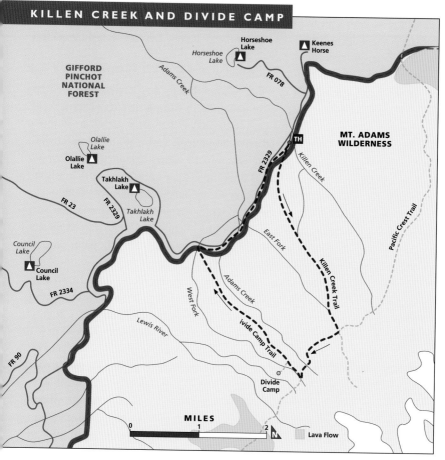

paintbrush exhibit their color with large bracts. **Mountain arnica** usually generates a single yellow ray flower on each stem. **Tiger** or **Columbia lily** presents a large, orange, speckled, hanging blossom with projecting stamens.

At mile 2.7, the path reaches the clear-running East Fork Adams Creek. Yellow **mountain monkey-flower** and fuchsia **Lewis' monkey-flower** display lovely trumpet-shaped blossoms. A small plant, **Cusick's speedwell**, or **Cusick's veronica**, exhibits four-petaled purple blossoms. Look for **mountain blue-eyed grass** with six small lavender petals around yellow centers. Leafless **naked broomrape** has lavender blossoms resembling those found on penstemons. This parasitic plant lives off plants such as stonecrops and saxifrages.

Members of the lousewort family congregate in wet areas. Conspicuous **elephant's head** shows many tiny pink blossoms. Look closely and you'll see their "trunks" and "ears." The curving, pink to white blossoms of **sickletop lousewort** resemble hand sickles. **Bracted lousewort** and **coiled-beak lousewort** bear curving flowers of a pale yellow to reddish hue.

Cinquefoils exhibit five petals on each yellow blossom. **Fan-leaved cinque-foil** has leaflets in threes, similar to strawberry leaves. **Diverse-leaved cinquefoil** has five to seven leaflets.

You'll find some excellent campsites on your way to the Pacific Crest Trail, but please be sure to search out a spot that will not damage fragile vegetation. Several types of purple asters and daisies reside along this upper stretch of trail. With large sawtooth-edged leaves, the purple-petaled **showy aster** prefers open forest and meadow edges. **Leafy bracted aster**, also purple with a yellow center, dwells in open meadows. **Cascade aster** presents 6 to 15 widely separated lavender rays. With 40 to 60 thin rays, **cut-leaved fleabane** is pink to lavender with a yellow center. The larger **subalpine daisy** bears white, purple, or pink blossoms.

You can't miss some of the bigger species that grow here. Sometimes reaching 6 feet tall in moist areas, **cow parsnip** sprouts a white, umbrella-shaped flower head and leaves that can span 10 inches. Large, strongly veined, flame-shaped leaves develop on **false hellebore**, or **corn lily**.

At mile 3.1, you reach the junction with the Pacific Crest Trail. Turn right (west) on the PCT and pass through verdant meadows blooming with most of the flowers you've seen so far. Also look for **pink mountain heather**, a woody shrub with numerous hanging bell-shaped flowers and evergreen needles.

At mile 4.1, you'll cross a branch of Adams Creek; at mile 4.3, you'll arrive at the main watercourse, the rushing Adams Creek. The stream runs swollen and gray from draining the massive Adams Glacier. The landscape here resembles a rocky moonscape, a harsh environment home to hardy survivors. **Alpine, dwarf mountain**, or **Lyall's lupine** flourishes in very little soil. **Cardwell's penstemon** and **cliff penstemon** brighten the barren ground with funnel-shaped pink to purple flowers. A small shrub, **shrubby cinquefoil** has five-petaled yellow blossoms and needlelike leaves.

Shortly after crossing Adams Creek, you'll come to a junction with the Divide Camp Trail (Trail No. 112), which descends to FR 2329. Return the same way you came, 4.3 miles back to the trailhead. Or complete the loop by turning right (north) and following the Divide Camp Trail 2.8 miles to the road, and then turning right (east) and hiking or hitching down the road 2.4 miles to your vehicle.

Plan to spend a couple days exploring this magnificent terrain. Mt. Rainier and the peaks of the Goat Rocks are clearly visible in fair weather. The flattened top of Mount St. Helens stands to the west. What a place this would have been to watch the blast! Will Mt. Adams follow suit? Camp here and you'll get to watch the sunset as it illuminates the mountain's glaciers with a pink glow.

Hellroaring Meadow

*Meadow near
Mt. Adams*

At 12,276 feet, Mt. Adams—Washington's second-highest mountain—spawns a web of glaciers and snowfields whose melt-off waters wildflowers in places like Hellroaring Meadow. Not only does this area nurture moisture-loving vegetation, it offers fabulous views of Mt. Adams' eastern flank.

This route travels the Heart Lake Trail (Trail No. 184) to Heart Lake. The nearly level trail begins by heading west through open forest of Douglas fir. In early summer you can find **western trillium**, with three white, tonguelike petals that fade to purple as the flower ages. Growing up to 3 feet tall, **Hooker's fairybell** reveals dangling white bells with long,

Trail Rating	Easy
Trail Length	2.4 miles round trip
Location	Yakama Indian Reservation, northeast of Trout Lake
Elevation	5,260 to 5,500 feet
Bloom Season	July to late September
Peak Bloom	Late July through late August
Contact	Gifford Pinchot National Forest, Mt. Adams Ranger District Office, (509) 395-3400
Directions	The Yakama Indian Reservation owns and manages the land where this hike is located. Stop in at the Mt. Adams Ranger District Office at 2455 Hwy. 141 in Trout Lake for maps and information on trail and road conditions.

From WA 141 in Trout Lake, drive north on FR 23 for 1.1 miles and turn right on FR 80. Go 0.6 mile, turn right on FR 82 (Mt. Adams Recreation Area Road), and set your odometer. Paved at first, FR 82 becomes very rough as it enters the Yakama Indian Reservation; high-clearance vehicles are recommended. Follow the signs for Bird Lake, clearly indicated at every junction, and proceed about 14.0 miles to Mirror Lake. There is a campground at Mirror Lake, which makes a good base camp. Continue straight for 1.8 miles to the Hellroaring Meadow trailhead parking area on the left.

protruding stamens. **Pipsissewa**, or **prince's pine**, shows three to eight loosely hanging pink blossoms and toothed evergreen leaves.

In a class of alienlike saprophytes that lack chlorophyll, **pinesap** relies on nutrients from decaying matter in the soil. Its nearly transparent, pale yellow to pinkish bell-shaped flowers hang from a fleshy stem.

At 0.7 mile, the forest begins to open and you'll reach a junction. Before heading right (north) to Heart Lake, take a brief detour and go straight for another 0.1 mile, where a spring harbors **mountain monkey-flower**. With tiny dots and a bearded throat, the five-petaled tubular flowers usually grow low to the ground in saturated areas, sometimes forming spectacular masses.

Now return to the Heart Lake Trail, which travels north across the rich, wet Hellroaring Meadow. Late in the summer, **mountain bog gentian**—one of the most elegant wildflowers—opens its giant purple buds to reveal trumpet-shaped blossoms with five deep blue petals. Nearly the same deep blue color but less conspicuous, **Cusick's speedwell**, or **Cusick's veronica**, has four small petals and two protruding stamens with one even longer pistil.

Many members of the lousewort family, which often sprout unusual flowers, thrive in damp areas. Perhaps the oddest looking is **elephant's head**, with miniature pink flowers resembling the head of said pachyderm—complete with ears and a trunk—on maroon, 8- to 20-inch, nonbranching stems. **Bracted lousewort** displays flowers that vary in color from white to yellow to maroon. Look for the curled, popcornlike white blossoms of **sickletop lousewort** near pockets of trees. Another flower found in moist terrain is the **white bog-orchid**, with sweet-smelling blossoms that look like white butterflies on a stick.

A common woody shrub in this wet area, **rosy spirea** has bright pink clusters of flowers with projecting stamens that look soft and fuzzy. An early flower, **sweet coltsfoot** displays blossoms with a mass of rays and large jagged leaves, which often fill out after the flower blooms. Several asters inhabit the area, including **leafy aster**, with about 30 slender purple rays around a yellow button center.

Continue following the trail to Heart Lake. Or, after hiking toward Heart Lake about 0.1 mile beyond the spring junction, if you have experience hiking off-trail, you might want to carefully ramble to the northwest for about 0.3 mile. Here, you'll enter meadows with great views of cascades plunging from the cliffs above. These meadows exhibit a good variety of wildflowers, but without a trail, the going is slow at times. **Pasqueflower**, or **western anemone**, transforms from a small and simple, white-petaled flower in early summer to a hairy, moplike seed head on a tall stem in late summer. Another early bloomer here, **glacier lily** has a nodding yellow blossom with six arching petals, six conspicuous stamens, and two broad, oval leaves at the base. With white cylinder-shaped flowers that wave in the breeze, **American bistort** has protruding stamens and a fuzzy appearance. Also fuzzy and white, **Sitka valerian** grows up to 40 inches tall. The tiny flowers of **cottongrass** often go unnoticed, but their seed heads are conspicuous, resembling tufts of white cotton.

MOUNTAIN BOG GENTIAN
Gentiana calycosa

HEIGHT: 4" to 12"
BLOOMS: Late summer

Common in the Olympics, mountain bog gentian favors deep soil in high-elevation wetland areas. The plant's single, trumpetlike, deep blue flower sprouts from a tall stem and opens to the sun. Pleats between petal lobes create a ruffled effect. The blossom closes into a large purple bud when the weather is cool and cloudy. The gentian's oval leaves climb in pairs all the way up the stem.

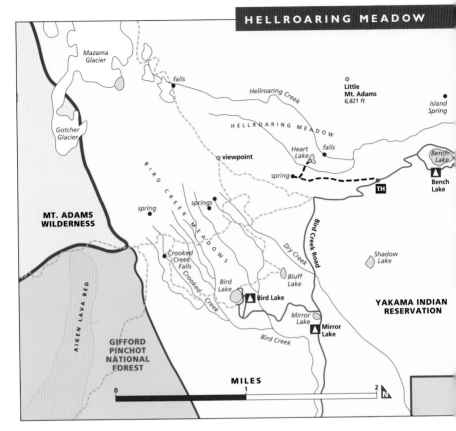

If you've made the optional ramble through the meadows, return to the trail and continue 0.1 mile to Heart Lake by crossing a stream. Or, if you have a topographic map, you should be able to find this lake while returning from the upper meadows. If you're feeling hot—and brave—cool off by taking a dip in Heart Lake.

A boot path starting at the east side of Heart Lake leads to the northeast about 0.1 mile to an overlook of Hellroaring Falls. You can't see much of this huge waterfall from the overlook, as it is in a deep gorge that hides it from view, but you can hear its thunder.

Take a moment to gaze at the volcano before you, and wonder about the landscape it has created. This mountain, in various forms, has existed for almost a million years. The area has undergone wild geologic activities, at times similar to the powerful more recent blast of neighboring Mount St. Helens.

Bird Creek Meadows

Wildflower
Hike 36

*Crooked Creek
Falls, Yakama
Indian Reservation*

Bird Creek Meadows is renowned for its wildflowers. A glance at a topographic map tells why: water. Bird Creek and Crooked Creek take in many tributaries as they traverse Bird Creek Meadows. At one point along the trail, you step over nine small streams in a mile.

This 3-mile loop encompasses an abundance of water-loving flowers. The total mileage of this hike also includes a 1.4-mile round-trip diversion to other magnificent wildflower meadows, leading to stunning views of 12,276-foot Mt. Adams, Washington's second-highest peak, as well as a 1.2-mile round-trip spur route to views of Mazama Glacier. For a shorter hike, you can just stick to the main loop.

Trail Rating	Moderate
Trail Length	5.6-mile loop
Location	Yakama Indian Reservation, northeast of Trout Lake
Elevation	5,590 to 5,660 feet
Bloom Season	July to late September
Peak Bloom	Late July to late August
Contact	Gifford Pinchot National Forest, Mt. Adams Ranger District Office, (509) 395-3400
Directions	The Yakama Indian Reservation owns and manages the land where this hike is located. The Mt. Adams ranger station in Trout Lake has a map and general information about the area, so stop in before your hike to pick up a map and to check road conditions.

From WA 141 in Trout Lake, drive north on FR 23 for 1.1 miles and turn right on FR 80. Go 0.6 mile, turn right on FR 82 (Mt. Adams Recreation Area Road), and set your odometer. Paved at first, FR 82 becomes very rough as it enters the Yakama Indian Reservation; high-clearance vehicles are recommended.

Proceed about 14.0 miles, following the signs for Bird Lake, clearly indicated at every junction. After you pass Mirror Lake, where there is a campground, turn left (west) on the marked road to Bird Lake. Continue 1.0 mile to Bird Lake, where there is another campground. If you are day-hiking, stay to the left at the campground entrance and park on the south side of the lake. This is the trailhead for Crooked Creek Falls, where you will start this hike through Bird Creek Meadows.

The hike begins on the south side of Bird Lake, at the trailhead for Crooked Creek Falls. At first, you pass by an unsightly area of administrative buildings, but you soon enter open forest and meadow. You'll hear the sound of cascading streams along much of the way to the falls.

You'll shortly cross a stream with an adjacent flower-speckled meadow. **Broadleaf lupine**, one of the most common flowers in subalpine environments, grows 1 to 2 feet tall in a rounded clump with many deep blue blossoms. Often found near lupine, **Sitka valerian** bears clusters of small white flowers with protruding stamens, making the blossoms look fuzzy. Bright **Indian paintbrush** has large scarlet bracts, which actually hide its smaller tube-shaped flowers. **Mountain arnica**, a yellow ray flower, can be recognized by its serrated petal tips and coarsely toothed leaves.

The trail skirts through forest, where **bunchberry** (also called **dwarf dogwood**) displays a white four-pointed flower framed by symmetrical, veined leaves. **Western trillium**, another forest flower, is also white, though it turns purple with age. You can identify the trillium by looking for threes: three leaves and three pointed petals around yellow stamens.

At about mile 0.5, you come upon Crooked Creek, flowing over many small cascades. The trail parallels the creek through forest and small meadows to reach Crooked Creek Falls at mile 1.0. Flowers fill the meadow below the falls. **American bistort** has a single, cylinder-shaped cluster of small white flowers with numerous stamens, giving them a downy appearance. Several types of aster grow here, including **Douglas' aster**, with masses of purple ray flower heads on each stem, and **leafy bracted aster**, also purple, with at least five varieties found in Washington.

Continue up the trail 0.2 mile from the falls to a T junction with the Round-the-Mountain Trail. Although our loop trip takes a right (east) at this junction, a left (west) will take you on the first diversion of this hike, a 1.4-mile round trip back to this point. This detour takes you to views of Mt. Adams and exceptional wildflower meadows, some of the largest in the area.

As you hike this detour, look for elegant **mountain bog gentian** in moist areas. This plant, which grows 4 to 12 inches tall, has deep blue tubular flowers and small smooth opposite leaves. Along stream banks, you'll likely see the bright pink of **Lewis' monkey-flower** and the yellow of **mountain monkey-flower**. Both have five-petaled trumpets and often grow in masses next to running water.

In the open meadows, early bloomers include **glacier lily**, with six brilliant yellow backward-curving tepals hanging on 6- to

STREAM VIOLET
Viola glabella

HEIGHT: 2" to 10"
BLOOMS: April to July

Even though it is a member of the violet family, the stream violet produces a yellow flower. Its five-petaled blossoms are small, with three lower petals marked in dark-colored veins toward their centers. The stream violet displays two or three alternating, heart-shaped serrated leaves near the top of its stem, and it bears brown seeds in capsules.

A common perennial, stream violet is found in many environments, from forests to marshy areas. Blooming just as the snow begins to melt, it grows predominantly in wet soils in the foothills and higher elevations of the Cascade and Olympic mountain ranges.

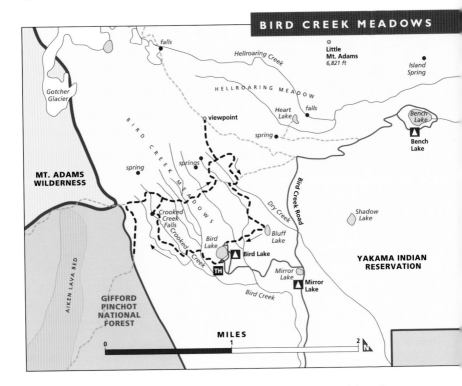

BIRD CREEK MEADOWS

10-inch stems. This lily and its cousin, the white **avalanche lily**, often carpet meadows soon after snowmelt. **Marsh marigold**, another early bloomer, has 5 to 11 white petal-like sepals. **Jeffrey's shooting star** appears in summer with a hanging flower head of elegant fuchsia petals pointing upward.

Bird's-beak lousewort, one of several louseworts found in moist subalpine habitats, produces clustered pink beaks at the stem top and fernlike leaves. Another lousewort, **elephant's head** has pink flower heads complete with elephant trunks and ears. **Sickletop lousewort** displays pinkish brown flowers on maroon stems and is usually found in the shade. Also common in moist meadows, **false hellebore**, or **corn lily**, grows spikes of fluffy looking flowers and beautiful masses of large, strongly veined, cabbagelike leaves on 2- to 5-foot-tall stalks.

After 0.3 mile on the Round-the-Mountain Trail, there is a junction with the Snipes Mountain Trail (Trail No. 11) on the left. Take a detour onto Snipes Mountain Trail (a detour on our detour) as the trail drops down for about 0.4 mile through some beautiful, large meadows. Just about every flower observed in the meadows on the loop hike can be found in this area, along with a few new ones.

In moist areas, look for **rosy spirea**. Much like the garden variety, this woody shrub exhibits pink flowers with projecting stamens that create a fuzzy appearance. Also in wet soils, **white bog-orchid** displays sweet-smelling, white larkspurlike blossoms. An early bloomer, small **spring beauty** shows five white petals, usually pink-veined.

Turn around after 0.4 mile on the Snipes Mountain Trail, where the path enters forested areas. Return to the junction where the Round-the-Mountain Trail meets the Crooked Creek Trail, just above Crooked Creek Falls.

From the junction, now proceed east on the Round-the-Mountain Trail, hiking through little meadows and across several small streams. **Cusick's veronica**, or **Cusick's speedwell**, grows here, with four deep violet petals and two long, delicate stamens. Look for yellow **stream violet**, with heart-shaped leaves. With limp clusters of light purple-blue flowers, **tall bluebell** also prefers wet areas.

At 0.6 mile from the junction, a trail departs to the left, leading to a dead-end point with amazing cliff-top views of the cascades pouring out of Mt. Adams' Mazama Glacier into Hellroaring Meadow (see Hike 35). This detour goes 0.3 mile across small meadows and streams to another left turn. Take this left and continue 0.3 mile more to the viewpoint.

The rocky ledges in this area harbor a number of wildflowers. Look for the neon pink to purple tubular flowers of **cliff penstemon** growing in low, shrubby mats. **Arctic sandwort** has small white star-shaped flowers. The needlelike evergreen leaves of **pink mountain heather** form a backdrop for its gracefully hanging, cup-shaped pink flowers. **Spreading phlox**, which prefers dry, rocky places, puts forth white, pink, or lavender blossoms.

From the viewpoint, return to the last junction, 0.3 mile back the way you came, and turn left (east). The trail curves south, passing the Bird Creek Meadows picnic area and several small meadows. With yellow buttercuplike flowers, **fan-leaved cinquefoil** blooms in late July and August. **Pasqueflower**, or **western anemone**, begins its cycle as a low-growing, five- to eight-petaled white flower. As it keeps growing and goes to seed, it produces a fuzzy mop head sometimes called "mouse-on-a-stick." Flamboyant **red columbine** and yellow-orange **tiger lily** attract hummingbirds. **Arrowleaf butterweed**, usually 2 to 3 feet tall, blooms with clusters of small yellow ray flowers. In the open forest, look for **woodland penstemon**, with bright pink-purple flowers on long, leaning stems. Deep purple **monkshood** looks similar to a larkspur but is poisonous.

In another 0.3 mile, you'll rejoin the Round-the-Mountain Trail. Turn right (west) at this T junction, and in 0.1 mile, take a left (east), leaving the Round-the-Mountain Trail to drop down to Bluff Lake. In the open forest, **elegant Jacob's-ladder** generates pale blue flowers and leaves that resemble those of the pea family. **Star-flowered false Solomon's seal** shows deeply veined, lance-shaped leaves and clusters of small cream-colored blossoms.

In 0.6 mile from the Round-the-Mountain Trail, Bluff Lake lies nestled under a steep ridge. Look for **vanilla leaf**, with giant shamrocklike leaves, and **queen's cup**, with a single white six-petaled blossom. On the west side of Bluff Lake, a trail leads 0.5 mile west, back to your vehicle at Bird Lake, where an icy dip revives the weary hiker.

Wildflower Hike 37 # Dog Mountain

Trail along Dog Mountain, Columbia Gorge

Trail Rating	Difficult
Trail Length	7.4 miles round trip
Location	Columbia River Gorge National Scenic Area, east of Carson
Elevation	190 to 2,948 feet
Bloom Season	March to late July
Peak Bloom	April to late May
Contact	Columbia River Gorge National Scenic Area, Hood River, Oregon, (541) 386-2333
Directions	From Carson, drive 9.0 miles east on WA 14. On the left (north) side of the road, look for a parking area big enough to accommodate about 40 cars.

og Mountain rises almost 3,000 feet above the Columbia River. The Dog Mountain Trail (Trail No. 147) leads to the summit of Dog Mountain and offers some of the best vistas of the Columbia Gorge. You'll see a great variety of wildflowers here, as the area lies at a commingling of habitats—where the dry country of eastern Washington meets the moist forests of western Washington. As spring progresses into summer, every week sees new plants blooming, providing a continually changing show of flowers.

This trail is popular. I recommend hiking it on weekdays or in the very early morning if you want to avoid throngs of hikers. Also, a few precautions are in order. While the lower portion of the trail is protected, the summit can get chilly and windy, so be prepared and take appropriate clothing. Keep an eye out for rattlesnakes, which inhabit the area. Patches of poison ivy grow along the lower section of trail; avoid these clusters of often-shiny leaves, which contain a chemical that causes itchy irritations.

From the parking area, find the large trailboard directing hikers to the Dog Mountain Trail. There is an outhouse available at the parking area, but no water. There are several junctions along the trail, so if you have children hiking with you, you'll want to keep them within sight. Also, this is a long, steep climb, so hiking poles would prove quite helpful in making the ascent.

The first half of the hike is mainly through mixed forest of Garry oak, ponderosa pine, Douglas fir, red alder, vine maple, and bigleaf maple. Several small flowering trees grow here. **Serviceberry**, also called **juneberry** or **Saskatoon berry**, usually stands 10 to 15 feet tall, with many clusters of five-petaled white blossoms and small, rounded leaves. **Western flowering dogwood** is stunning in May when blossoms of four white petal-like bracts cover its 20- to 50-foot canopy. Spiny **black hawthorn's** five-petaled flowers form white clusters, maturing

GRASS WIDOW
Sisyrinchium inflatum

HEIGHT: 6" to 16"

BLOOMS: April to early May

A member of the iris family with grasslike leaves, grass widow has a single stem from which it puts forth a single flower. Its name originates from the way the little flower bows its head as though in mourning. Its small flowers are blue, purple, and even reddish on occasion.

Usually growing in tufts with tall stems, grass widow is abundant in sagebrush and ponderosa pine regions. Also known as purple-eyed grass, it thrives in moist environments, appearing soon after snow disappears.

in April and May. Branching stems of blossoms bloom on **bitter cherry**, whose five-petaled white flowers are very fragrant.

A number of woody-stemmed plants thrive on the forest floor. **Oregon grape**, an evergreen with hollylike leaves, displays sweet-smelling, fuzzy yellow blossoms in May and June. Also in May and June, look for **wild rose**, with lovely pink blossoms and a mass of yellow stamens. **Thimbleberry** bears white tissuey flowers, large maplelike leaves, and, in late summer, edible red berries. Never consume any wild plant without absolute certainty as to its identity.

The first 0.5 mile of trail passes some beautiful Garry oaks with **broadleaf lupine** and **deltoid balsamroot** growing underneath. These partner plants add great splashes of blue and yellow throughout the gorge. **American vetch** and **woolly vetch** are abundant in forest openings. Bearing clusters of purple pealike flowers and compound leaves in pairs, vetches add vital nitrogen to the soil. Also widespread, **desert-parsley** has a yellow flower head that looks like exploding fireworks. In low-elevation openings, early flowers include pink to lavender **grass widow** and **yellow bell**, which, not surprisingly, is yellow and bell-shaped.

At mile 0.6, there is a junction. Both trails lead to the top—the left fork through forest and the right fork mostly in the open, which is the better choice for enjoying flowers and views. Stay to the right here.

Look for the small **wild strawberry** growing on the forest floor, presenting five-petaled white flowers and jagged leaves. With elegant lance-shaped leaves, **star-flowered false Solomon's seal** reveals clusters of tiny white starburst blossoms. **Broad-leaved starflower** has a single white bloom in the center of leaf whorls. Another forest dweller, **Hooker's fairybell** produces two or three hanging white blossoms with protruding stamens.

At mile 1.6, the trail leaves the forest, opening up to exceptional views of the Columbia River. The flowers thicken here. In May, you'll see a profusion of lupine and balsamroot. The orange-red bracts of **harsh paintbrush** decorate the way here to the summit. **Nuttall's larkspur**, a member of the delphinium family, boasts a graceful blue-purple five-petaled blossom. **Western spring beauty** bears star-shaped white blossoms.

At mile 2.0, the path joins with the northern end of the trail you bypassed at mile 0.6. Stay to the right here, following the sign to Dog Mountain. The trail enters forest again, where open areas host **ballhead waterleaf**, displaying balls of many tiny purple flowers. **Phantom orchid**, entirely white, grows in moist, shady spots. A saprophyte, it relies on decayed matter in the soil for its nutrients. **Stream violet**, with yellow pansylike flowers and heart-shaped leaves, also resides in moist areas. Forest-dwelling **three-leaved anemone** presents a single white five-petaled blossom. Along the edges of the forest, **prairie star** sprouts small thin-petaled flowers and grassy leaves. Thimbleberry and Oregon grape are widespread in this area.

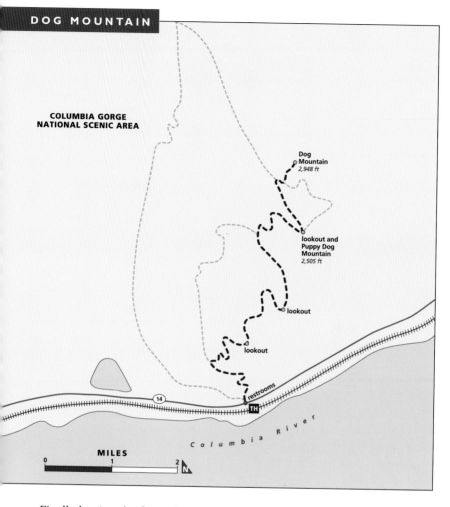

Finally leaving the forest for good, the trail traverses meadows on the high slopes of the mountain. At mile 2.5, the trail forks again. Go left for the best views of flower-filled meadows. In addition to many of the wildflowers already noted, several types of phlox grow here, including **spreading** and **showy phlox**. Their five-petaled flowers might be pink or purple and usually grow in thick mats. Purple **leafy aster** blooms toward midsummer, along with **showy fleabane**, another lavender ray flower. The crimson trumpets of **skyrocket**, also known as **scarlet gilia**, dot the landscape.

Early in the season, different groupings of flowers bloom in the mountain-top meadows. One of the first to bloom, **buttercup** produces shiny yellow bowls and sometimes covers areas en masse. Purplish **early blue violet**, which closely resembles the garden variety, flowers in May. Often blooming soon after snowmelt, the small yellow **glacier lily** displays arching petals and projecting stamens.

Mile 3.4 brings you to another trail junction. Following the sign, stay on the middle of three forks to reach the summit of Dog Mountain. Several other members of the lily family reside in the upper meadows and bloom later in the season. With fascinating color and shape, **chocolate lily** is one of the only brown flowers in the state. The flower heads hang down with green-yellow mottling on the six brown petals. **Howell's triteleia**, another lily, has tubular, six-petaled blossoms in clusters that range from blue to white in color. **Columbia lily**, or **tiger lily**, exhibits its exotic spotted yellow-orange flower from June into July.

At mile 3.7, you reach the summit, almost 3,000 feet above the Columbia River. Vast meadows wrap around Dog Mountain and, in the distance, Mt. Hood peeks above the horizon. Before returning the way you came, take some time to enjoy this spot, especially the views of the gorge.

The Columbia River Gorge, a designated national scenic area, is a corridor of historical significance as well as natural beauty. This is the Northwest's only low-elevation route to the Pacific. Lewis and Clark and their Corps of Discovery traveled through here in 1805. As you stand at the summit of Dog Mountain, imagine yourself two centuries back in time, looking down on the gorge and seeing their boats drifting by on the river below, dwarfed by the magnificent scenery.

Arrowleaf balsamroot on Dog Mountain, Columbia Gorge

Catherine Creek

Wildflower Hike 38

Oregon white oaks along Catherine Creek, Columbia Gorge

Easy	***Trail Rating***
1.6 miles round trip	***Trail Length***
Columbia River Gorge National Scenic Area, east of White Salmon	***Location***
250 to 500 feet	***Elevation***
February to late June	***Bloom Season***
April to late May	***Peak Bloom***
Columbia River Gorge National Scenic Area, Hood River, Oregon, (541) 386-2333	***Contact***

From Hood River, go north on the toll bridge. Turn right (east) on WA 14. Drive 5.8 miles. Turn left just before Rowland Lake. Take this old highway, now a county road, 1.2 miles to a parking area on the left. Water and restrooms are not available here. Be sure not to confuse this trail with the short paved trail on the south side of the road, which is signed Catherine Creek. — ***Directions***

The Catherine Creek valley is a magical place, reminiscent of the Sierra foothills. Catherine Creek, a seasonal stream, runs through meadows and beneath sprawling oaks. Basalt walls conceal the valley. Hobbits would enjoy this landscape!

This is one of the better areas in Washington to witness Garry oak (also called Oregon white oak) habitat. From the valley, you might choose to explore the upper plateau lands, which reveal open terrain with splendid views. Keep a sharp eye out though, as poison ivy, poison oak, and rattlesnakes are found here.

Beginning at the parking area on the north side of the road (not the larger parking area on the road's south side), pass through the gate to follow an old dirt road north into the valley. The rocky soil at the beginning of the trail yields an assortment of edible plants, some of which were an important food source for American Indians. Many tribes in the Northwest harvested **bitterroot**. Sometimes growing in what looks to be solid rock, the plant is fairly inconspicuous until its pink, roselike blossoms open in the spring.

Many flowers of the lily family also have edible roots. You can often smell **narrow-leaf, Douglas', and Hooker's onion** before you see their pink to lavender, ball-shaped flowers. Also in the lily family are several types of brodiaea, which exhibit clusters of six-petaled, trumpet-shaped blossoms on bare stems. **Howell's brodiaea** grows about 2 feet tall with white to sky blue flowers. Purple brodiaeas include **harvest brodiaea** and **ball-head cluster**

BITTERROOT
Lewisia rediviva

HEIGHT: 1" to 3"
BLOOMS: April to mid-May

Bitterroot has large purple-pink, roselike blossoms and thin, sage-colored leaves. It grows low to the ground in arid areas on the east side of the Cascades. The Latin name for bitterroot comes from explorer Meriwether Lewis, who first described it in his journals during the 1804 to 1806 overland expedition to the Pacific. He collected the plant in the Bitterroot Valley of Montana.

American Indians valued it highly as a food, and although it is nutritious, it tastes bitter. According to Flathead myth, the plant grew from the tears of a starving old woman, and its roots are bitter because of her sorrow. The large, fleshy roots were harvested just as the blossoms began to bud, and, after being boiled, became jellylike and less bitter.

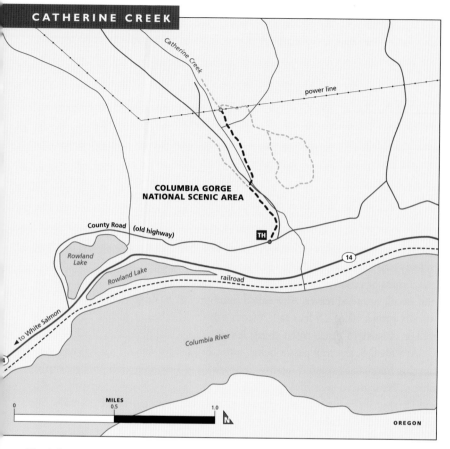

CATHERINE CREEK

Catherine Creek

power line

COLUMBIA GORGE
NATIONAL SCENIC AREA

County Road (old highway)

TH

14

Rowland
Lake

Rowland Lake

railroad

to White Salmon

Columbia River

MILES
0   0.5   1.0

N

OREGON

lily. The very poisonous **death camas** grows here as well, with a cream-colored, cone-shaped flower cluster. Never sample any plant without positive identification.

Buckwheats are also common in the area. With deep, edible taproots, buckwheats are well adapted to harsh environments. Identifying them can be tricky because there are more than 24 kinds in Washington, with several color variations within species. All buckwheats have short, woody stems and masses of tightly clustered, often fluffy looking, flower heads above a low mat of leaves. Colors range from white, cream, or yellow to pinkish. Common varieties in the Catherine Creek area include **heart-leaf**, **Douglas'**, and **strict buckwheat**.

The trail quickly reaches Catherine Creek and follows it upstream into the oak-filled valley. Look for members of the parsley family—another large group of common plants. Desert-parsleys are white, cream, or yellow with umbellate flower heads. **Large-fruited desert-parsley**, or **biscuitroot**, bears dirty-white flower clusters. Yellow desert-parsleys include **Gray's**, **barestem**, **nine-leaf**, and **narrow-leaved**. American Indians pounded the taproots of desert-parsleys into a flour-paste, which they then cooked. All parts of desert-parsleys are considered edible, though other toxic plants, such as poison hemlock, may resemble them.

At mile 0.3, the trail reaches a junction. Stay to the right, cross the creek, and you'll soon pass an old barn and corral. Stalks of **lupine** generate purple-blue blossoms. A member of the pea family, this fragrant plant enriches the soil with nitrogen it converts from the air. **Larkspur**, another purple-blue flower, has winged blossoms on erect stems.

Several types of clover dwell in the valley. **Sand**, **small-head**, and **white-tip clover** grow 4 to 14 inches tall and bear rounded multiblossomed flower heads. You'll pass an arch in the basalt wall on the right. Look for the lavender, funnel-shaped flowers of **Barrett's penstemon** along these cliffs.

In April, **grass widow** opens a six-petaled, pink to purple flower that fades in the first heat wave. **Yellow bell**, also an early bloomer, has hanging blossoms. Another yellow flower, **cut-leaf violet** blooms in the spring, as well.

A number of woody-stemmed plants thrive on the forest floor. **Oregon grape**, an evergreen with hollylike leaves, displays sweet-smelling, fuzzy yellow blossoms in May and June. Around the same time, **wild rose** offers lovely pink blossoms and a mass of yellow stamens. **Serviceberry** has clusters of five-petaled blossoms and small, rounded leaves. Also called **juneberry** or **Saskatoon berry**, this shrub usually grows 10 to 15 feet tall. Watch out for patches of poison ivy, with its telltale clusters of three, often shiny, leaves.

At mile 0.8, the trail passes below a power line, the official turnaround spot for this hike—although a nearby network of old roads invites further exploration. Near the power line, you'll see the lacy white heads of **yarrow**, along with many of the other flowers you've already encountered along the trail. Also look for **wild cucumber**, or **big root**, which grows on a vine with small, star-shaped white flowers and maplelike leaves. Another small flower, **baby stars**, is from the phlox family and has small pink blossoms and spiny leaves. The larger **showy phlox** is also pink, with five-petaled flowers.

Many small flowers begin blooming here in early spring. Displaying yellow disks, **western buttercup** is usually the first to bloom, often after a warm spell in February. **Glacier lily** resides in an amazing variety of habitats, from low to high elevations. Here it blossoms in March, presenting yellow arching petals and protruding stamens. **Shooting star**, an April bloomer, boasts brilliant pink petals and a projecting anther tube.

If you choose to do some more hiking, just past the power line is a junction, at mile 0.9. Stay to the right and switchback up to a large plateau: the Major Creek Plateau. Here you'll find a network of old roads to explore. One leads northeast to a rim overlooking Major Creek, a large, deep drainage. Another leads southeast to views of the Columbia River and Mt. Hood.

Throughout the spring, you'll find a parade of flowers on the plateau. Ponderosa pines dot the meadows. This spacious area makes a great place for a picnic or for close-up flower photography.

Columbia Hills State Park

Wildflower Hike 39

Arrowleaf balsamroot and lupine at Columbia Hills State Park

In the early 1990s, the State of Washington acquired Dalles Mountain Ranch, a 6,000-acre chunk of land at the eastern end of the Columbia Gorge. The Washington Department of Natural Resources manages the northern section as Columbia Hills Natural Area Preserve, while Washington State Parks administers this former ranch as a part of Columbia Hills State Park. In the coming years, new hiking trails will be developed in the area formerly known as Dalles Mountain Ranch State Park. The area adjacent to the Columbia River previously known as Horsethief Lake State Park is now also part of Columbia Hills State Park.

Trail Rating	Moderate
Trail Length	7 miles round trip
Location	Columbia Hills State Park, north of The Dalles, Oregon
Elevation	1,250 to 3,200 feet
Bloom Season	February to late June
Peak Bloom	April to early June
Contact	Columbia Hills State Park, (509) 767-1159
Directions	From the east end of The Dalles, Oregon, drive north on US 197, crossing the Columbia River. Go 3 miles to a T intersection with WA 14. Turn right (east), continue 0.9 mile and turn left (north) on Dalles Mountain Road. (Going straight here leads you to another section of Columbia Hills State Park, the popular boat launch area on Horsethief Lake.) Drive this dirt road—past wonderful displays of lupine and balsamroot—for 3.5 miles and look for a sign at a junction with ranch buildings; turn left onto another dirt road and park in the small parking area.

This area offers a sheer abundance of springtime wildflowers, as well as a diversity of species to observe. Whole hillsides of yellow and blue make this place a hotspot for photographers of all levels.

Bring plenty of water, as none is available. There is an outhouse. At nearby Horsethief Lake, the park offers boating, picnicking, and camping, which can be quite windy. My tent rattled through the night.

Near the small parking area, an old farmstead provides a glimpse into the past. Ranchers have long taken advantage of the area's open grasslands for grazing cattle. Hike north up the road toward the private residence, 0.2 mile away. Stay on the road, passing the house on your left. Follow the dirt road into the spacious hills.

In late April, and in some years on into early May, the large sunflower heads of **arrowleaf balsamroot** carpet the slopes with golden yellow. After a wet winter, this spot ranks as one of the most spectacular flower shows in the state. Call the rangers at Columbia Hills State Park to check on the progress of the balsamroot bloom, and time your trip with its peak.

Desert-parsleys are common here. The flowers host a spray of tiny blossoms in an umbrellalike arrangement. Though mostly yellow, you'll also see white or purplish blooms. Look for the yellow **barestem desert-parsley**, which has oval basal leaves, and for **slender-fruited desert-parsley**, with its spindly, dissected leaves. American Indians consumed the edible roots, stems, and leaves of these plants.

Lupine, another common, showy flower in these hills, blooms in April and May. A member of the pea family, lupine takes nitrogen from the air and adds it to the earth, enriching the soil for neighboring plants. Lupines can be hard to differentiate and often require careful study of flower parts and seeds to identify.

Here you'll see **broadleaf** and **prairie lupine**, both of which bear blue to purple vertical spikes of blossoms. A blue variety of **sulphur lupine** also grows in the area.

The road passes below power lines, curves northeast, and then crosses over Eightmile Creek at mile 0.7. This lovely, oak-filled valley makes a great spot for a picnic. Garry oaks, sometimes called Oregon white oaks, are the only native oaks in Washington. With beautiful gnarled limbs, they grow in parklands in much of the eastern section of the Columbia Gorge. Some oaks in this area tower more than 100 feet and have been estimated to be 500-plus years old. Early inhabitants gathered the acorns for food.

The oaks shelter **Howell's brodiaea**, a member of the lily family that bears clusters of white to purplish blossoms and has an edible bulb. In the iris family, **grass widow** shows a six-petaled pink to purple flower in spring. **Nuttall's larkspur** displays stalks of winged, purple blooms. **Prairie star**, also found beneath the oaks, has a small white blossom with five, three-fingered petals. **Chokecherry** is a large white-flowering shrub.

The road climbs, arriving at a gate at mile 1.5. The gate, which marks the boundary with Columbia Hills Natural Area Preserve, is meant to keep out motorized traffic, but hikers may proceed beyond this point as long as they keep to the road. Along this stretch, you'll see magnificent views of flowered slopes with snowcapped Mt. Hood rising to the southeast. Milk-vetch, a member of the pea family, grows

ARROWLEAF BALSAMROOT
Balsamorhiza sagittata

HEIGHT: 30"

BLOOMS: May

With large sunflowerlike blooms, arrowleaf balsamroot is hard to miss. There may be as many as 20 flowers per plant, each on a separate stalk. The plant's Latin name, *sagittata*—a reference to the constellation Sagittarius, the archer—alludes to the arrow shape of its leaves, which are fuzzy and grow out from the root.

Both the seeds and roots of arrowleaf balsamroot are edible and highly nutritious. The plant is common in dry, open areas across eastern Washington.

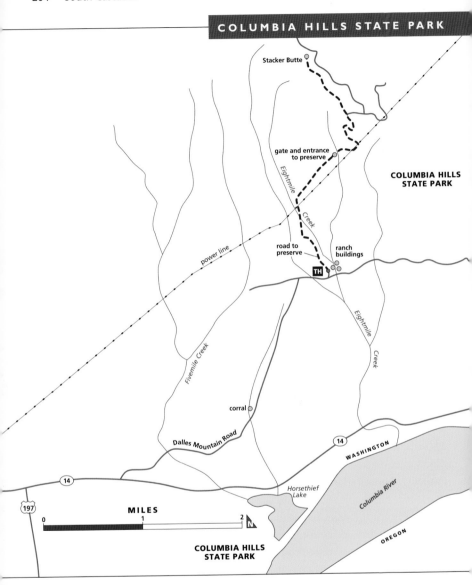

here, including **Hood River** and **Yakima milk-vetch**, both displaying shaggy, creamy white flower clusters.

At the top of a ridge, look for plants that have adapted to a harsh, exposed environment—baked by the summer sun and dried out even more by nearly constant winds. Bearing creamy to lemon yellow flower heads in a low-growing mat, **Douglas' buckwheat** has woody stems and deep taproots. Usually pink, though sometimes lavender or white, **spreading phlox** also grows low to the ground. **Hood's phlox** is generally white, but might have a pink or blue tint.

Washington hosts more than a dozen types of phlox, all with five-petaled, star-shaped blossoms.

An endemic species, **Dalles Mountain buttercup** opens in March with a yellow disk-shaped flower. Look for it on hilltops. White-flowering **Canby's desert-parsley** generates a dirty-white, umbrella-shaped flower head. The tiny, four-petaled white blossom of **spring whitlow-grass** (not a grass, but a member of the mustard family) blooms in March. In rocky areas, **bitterroot** remains inconspicuous until opening its attractive roselike flower.

Continue hiking all the way to the top of 3,200-foot Stacker Butte, a total of 3.5 miles from where you started. The butte is marked with a radio tower. Views are grand here, if you can stand still long enough in this windy place to enjoy them.

Springtime scene in Columbia Hills State Park

*Wildflower
Hike 40*

Sawtooth Ridge

*Penstemon
and lupine,
Wenaha-
Tucannon
Wilderness*

T he Sawtooth Ridge Trail (Trail No. 3256) is one of my favorites in the Blue Mountains. In some places, sandwort grows in the middle of this little-used, ridge-top route, where elk tracks are more common than human footprints. It meanders through forests and flowery meadows on a gradual grade, so kids should be able to hike out a few miles.

When I hiked it, Sawtooth Ridge had the best display of flowers out of the five hikes in the Blue Mountains that I have included in this guide. Although the soil is quite dry here, many flowers have adapted to these conditions. Some rely on moisture from melting snow or the occasional summer thunderstorm. Others have deep taproots or small water-conserving leaves. You should definitely carry your own water, as none is available unless you detour at mile 1.7 to Lady Spring.

Trail Rating	Moderate
Trail Length	8 miles round trip
Location	Wenaha-Tucannon Wilderness, southeast of Dayton
Elevation	5,450 to 5,980 feet
Bloom Season	June to late August
Peak Bloom	Late June to mid-July
Contact	Umatilla National Forest, Pomeroy Ranger District Office, (509) 843-1891
Directions	From US 12 in Dayton, follow the Bluewood Ski Area signs south from town. Two miles out of town, stay left at a fork, on the North Fork Touchet River Road. This road enters the Umatilla National Forest and becomes FR 64. Keep right on FR 64 at the Bluewood Ski Area road, which is on the left. Three miles after the Bluewood junction, turn left (east) on FR 46. This stretch of road is also known as the Kendall Skyline Road. In about 4 miles, look for FR 420 on the right (south). Take FR 420 for 0.3 mile to the road's end and trailhead, marked by a Wenaha-Tucannon Wilderness sign.

From the end of the road, the trail departs to the south. The trail is wooded for about 100 yards, and then opens to a large meadow the size of a football field. **Lupine**, with bright purple-blue blossoms, grows abundantly. Mixed in with the lupine is purple-blue **small-flowered penstemon**. This common flower bears whorls of trumpet-shaped blossoms. Fragrant **mint**, with small white to pale pink or purple blossoms, also resides here.

A number of white flowers brighten the meadow. **Yarrow** generates lacy flowers and feathery leaves. **Thread-leaved sandwort** displays small, five-petaled blossoms and grasslike leaves. **Pearly everlasting** has ball-shaped flowers and sage green leaves.

Though not the most attractive flowers in the meadow, buckwheats have clusters of tiny blossoms with protruding stamens. **Creamy** and **cushion buckwheat** are two common white buckwheats found on this ridge. Yellow **sulfur buckwheat** grows here—and across the Blue Mountains—and in good years proliferates in open meadows.

The trail enters the woods again. Look for patches of **Nuttall's larkspur**, a delphinium that bears purple, winged blossoms. At mile 0.4, the trail passes through another meadow. Smooth, rounded boulders interspersed with thread-leaved sandwort create a rock-garden effect. You'll also notice the bright red bracts of **Indian paintbrush**. A thick patch of bracken fern grows at the end of the meadow.

The trail passes through forest once again and then breaks out into another meadow. Views open to the southwest. An ancient, twisted ponderosa pine stands like a sentinel. Among the buckwheat, yarrow, paintbrush, penstemon, and pearly everlasting, look for **fan-leaved cinquefoil**, which has five-petaled yellow flowers and leaflets in threes. **Leafy aster** displays purple rays around a yellow center.

The trail continues to go in and out of forest and meadows. In the forest, look for **arnica**, a composite with 10 to 15 large yellow rays, and **wild strawberry**, showing five small white petals around a yellow center. To the south, you'll see the high peaks of the Wallowa Mountains, which hold snow much of the summer. At mile 1.7 a trail to the left leads to Lady Spring and Lady Camp, which is 0.8 mile away. Keep right to stay on Sawtooth Ridge Trail.

SUBALPINE MARIPOSA LILY

Calochortus subalpinus

HEIGHT: 4"

BLOOMS: May to July

Subalpine mariposa lily flaunts a gorgeous yellowish white flower with purple markings and triangular-shaped petals. This delicate flower develops a purple tint as it matures. Its one long, thin leaf is usually light green.

Subalpine mariposa lily dwells in open, mid- to high-elevation forests and meadows in Washington and Oregon. Along with trillium, they are the most common three-petaled white flowers.

From here you cross the level, lodgepole pine–covered Burnt Flat, then pass through outstanding open country with expansive views. This area makes a fine camping spot if you don't mind carrying enough water. The meadows here are drier than those you first encountered on this hike. **Skyrocket**, or **scarlet gilia**, displays small trumpet-shaped crimson blossoms. Low-growing **shrubby penstemon** has woody growth and bears lavender, snapdragonlike blossoms. Common in rocky soil, **Oregon sunshine** produces yellow ray flowers and sage green, dissected leaves.

The route drops down through some trees, and then passes lush areas bursting with wildflowers. Look for **blackhead** or **dark coneflower**, brown with green sepals. Early in summer, **subalpine mariposa lily** boasts an elegant blossom.

As the trail continues down the ridge, it enters a more forested setting and the wildflowers begin to diminish. Turn around at 4.0 miles from the trailhead and head back the way you came.

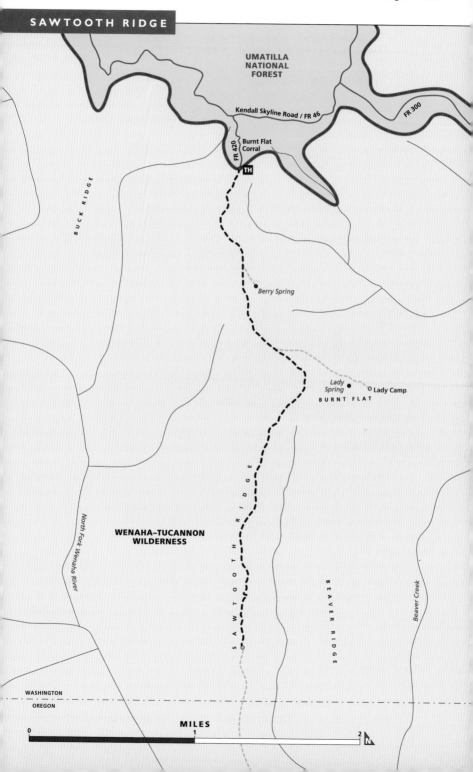

SAWTOOTH RIDGE

UMATILLA
NATIONAL
FOREST

Kendall Skyline Road / FR 46

FR 300

FR 420

Burnt Flat
Corral

TH

BUCK RIDGE

Berry Spring

Lady
Spring   ○ Lady Camp
BURNT FLAT

SAWTOOTH RIDGE

WENAHA–TUCANNON
WILDERNESS

North Fork Wenaha River

BEAVER RIDGE

Beaver Creek

WASHINGTON
OREGON

MILES

0   1   2

N

Grizzly Bear Ridge

*Buckwheat
in bloom,
Wenaha-
Tucannon
Wilderness*

G rizzly Bear Ridge Trail (Trail No. 3103) is a remote route that leads gradually down a ridge through forests and meadows. Thick with wildflowers, these open meadows offer views across the Wenaha-Tucannon Wilderness, a 177,465-acre preserve that spans the Washington-Oregon border. Ranging in elevation from 1,700 to 6,387 feet, this wilderness is cut by small rivers and streams, which have created deep valleys with long ridges in between.

The area, averaging 24 to 32 inches of precipitation annually, is much drier than the Cascades, so be sure to bring in plenty of water when hiking here. Summer days can be hot, with occasional afternoon thunderstorms.

Trail Rating	Moderate
Trail Length	6 miles round trip
Location	Wenaha-Tucannon Wilderness, southeast of Dayton
Elevation	4,900 to 5,400 feet
Bloom Season	June to late August
Peak Bloom	Late June to mid-July
Contact	Umatilla National Forest, Pomeroy Ranger District Office, (509) 843-1891
Directions	From US 12 in Dayton, follow the Bluewood Ski Area signs south from town. Two miles out of town, stay left at a fork, on the North Fork Touchet River Road. This road enters the Umatilla National Forest and becomes FR 64. Keep right on FR 64 at the Bluewood Ski Area road, which is on the left. Three miles after the Bluewood junction, turn left (east) on FR 46. This stretch of road is also known as the Kendall Skyline Road. Follow FR 46 about 6 miles to FR 300. Turn right (southeast) on FR 300 and keep left after 5 miles, staying on FR 300. In 0.5 mile, you'll reach the road's end, a parking area, and the trailhead, where there is a Wenaha-Tucannon Wilderness sign but no trail sign.

Elk, cougar, and black bear reside here, though you don't need to worry about grizzly bears—the nearest grizzly lives hundreds of miles to the west in the North Cascades, across the Washington desert and wheat fields.

Starting at the Wenaha-Tucannon Wilderness sign, follow the trail, which heads east, passing a number of flowers that you'll see many times on this hike. **Pearly everlasting** is named for its white, pearl-like blossoms, which stay in bloom week after week. This common roadside plant has sage green leaves and grows 12 to 28 inches tall. **Heart-leaf arnica**, also common here, puts forth sunflowers 1 to 2 inches across.

Wild strawberry bears small white flowers and edible miniature fruit. With blossoms consisting mostly of numerous hairlike white stamens, **false bugbane** is a large plant, with leaves growing 6 to 10 inches across. **Yarrow**, also common here, has off-white clustered heads and feathery leaves. **Blackhead** or **dark cone-flower**, brown with green sepals, grows in shady areas.

Less than 0.1 mile after the start of the trail, the route divides. There is a very old trail sign on a tree at this junction. The East Butte Creek Trail (Trail No. 3112) forks left. Take the right fork for the Grizzly Bear Ridge Trail, which heads south. The path leads through open forest. Look for two varieties of columbine, which are similar to the garden variety. Depending on soil and moisture conditions, **yellow columbine** grows 4 to 30 inches tall. Ornate **red columbine** boasts a long yellow cluster of stamens. Hummingbirds often pollinate both types of columbine.

FALSE BUGBANE
Trautvetteria caroliniensis

HEIGHT: 10" to 30"
BLOOMS: May to July

A member of the buttercup family, false bugbane has a head of many tiny flowers consisting of a mass of white stamens. Its leaves are lobed, with V-shaped clefts, and resemble maple leaves. These large, conspicuous leaves may grow to 10 inches across.

False bugbane prefers moist, nitrogenous soils. It possesses a chemical compound that causes skin irritation on contact. Baneberry, a close relative with smaller leaves, was used as a tonic, but was also a violent laxative. These strikingly similar plants are often confused with one another.

You'll enter a small meadow where Indian paintbrush grows abundantly. **Scarlet paintbrush**, 20 to 30 inches tall, is the most common variety found here. **Small-flowered paintbrush** and **magenta paintbrush** bloom nearby in richer, moister soil. Also prevalent, **small-flowered penstemon** has purple clusters of trumpetlike blossoms arranged in a ball shape. Sweet-smelling **mint** and purple **larkspur** reside in this meadow. **Leafy aster**, one of several purple ray flowers with yellow centers, dwells on the ridge, too.

The trail ducks back into the trees, where **western mountain ash** and **elderberry** host sprays of white blossoms. In late summer, elderberries yield edible fruit, which can be made into jam. **Oregon grape** is a smaller, woody shrub with yellow flowers and hollylike leaves. Another common yellow flower, **fan-leaved cinquefoil** displays a disk-shaped blossom with five petals and strawberrylike leaves.

At mile 0.4, the trail enters a large meadow. With deep taproots, buckwheats are able to survive in dry soil by reaching far down for moisture. **Sulfur buckwheat**, prevalent here, dots the field with yellow blossoms. **Creamy buckwheat** and **strict buckwheat**, both white, grow here and in other dry, sunlit places on the ridge.

After passing through forest, the trail enters another meadow. **Lupine** displays stalks covered with purple-blue blossoms. Yarrow, small-flowered penstemon, and

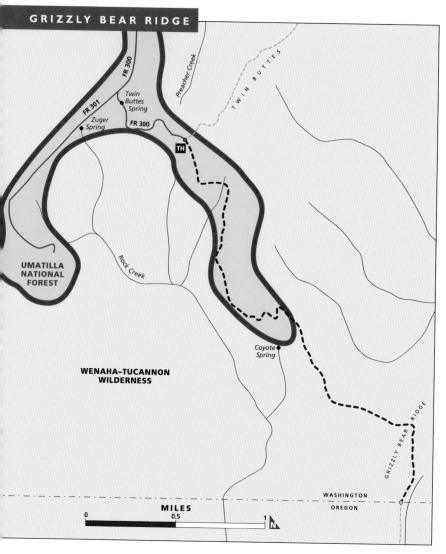

GRIZZLY BEAR RIDGE

paintbrush also add color. Views open to the south, where the Wenaha River runs through a valley 4,000 feet below. On the southern horizon, snowfields linger in the Wallowa Mountains, which are 4,000 feet higher than the Blue Mountains.

With a fairly dry climate, the Blue Mountains, here about 5,200 feet high, are home to a number of plants usually found only at the lower elevations of eastern Washington. Massive ponderosa pines tower above the meadows, and sagebrush also grows along the ridge. **Sticky geranium**, another plant usually found at lower elevations, resides in open forest, presenting a lovely, five-petaled pink blossom. With a small, five-petaled white flower, **prairie star** is usually a lowlander, as well.

For the next mile, you'll continue through woods and meadows, seeing many of the flowers already noted, in addition to new ones. **Corn lily**, or **false hellebore**, resides in pockets of moist soil, showing large, heavily veined leaves. **Mountain arnica**, with yellow composite blossoms, also grows in the richer soil here. Forming a mat of dense, woolly leaves, **rosy pussytoes** has clusters of rounded pink blossoms. **Thread-leaved sandwort** bears small white flowers and sprouts grasslike leaves. **Longleaf phlox** displays a pink to lavender, five-petaled flower.

In rocky areas, in addition to buckwheats, low-growing **stonecrop** appears among bare rock with five, pointed yellow petals and a mass of protruding stamens. In the same habitat, **Oregon sunshine** reveals small yellow sunflowers and sage green leaves. A treasure of the Blue Mountains, and probably the tallest penstemon in the Northwest, **royal penstemon** generates a mass of flower-covered stems up to 3 feet tall.

For the last mile of trail, columbine, penstemon, aster, paintbrush, arnica, yarrow, and buckwheat continue to decorate the route. In the open, dry areas, **elkhorn clarkia** displays an odd, three-lobed blossom that resembles antlers. In partial shade, look for **old-man's whiskers**, featuring pink to purple globes with five arching sepals.

At around mile 3.0, near the Oregon border, the meadows begin to taper off as the trail drops in elevation. The path continues on and begins descending steeply, mostly through forest, to the Wenaha River. The trail's descent makes a good turnaround spot.

Squaw Spring

Wildflower medley, Wenaha-Tucannon Wilderness

Moderate	*Trail Rating*
5.4 miles round trip	*Trail Length*
Wenaha-Tucannon Wilderness, south of Pomeroy	*Location*
5,880 to 6,330 feet	*Elevation*
June to late August	*Bloom Season*
Late June to mid-July	*Peak Bloom*
Umatilla National Forest, Pomeroy Ranger District Office, (509) 843-1891	*Contact*

Directions

Stop by the Forest Service office in Pomeroy for maps and information on road and trail conditions. Armed with plenty of gas and a Forest Service map, head south from Pomeroy on CR 128 (Peola Road). In 8 miles, the road comes to a Y. Stay to the right, on Mountain Road, which becomes FR 40 when it enters the Umatilla National Forest. Drive 17 miles to a junction at Mt. Misery. Turn right (west) on FR 4030 and drive 5 miles to the end of the road.

The Squaw Spring Trail starts at the same place as Jelly Spring Trail (see Hike 43) and follows Trail No. 3113 the entire route. Because much of the trail is fairly level, this hike is a good one for children. Be prepared for thunderstorms, which might develop in the afternoon. Treat any water drawn from springs in this area.

The trail enters and remains in the Wenaha-Tucannon Wilderness, named for the area's two largest rivers. Home to elk, bear, and cougar, this 177,465-acre wilderness protects much of the Blue Mountains. You'll surely find solitude as you explore the wilderness' many ridges dissected by deep, wooded valleys. This trail quickly accesses ridge tops, offering expansive views.

An interesting intersection of habitats meets in the Blue Mountains: Plants commonly found in sagebrush country mingle with those of subalpine mountain environments, so you'll find low-elevation dryland flowers rubbing shoulders with species generally associated with the Cascade Range. Some plants bloom within two or three weeks after snowmelt; others rely on the sometimes infrequent summer rain showers. Many have adapted to the parched, rocky soils, blooming profusely in spite of the harsh habitat. You'll see an array of wildflowers here in early and midsummer.

The Squaw Spring Trail begins at almost 6,000 feet. From the parking area near the end of the road, look for a steep path (unmarked when I visited) heading south. The trail climbs up through forest and, at about 200 yards, opens on a ridge. Here you'll come upon a T junction at a well-worn east-west trail, used for both hiking and pack animals. Turn right (west) at this junction.

With its numerous yellow ray flower heads and olive green leaves, **Oregon sunshine**, also known as **woolly sunflower**, grows on stony knobs. Smallish **stonecrop** also resides in rocks, exhibiting five yellow petals and a spray of yellow stamens. Look for **skullcap**, with a small four-lobed purple blossom.

Heading west, the route passes north of Diamond Peak and into forest. Flowering shrubs bloom here in late June and July. **Thimbleberry** grows abundantly, revealing white tissuelike blossoms and large leaves reminiscent of maples. Also found here, and across much of the Blue Mountains, **wild rose** flaunts pink five-petaled blossoms with yellow stamens. **Oregon grape**, another forest shrub, is named for its purple berries, noticeable in late summer. It has clusters of yellow blossoms and hollylike evergreen leaves.

White flowers dominate the forest floor. **Prairie star** displays a small five-petaled blossom. **Mariposa lily**, also low growing, has three triangle-shaped white petals and three narrower sepals. **Yarrow** puts forth clusters of lacy white blossoms and feathery leaves.

The trail climbs through an open, rocky landscape to a wide ridge. Look for penstemons with blue, lavender, or pinkish funnel-shaped blossoms. Most plentiful is **small-flowered penstemon**, bearing whorls of purple blossoms. Some

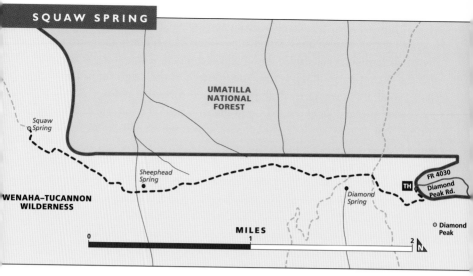

penstemons generate woody stems. **Shrubby, Scouler's,** and **Davidson's pen-stemon** grow in rocky areas with low mats of leaves and pink to purple flowers.

At mile 0.6, the trail reaches a large, level meadow displaying more than a dozen flower varieties in July. Buckwheats, having adapted well to dry soil, display clusters of tiny blossoms with protruding stamens. In some years, **sulfur buckwheat** blankets whole areas in lemon yellow. **Creamy buckwheat** and **cushion buckwheat** are two common white buckwheats growing here.

Many other low-moisture plants inhabit this grand meadow. Lomatiums, or parsleys, grow profusely, sprouting umbrella-shaped flower heads of many small blooms. Parsleys once held an important place in the diet of American Indians. **Gray's, narrow-leaved,** and **barestem desert-parsley**—all with yellow flowers—appear in most of the ridge-top meadows. Also yellow, **wallflower** shows a clustered head of four-petaled blossoms.

It's hard to miss the Indian paintbrush growing in this meadow, as well as along much of the trail. Found in sunny areas, **harsh paintbrush** and **scarlet paintbrush** sprout spiky crimson bracts. Less than 6 inches high, **showy paint-brush** may be reddish, purple, or yellow.

Lupine and **Nuttall's larkspur** add splashes of purple and blue to the meadow. Important to this ecosystem, lupine adds nitrogen to the soil. Nutall's larkspur's wing-tipped flowers bloom on 16-inch stems. Several asters with purple rays and yellow centers reside here. **Showy aster,** which dwells in forest openings and along meadow edges, has 6-inch leaves and generates many purple ray flowers at the top of each stem. Also found in forest clearings, **leafy aster** has narrower leaves, but a similar ray flower.

In early summer, several small flowers take advantage of the moist soil soon after snowmelt. One of the first to bloom, **buttercup** follows snowmelt with yellow, bowl-shaped flowers. **Shooting star** boasts a brilliant pink hanging blossom with a conspicuous anther tube. Phlox also blooms fairly early, with five petals forming a star-shaped flower. Phlox comes in a variety of colors within species, including pink, lavender, and white. On the ridge, and in partial shade, you'll likely see **narrowleaf, longleaf,** and **spreading phlox.**

Toward the middle of the ridge-top meadow is a junction where the Jelly Spring Trail departs to the right (north). Continue straight (west) on Trail No. 3113, as you enter a mostly wooded area. In July, you can sample the ripened fruit of **wild strawberry**, always a delightful treat when hiking—just make sure you can positively identify wild plants before consuming them. Low-growing **long-flowered bluebell** displays hanging clusters of pink to lavender tubular blossoms. The graceful **yellow columbine** is similar to the garden variety. Growing in clearings, **orange honeysuckle** bears clusters of long tubular blossoms framed by a pair of smooth, rounded leaves.

NUTTALL'S LARKSPUR
Delphinium nuttallianum

HEIGHT: 16"
BLOOMS: June to August

Many varieties of larkspur grow throughout the country. Nuttall's larkspur is the variety commonly found east of the Cascades. Its deep blue flowers bear a classic delphinium shape, with five spreading sepals forming a star-shaped blossom. The slender, tubular upper sepal protrudes from the flower like a spur. Its leaves are muted green with long, rounded lobes.

American Indians traditionally used larkspur to treat sores, but the skin-irritating chemicals in the plant rendered the remedy quite painful. Nuttall's larkspur is poisonous to cattle.

At mile 1.0, the trail reaches another large, flower-filled meadow. At times sulfur buckwheat seems to turn the whole field yellow. Along the meadow's south edge, **elkhorn clarkia** sprouts a pink, branching, antler-shaped flower.

During the next mile, the trail dips in and out of forest. The flowers in pocket meadows peak in late June or early July, depending on the snowpack and spring melt. At mile 1.8, just off the trail to the right, is Sheephead Spring. The spring is swampy and the water is better at Squaw Spring, another mile ahead. There is also a corral near Sheephead Spring, where I met a friendly group on horseback. They gave me a bag of fresh peas from their garden—the best I've ever tasted.

From Sheephead Spring, the path climbs to a tabletop mesa. Nuttall's lark-spur appears in early summer with purple, butterflylike blossoms. Also out in the open, **scarlet gilia**, or **skyrocket**, is a spindly plant with crimson, trumpet-shaped blossoms. Sprawling **Gray's lovage** displays compound, umbrella-shaped white flower heads and carrotlike leaves.

Yellow composites grow in many of the ridge-top meadows. **Western butter-weed**, or **western groundsel**, is fairly tall with many smallish ray flower heads on each stem. With larger flower heads, **little sunflower** blooms in early summer along meadow edges in partial shade. Another yellow ray flower, arnica displays 10 to 15 yellow petals. **Heart-leaf arnica** dwells in wooded areas, while **moun-tain arnica** prefers open meadows.

Squaw Spring is on the right at mile 2.7. **Jacob's-ladder** dwells here, with clusters of five-petaled, light blue blossoms and ladderlike leaves. Featuring rose-purple globes with arching sepals, **long-plumed avens**, or **old-man's whiskers**, grows along the forest edges.

There are some good campsites near Squaw Spring. You can camp here for the night, or turn around at the spring and head back to the trailhead.

Indian paintbrush,
Wenaha-Tucannon
Wilderness

Wildflower Hike 43

Jelly Spring

Penstemon bloom in the Blue Mountains, Wenaha-Tucannon Wilderness

Trail Rating	Moderate
Trail Length	8 miles round trip
Location	Umatilla National Forest, south of Pomeroy
Elevation	5,880 to 6,330 feet
Bloom Season	June to late August
Peak Bloom	Late June to mid-July
Contact	Umatilla National Forest, Pomeroy Ranger District Office, (509) 843-1891
Directions	Stop by the Forest Service office in Pomeroy for maps and information on road and trail conditions. With plenty of gas in your tank and a Forest Service map in your hand, head south from Pomeroy on CR 128 (Peola Road). In 8 miles, the road comes to a Y. Stay to the right, on Mountain Road, which becomes FR 40 when it enters the Umatilla National Forest. Drive 17 miles to a junction at Mt. Misery. Turn right (west) on FR 4030 and drive 5 miles to the end of the road.

This hike starts at the same place as Hike 42, Squaw Spring. Like most ridge-top trails in the Blue Mountains, the Jelly Spring Trail provides long, sweeping views across the Wenaha-Tucannon Wilderness. The route—which follows Trail No. 3113, then Trail No. 3110—begins at almost 6,000 feet, providing quick access to the high and dry landscape. Jelly Spring has a very small flow, so it's a good idea to carry all the water you'll need for this trip. If you do obtain water from any of the springs in this area, consider it nonpotable and treat it before consumption.

From the parking area at the end of the road, a steep and unmarked path leads south, climbing through forest. In about 200 yards it reaches a ridge and the T junction with a well-traveled, east-west trail. Go right (west), passing the north side of Diamond Peak.

Some flowers bloom here within two or three weeks after snowmelt, whereas others rely on the sometimes infrequent summer rains. But many of the plants you'll see here have adapted to parched, rocky soils, blooming profusely in spite of the harsh habitat. **Stonecrop** has pointed yellow petals, a mass of fuzzy stamens, and a fleshy brownish stem. Also found among the rocks, **Oregon sunshine**, or **woolly sunflower**, produces yellow ray flower heads and olive green leaves. Purple-flowering **skullcap** is another plant that thrives in stony soil.

A mix of open forest and meadow harbors **yarrow**, with its lacy white blossoms and feathery leaves. At home in many environments, yarrow can be found from sagebrush to subalpine habitats. A standard in the Blue Mountains, **Indian paintbrush** brightens open areas along much of the trail. Showing spiky crimson bracts, **harsh** and **scarlet paintbrush** are common in the region.

Along more shaded sections of the trail, you'll see the unmistakable **Oregon grape**, the state flower of Oregon. This woody evergreen shrub bears clusters of yellow blossoms and hollylike leaves, with blue-purple berries in late summer and fall. Another common flowering shrub, **thimbleberry** reveals white tissue-like blossoms and large maplelike leaves. Found in this area and across much of the Blue Mountains, **wild rose** displays five-petaled pink blossoms with yellow stamens.

The low-growing **mariposa lily**, a floral gem with three triangle-shaped petals and three narrower sepals, grows in forest openings and is usually white. Keep an eye out for it from late May to early July. Sprawling **Gray's lovage** displays white, compound, umbrella-shaped flower heads and foliage resembling that of a carrot. A small white flower, **prairie star** presents five petals with three notches at each tip. A favorite of hummingbirds, **orange honeysuckle** grows in clearings and bears clusters of long tubular blossoms framed by a pair of smooth, rounded leaves.

A short, steep section of trail opens up as it ascends to a ridge. Many kinds of penstemons thrive in these dry, rocky habitats. The largest genus of plants in North America—with approximately 270 different species—penstemons can be tricky to differentiate because of their individual diversity in size, color, and range. All penstemons have five-lobed blossoms in a trumpet- or funnel-like shape. **Davidson's penstemon** often blankets small areas in a groundcover of leaves and pink to lavender blossoms. Growing more sparsely, pink to purple **Gairdner's** and **Scouler's penstemon** can be recognized by their needlelike leaves. Preferring better soil, **small-flowered penstemon** produces purple blossoms in ball-shaped clusters and is common in this region.

ELKHORN CLARKIA

Clarkia pulchella

HEIGHT: 6" to 16"

BLOOMS: June to August

Elkhorn clarkia's common name pays homage to explorer William Clark and to the blossom's antler shape. *Pulchella*, its Latin name, means "beautiful." Also called pink fairies, this flower has four deeply lobed, leaflike petals in a soft, pastel pink. Its leaves are a dull green. Elkhorn clarkia resides in dry, exposed areas, thriving near sagebrush. It grows east of the Cascades, abundantly in the Blue Mountains.

At mile 0.6, the trail levels out at a wide-open ridge-top meadow. In July, thousands of lemon yellow **sulfur buckwheat** fill the meadow, which comes alive with color. Like most of the buckwheats in the area, these fuzzy-looking flowers survive on exceptionally dry ridges. Usually cream-colored, **creamy buckwheat** and **cushion buckwheat** can vary in color, depending on soil, precipitation, and age.

Many other plants adapted to arid conditions inhabit this huge meadow. Presenting a clump of many four-petaled blossoms, yellow **wallflower** blooms from late June through July. Several edible parsleys, or lomatiums, commonly grow here, all with compound, umbellate flower heads. Yellow-blooming **Gray's**, **narrow-leaved**, and **barestem desert-parsley** grow in the area, depending on elevation and soil conditions.

Early in the summer, look for varieties of phlox, with five petals. Phlox exhibits a variety of colors within species, ranging from pink to lavender to white. You'll likely see **narrowleaf**, **longleaf**, and **spreading phlox** on the ridge.

Toward the middle of this large, ridge-top meadow, you'll find the

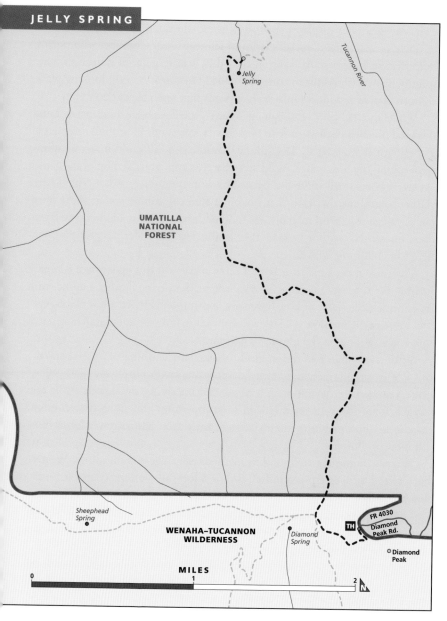

junction where the Jelly Spring Trail (Trail No. 3110) heads north. When I was there, the sign was turned 90 degrees to confuse things. Take a right on Jelly Spring Trail and you'll enjoy a clear-sailing, open ridge trail that gradually descends to the Tucannon River. The trail occasionally tracks through woods, though more often it continues across dry meadowlands with abundant wildflowers.

Most meadows display paintbrush, small-flowered penstemon, yarrow, buckwheat, and phlox. **Nuttall's larkspur** appears in early summer with purple, butterflylike blossoms. Also out in the open, **scarlet gilia**, or **skyrocket**, is a spindly plant with crimson, trumpet-shaped blossoms. An odd-looking plant, **elkhorn clarkia** produces pink, leaflike petals that resemble antlers.

Where the trail passes through open forest, the flowers are a bit sparse. **Long-flowered bluebell** displays pink to blue tubular blossoms. Presenting rose-purple globes with arching sepals, **long-plumed avens**, also called **old-man's whiskers**, grows along the forest edge. **Wild strawberry**, a miniature version of the garden variety, features small white five-petaled blossoms. Another garden-type flower, **yellow columbine** dwells in shady habitat. **Red columbine** prefers more open pocket meadows. With fragrant, sawtoothed leaves, **mint** is another dweller of open forests. Named for its ladderlike leaves, **Jacob's-ladder** has groupings of light blue blossoms with five petals.

The trail enters a meadow several acres in size. All this open space is plenty inviting for a picnic, a nap, taking pictures, or identifying flowers. **Lupine**, with its unmistakable stalks of blue blossoms, is common here. In a few places, the trail through the meadow is a little inconspicuous, but with some searching you'll find it continuing on the meadow's far side.

With more than two dozen kinds of asters in Washington, members of this family can be tricky to identify. Several asters with purple rays and yellow centers reside here. With 6-inch leaves and many purple ray flowers at the top of each stem, **showy aster** dwells in forest openings and along the edges of meadows. Also inhabiting forest clearings, **leafy aster** has narrower leaves but a similar ray flower.

Yellow composites are found in many of the ridge-top meadows. **Western butterweed**, or **western groundsel**, is 2 to 3 feet tall with many smallish ray flower heads on each stem. **Little sunflower** has larger flower heads and blooms along the fringes of meadows in early summer. Arnica, another yellow ray flower, displays 10 to 15 yellow petals. **Heart-leaf arnica** dwells in wooded areas, while **mountain arnica** prefers moist, open terrain.

As you leave the last meadows along the ridge, the trail descends toward the Tucannon River. Look for **large-leaved avens** with five rounded yellow petals and jagged strawberrylike leaves. The trail enters forest a final time, angling northeast and dropping to unspectacular Jelly Spring on the right, which was barely flowing when I was there in July. At mile 4.0, this is your turnaround point.

Puffer Butte

*Fields Spring
State Park*

Tucked in out-of-the-way southeast Washington, Fields Spring State
Park perches high above the Grande Ronde River canyon. Besides a
pleasant campground, a picnic area, a lodge, and cabins for rent, the park
offers a network of trails and open country for roaming. At 3,000 to
4,000 feet in elevation, the area receives enough winter snow for excellent cross-country skiing and snowshoeing. Summer nights usually cool
off nicely. You'll find quite a diversity of flowers here, with many subalpine
species as well as those found in sagebrush habitats.

The Snowshoe Trail starts on the west side of the parking lot. A trailhead sign displays a map and a description of the hike, which takes you
to the top of Puffer Butte. Just follow the blue diamonds.

Trail Rating	Easy
Trail Length	3-mile loop
Location	Fields Spring State Park, south of Clarkston
Elevation	2,960 to 3,700 feet
Bloom Season	May to late August
Peak Bloom	May to early July
Contact	Fields Spring State Park, (509) 256-3332
Directions	From Clarkston, drive south on WA 129 for about 25 miles. You'll pass through Anatone, where the welcome sign informs of the town's inhabitants: 48 people, 17 cats, 18 dogs, and 21 horses. Continue 4 miles past Anatone and look for the Fields Spring State Park entrance on the left (east). Follow the signs to the campground and park in the large parking lot near the restrooms. The Snowshoe Trail, which you will follow for this hike, starts at the west side of the parking area.

Near the trailhead you'll see lacy white **yarrow** and **heart-leaf arnica**, a yellow ray flower. Meandering through an open forest of grand fir, larch, Douglas maple, and ponderosa pine, the trail passes several flowering bushes. **Wild rose**, a shrub bearing blossoms with five pink petals surrounding a cluster of yellow stamens and pistils, commonly grows here and across eastern Washington. **Sticky currant** bears clusters of five-petaled white blossoms on bushes 3 to 4 feet tall. **Thimbleberry**, recognized by its pure white, tissuelike flowers and large maplelike leaves, yields edible red berries in late summer. **Oregon grape**, a bush commonly found on forest floors, has hollylike evergreen leaves, a cluster of sweet-smelling yellow blossoms in early summer, and dark blue berries in August.

About 100 yards up the trail, look for **mountain lady's slipper**, a rare and beautiful floral gem. Its flower resembles a hanging white pouch, with copper-colored or brownish purple sepals twisting away from the pouch. Also growing on the forest floor, **wild strawberry** yields edible fruit in late summer. **Kinnikinnick** is another ground cover, spreading over large areas with a mat of small leathery evergreen leaves; tiny pink bell-shaped flowers are followed by red berries later in the season. A beauty of the forest, **queen's cup** displays a white, six-petaled flower and large, shiny, green, tonguelike leaves. **Star-flowered false Solomon's seal** has tiny white star-shaped blossoms and elegant, lance-shaped leaves.

The trail steadily climbs, crossing several roads on its way to the top of Puffer Butte. Several yellow flowering plants dwell in forest clearings. Large, strawberrylike leaves and five yellow rounded and separated petals distinguish **large-leaved avens. Silvercrown,** also with large strawberrylike leaves, has clusters of half-inch flower heads with about 20 narrow, spiky rays that later turn into dandelionlike seed heads. **Yellow salsify** shows a large dandelionlike blossom and seed head on a single stem. With five petals forming a disk, cream-colored **cinquefoil** grows to 40 inches.

At mile 0.6, **sticky geranium** becomes prevalent here in June and early July, with beautiful pink, veined flowers and large, deeply segmented leaves. Framed by two smooth, round leaves, **orange honeysuckle** has clusters of long tubular blossoms that hummingbirds find attractive. Fragrant blue **lupine** appears as the trail opens up near the top of the butte.

One of several penstemons in the area, **small-flowered penstemon** has whorled clusters of deep purple trumpets. **Woodland penstemon** has rose to purple trumpets on 20- to 30-inch leaning stems. Another purple flower found in open areas, **Nuttall's larkspur** has wing-tipped blossoms that open in late spring to early summer. With purple clustered balls, **ballhead waterleaf** dwells under the pines, often with **western spring beauty**, a small, star-shaped white flower.

In the spring, you'll find a different grouping of blossoms here. One of the earliest to bloom, **buttercup** displays bright yellow, varnished blossoms that signify the coming of spring. **Yellow bell,** a small lily, has a single, hanging flower originating from an edible bulb once consumed by American Indians. **Douglas' brodiaea,** also with edible bulbs, displays clusters of horizontal, lavender trumpets. **Shooting star** is

MOUNTAIN LADY'S SLIPPER
Cypripedium montanum

HEIGHT: Up to 2'
BLOOMS: May to June

Mountain lady's slippers are renowned for their beauty and showiness, flaunting a large white, purple-veined flower, which grows one or two per stem. Its lip is puffed into a slipperlike pouch, and brownish purple or copper-colored sepals and petals twist in spirals. Its thick, waxy leaves are alternating and egg-shaped.

A rare mountain orchid, mountain lady's slippers take more than 12 years to grow to maturity, and they are unable to regenerate as quickly as a common wildflower. Quite fragrant, they flourish in open woodlands of the foothills at low to middle elevations.

another small gem found here, with arching, fuchsia petals. An odd-looking plant, **elkhorn clarkia** has lobed pink flowers that resemble antlers.

With five small white petals, **prairie star** sprouts grasslike leaves. **Long-flowered bluebell**, recognizable by its clusters of pink to blue tubular flowers, prefers partial shade. Two types of camas dwell here: one edible, the other deadly. **Common camas** has six purple-blue petals with a small yellow center and edible bulbs. The lethal **death camas** has a fuzzy, cream-colored blossom. This plant is one reason to never sample any plant without positive identification.

At the top of Puffer Butte, a large field of sunflowers greets hikers. The trees are now behind you and the ridge opens to inspiring views. The Grande Ronde River winds through the canyon, 3,000 feet below. The ridge of the Blue Mountains extends along the southwest horizon, and far to the south you can see the snow-covered crags of the Wallowa Range. Notice the abrupt change in flower types here. This is a dry, rocky habitat. The open country is perfect for picnics and careful rambling as you enjoy the great show of blossoms.

Many plants here bloom in late May through early July. An amazing-looking plant, **skyrocket**, or **scarlet gilia**, is unmistakable because of its bright red clusters of five-petaled trumpets. It can bloom from May into October. Stonecrops grow abundantly on the ridge. With five pointed yellow petals and protruding stamens, these low-growing plants have small, fleshy, edible leaves. **Lance-leaved stonecrop** and **worm-leaved stonecrop** grow here. **Skullcap**, resembling a small penstemon, has four purple lobes and dwells in rocky areas. Displaying brilliant red bracts, **scarlet** and **harsh paintbrush** bloom in May and June.

With long taproots that reach down deep for moisture, buckwheats love this dry, rocky environment. In late May and June, they are the showiest flowers on the ridge. Buckwheats have short, woody stems and masses of tightly clustered flower heads, often fluffy-looking, above a low mat of leaves. Colors range from white or cream to yellow or pinkish. The common varieties you'll see on the butte include **creamy**, **cushion**, **sulfur**, and **heart-leaf buckwheat**.

Phlox also seems to enjoy a challenging habitat, though it blooms early and wilts in the first heat waves. With five petals, phlox ranges from white to pink to lavender, often within the same species. **Narrowleaf**, **longleaf**, and **showy phlox** bloom on these open slopes in early summer.

Other early flowers of the area include **arrowleaf balsamroot**, with large yellow sunflower heads and spade-shaped leaves. A smaller sunflower, widespread in the state's dry areas, **Oregon sunshine** (also called **woolly sunflower**) has 8 to 13 rays and olive green leaves. An unusual white penstemon, **hot-rock** or **scorched penstemon** prefers dry, rocky areas, as does the **wallflower**, a member of the mustard family with clusters of four-petaled yellow flowers.

Many desert-parsleys, or lomatiums, reside in the vicinity, with branching, umbrellalike flower heads consisting of many tiny flowers. American Indians

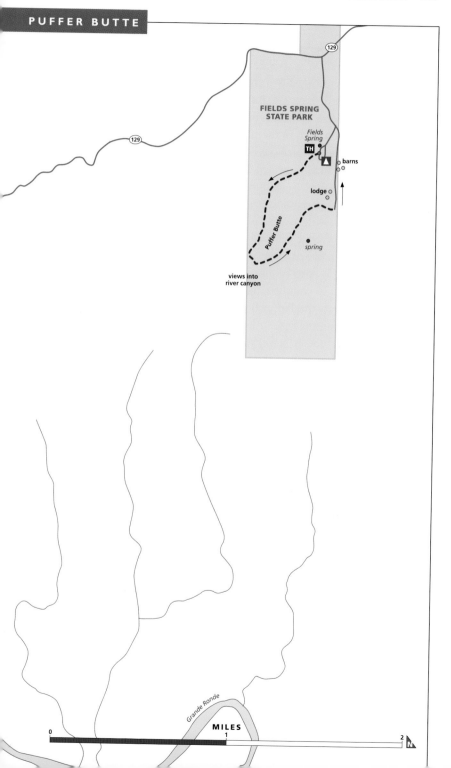

129

FIELDS SPRING
STATE PARK

Fields
Spring
TH
barns

lodge

Puffer Butte

spring

views into
river canyon

129

Grande Ronde

MILES

0   1   2

N

prized the more than 30 varieties of desert-parsley for their large, edible taproots. Usually blooming in May and June, **narrow-leaved**, **barestem**, and **Gray's desert-parsley** all display yellow umbellate flower heads.

The trail gently drops down the ridge, and then switchbacks left (east), heading back toward the trees. But first, you might want to do some more exploring on the butte, where the previously mentioned flowers are plentiful.

Back on the main trail, in the protection and shade of scattered trees, look for **Payette penstemon**, which has blue-purple trumpets and flowers larger than those of its cousins, **small-flowered** and **woodland penstemon**, which also grow here. Large-leaved avens are common along this section of trail, along with another, but quite different looking, avens—**long-plumed avens**, also called **old-man's whiskers**, with rose-purple globes and five arching sepals.

In a wide, grassy area, the trail crosses a road. Continue straight and in 100 yards you will come to a parking area and trailhead. A gated road leading to the right (south) is open to hikers and accesses several trails to overlooks of the Grande Ronde. To complete this loop hike, however, follow the road left (north). You will pass the Puffer Butte Lodge, cabins, and a ball field on the left, and old barns on the right. Also on the right, a beautiful clump of **false hellebore** shows off lovely large, veined leaves and stalky, off-white flower heads. The first main road to the left will take you back to the campground and your vehicle.

Pine Ridge

*Wildflower
Hike 45*

*Paintbrush on
Kamiak Butte,
Palouse Hills*

Outside of the Moscow-Pullman area, Kamiak Butte is little known
to most Washingtonians. Set among the rolling hills of the Palouse
Prairie, the butte rises to 3,641 feet above the surrounding wheat fields.
On a clear day, you can see great views from the ridge. The north slope
of this ridge is mostly wooded, while the south face opens to meadows
with grasses and flowering plants. Most of the area is within the 300-acre
Kamiak Butte County Park. Both park and butte are named for Chief
Kamiakin of the Yakama tribe. The park has a campground and picnic
area, with restrooms and potable water. **From late July to mid-September,
check for park closures from fire danger.**

Trail Rating	Easy
Trail Length	3-mile loop
Location	Kamiak Butte County Park, east of Colfax
Elevation	2,500 to 3,641 feet
Bloom Season	March to late July
Peak Bloom	Late April to mid-June
Contact	Kamiak Butte County Park, (509) 878-1869
Directions	From Colfax on US 195, turn east on Canyon Street and set your odometer. The road climbs out of town, becoming WA 272. Drive 5.5 miles, turn right (south) on Clear Creek Road, and reset your odometer. Drive another 8.2 miles to a sign for Kamiak Butte and take a sharp right turn onto Fugate Road. In less than a mile, another sign directs you to turn left into the park. Go 0.8 mile to the parking lot at the trailhead and picnic area.

Hosting 130 bird and 30 mammal species, as well as 170 different plant types, Kamiak Butte has been designated a national natural landmark—a fairly limited and prestigious classification. This hike is on the Pine Ridge Trail, a national recreation trail; the uniqueness of the ridge it follows above the surrounding prairiescape rich with flora earned it such a designation. The top of the ridge, or butte—accessible via a relatively short hike—is a great spot to contemplate. You might want to bring a journal, a picnic, or even a hang glider!

The loop hike on the Pine Ridge Trail begins by heading south, up the hill toward the ridge top, through woods of ponderosa pine, Douglas fir, and the occasional **chokecherry**, which has creamy, cylindrical flower clusters in early summer. With rounded, white balls of five-petaled flowers, **ninebark** resembles a currant and is a common shrub on the butte's northern slopes. Another prevalent bush, **wild rose** displays five pink petals around yellow stamens, with scarlet hips in the fall. Possibly the most plentiful flowering shrub on the ridge is **thimbleberry**, with large maplelike leaves, white tissuelike blossoms in the spring, and edible red berries in late summer.

On the forest floor dwell white-blooming **wild strawberry** and **star-flowered false Solomon's seal**, with tiny white star-shaped flowers and attractive, lance-shaped leaves. Having woody stems and hollylike evergreen leaves, **Oregon grape** exhibits fragrant clusters of yellow blossoms, and deep blue berry clusters in late summer. The presence of ferns is a telltale sign that the area stays cool and shady during the summer—a far cry from the ridge's southern slope. Also found in partial shade, **yellow columbine** produces a delicate, hanging flower.

Toward the top of the hill at mile 0.5, the forest opens slightly. **Prairie star** displays small white, five-petaled blossoms in May and June. With strawberrylike leaves, **large-leaved avens** exhibit five rounded yellow petals around greenish centers. Also in the area, **long-plumed avens**, also called **old-man's whiskers**, looks very different from the long-plumed variety, with hanging, rose-purple globes and arching sepals. An extremely adaptable species, **yarrow** inhabits these upper slopes; its white, filigreed flower heads can be found from the desert to subalpine habitats in Washington. With notched petals, **heart-leaf arnica** is a yellow ray flower widespread in the vicinity.

At mile 0.6, the trail levels off atop the open ridge, where a profusion of sun-dwelling flowers greets hikers. **Western butterweed**, or **western groundsel**, presents many small, yellow ray flowers on each stem. With blue-purple, wing-tipped blossoms, the elegant **Nuttall's larkspur** grows abundantly here and across eastern Washington. **Douglas' brodiaea** shows off clusters of horizontal, six-petaled lavender trumpets on leafless stems. A prolific May bloomer, **narrow-leaved desert-parsley** displays tiny, umbrellalike flower heads of yellow blossoms. Fragrant blue **lupine**, also common across the state, enriches the soil with nitrogen.

Several showy yellow composites are commonly found on the ridge. A big yellow sunflower with large leaves, **arrow-leaf balsamroot** is a regular resident of the area. **Mule's ear** has similar looking flowers but with glossy, more symmetrically shaped leaves. With smaller flower heads and skinny leaves, **little sunflower** (also called **helianthella**) grows abundantly here. In June, look for **blanket flower**, or **brown-eyed Susan**, displaying notched yellow rays around a reddish-brown center.

COMMON CAMAS
Camassia quamash

HEIGHT: 1' to 2'

BLOOMS: April to June

A member of the lily family, common camas produces a light blue to purple flower. Its sepals and petals measure a little more than an inch across. This camas has thin, grasslike leaves on tall, strong stems. It grows in the grassy meadows and dry lands of eastern Washington.

This plant was of vital importance to native peoples of the Pacific Northwest, who considered it a food staple. American Indians dug up the bulbs and boiled them. The bulb of the common camas has a pleasant taste, similar to that of a chestnut.

Where the trail reaches the top of Kamiak Butte, a few trails branch off from the main route to overlooks. Views to the south are stupendous. The velvet-green fields stretch for miles, dotted with farms and small towns. On a clear day, you can see the dark rise of the Blue Mountains, about 75 miles south.

Follow the main trail, heading west through patches of butterweed, desert-parsley, yarrow, and larkspur. Two types of camas, one edible and one deadly, dwell in the area. Luckily, they look very different. **Common camas**, which has edible bulbs, exhibits six purple-blue petals around a small yellow center. The lethal **death camas** has a creamy white, cone-shaped cluster of flowers. Never consume any plant without absolute certainty of its identification.

The trail meanders west around scattered trees where, in late May and June, you'll see **long-flowered bluebell**, with its clusters of pink to blue tubes. **Ballhead waterleaf** also likes some shade. Its round, purple flower clusters often bloom near **western spring beauty**, a simple, white star-shaped flower. An elegant plant, **sticky geranium** has large, deeply segmented leaves framing bright pink, veined blossoms.

Earlier in the year, a different group of blossoms thrives here. Often blooming soon after snowmelt, **buttercup** sprouts in sunny spots, with varnished, disk-shaped yellow flowers. In April, look for two kinds of yellow lilies. Displaying a downward-hanging single blossom, **yellow bell** originates from a bulb once part of indigenous diets. Also hanging downward, **glacier lily**, also called **fawn lily** or **dogtooth violet**, has six yellow petals arching upward from protruding stamens with conspicuous anthers. Fuchsia **shooting star**, another early flower with arching petals, has a yellow ring around the anther tube. In April and early May, look for **grass widow**, a member of the iris family, with six pink to lavender petals surrounding yellow stamens.

As you continue west, the trail gradually climbs. You'll now encounter a number of plants that have adapted to dry and rocky habitats. With five-petaled red trumpets, **skyrocket**, or **scarlet gilia**, blooms anytime from June to late September. Look for **Oregon sunshine**, also called **woolly sunflower**, growing in bouquets of yellow ray flowers above olive green leaves. With pink-lobed, leaflike flowers resembling antlers, **elkhorn clarkia** also survives in arid soil. Bountiful in sunny areas, the dazzling bracts of paintbrush display shades of red and orange. **Scarlet** and **harsh paintbrush** are the two most commonly found here.

Having deep taproots enabling them to thrive in barren soil, buckwheats grow profusely, with more than 24 types found in Washington. Usually displaying a low mat of leaves and woody stems, buckwheats come in many colors: white, cream, yellow, or pinkish. Two varieties you'll find here are **cushion** and **creamy buckwheat**.

After about a mile on the ridge, the trail forks. You will return to this junction to finish the loop hike, but go left here, following the "summit spur" sign for a diversion of 0.5 mile. As you hike through trees, look for thimbleberry,

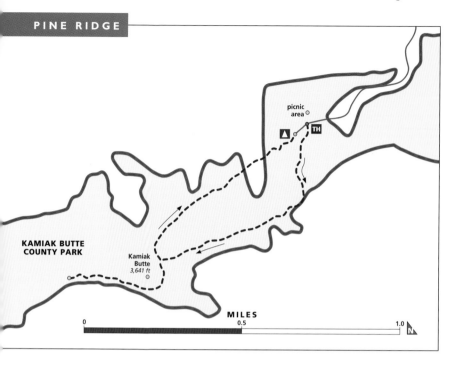

Oregon grape, arnica, and **elderberry**, a small tree that produces edible, light purple berries in the fall. The tiny **small-flowered blue-eyed Mary** resembles a miniature penstemon. Blue-purple **early blue violet** has many heart-shaped leaves and blooms here in June.

The trail levels out at 3,641 feet and continues west toward radio towers. Look for **stonecrop**, with fleshy, tiny, brownish leaves, and blossoms sporting five yellow, pointed petals and protruding yellow stamens. Also found in rocky soil, **longleaf phlox** has grasslike leaves and five-petaled, white to deep pink flowers that bloom in May. Soon you'll see a sign that says, "Trail ends, turn around now." Return to the last junction, where the trail forked, and turn left (north), dropping into forest.

Shade-loving plants grow on the ridge's forested north face. Here, you'll find **prairie star**, wild strawberry, thimbleberry, and arnica. Two types of Solomon's seal dwell in this forest. With 5 to 10 white, starlike blossoms, beautiful star-flowered false Solomon's seal exhibits 4-inch, lance-shaped veined leaves. Its cousin, **false Solomon's seal**, also a resident of shady forests, has larger leaves and a cluster containing dozens of sweet-scented, creamy stars.

The trail traverses eastward through the forest, passing above the campground at mile 2.8. Aspens inhabit the area as well as thimbleberry and ferns. Ninebark, a cascade of white when in full bloom in June, covers the hillside near the campground. In another 0.2 mile, you'll be back to your car, possibly wondering why you didn't spend more time on the ridge.

*Wildflower
Hike 46* Fishtrap Lake

*Arrowleaf bal-
samroot in
bloom beside
Fishtrap Lake*

The name Fishtrap Lake comes from the American Indian practice of
trapping fish in the lake's upper reaches. The lake lies on the edge of two
ecosystems. To the east stand ponderosa pine forests, while sagebrush fans
out to the south and west. Because of the overlap of these two ecosystems,
you'll find a variety of wildflowers here—more than 100 different species—
even though the area receives less than 12 inches of precipitation annually.
This is a great place to wander in solitude under the open sky.

Fishtrap Lake is a fairly recent acquisition by the Bureau of Land Management, and the BLM is just beginning to develop a trail system here. The loop
trail passes several ponds and reaches the southern end of long, narrow Fishtrap
Lake. Unless you want to filter water from the lake, be sure to carry your own.

Trail Rating	Easy
Trail Length	4.5-mile loop
Location	Southwest of Spokane
Elevation	2,150 to 1,975 feet
Bloom Season	March to late July
Peak Bloom	May to mid-June
Contact	Bureau of Land Management, Spokane District Office, (509) 536-1200
Directions	From Spokane, drive southwest on I-90 about 30 miles to the Fishtrap exit (Exit 254). Head south on Sprague Highway Road. In 2.4 miles, you'll come to a junction where Fishtrap Road heads left, but stay straight and continue another 1.3 miles to Miller Ranch Road. Turn left onto Miller Ranch Road, a gravel road, and drive 0.2 mile to the parking area near the farmhouse.

The trail passes through a geologic landscape known as the channeled scablands. Two to three million years ago, intermittent lava flows deposited vast amounts of basalt. During the last ice age, 10,000 to 15,000 years ago, advancing glaciers blocked rivers, creating glacial lakes. Filling to gigantic proportions, these lakes finally burst through the ice dams, creating the largest floods known. The flood from ancient Lake Missoula in present-day Montana is estimated to have carried half of the volume of Lake Superior. The raging waters scoured the basalt to create these channeled scablands, including the canyons and potholes seen today in places such as Grand Coulee, Moses Coulee, Dry Falls, the Palouse River Canyon at Palouse Falls, and many other sites.

Just south of the parking area, a trail board warns of rattlesnakes and also highlights some of the region's wildlife: sharp-tailed grouse, burrowing owls, jackrabbits, and yellow-headed blackbirds. From here, walk northeast past the farmhouse, along an old railroad bed. At mile 0.1, look for a two-track trail on the right leading up the hill, just past the tree line at the edge of the farm. Turn here and follow the trail up through a gate, then wind around the east side of a grassy knoll.

With flat to rolling terrain covered in bunchgrass, much of this spacious landscape feels more like parts of Wyoming or central Montana than Washington. Views soon open to the south, where a distant line of ponderosa pines marks Fishtrap Lake. A number of edible plants grow in the dry soil here. You'll see several types of desert-parsley, all of which are considered edible. With showy, umbrellalike clusters of tiny yellow flowers, **narrow-leaved desert-parsley** blooms in mid- to late May. **Large-fruited desert-parsley**, or **biscuitroot**, has greenish white flowers. It often grows in rocky soil, making the harvest of its tuberous roots a challenge.

FIDDLENECK
Amsinckia intermedia

HEIGHT: 8" to 32"
BLOOMS: May to mid-June
The tightly furled top of the fiddleneck resembles the scroll of a violin, thus the plant's name. Its small, delicate, yellow-orange blossoms follow the outer edge of the curl. Fiddleneck grows mostly in the shrub grasslands of eastern Washington. With weedlike tendencies, fiddleneck takes over areas, often displacing other plants. This lanky plant's hairs may irritate the skin, and its flowers are poisonous to cattle and horses.

The trail passes through a slight depression where **Hooker's onion** and purple-blue **common camas** bloom from late April through May. Their bulbs were a source of food for indigenous peoples. Displaying horizontal, lavender trumpets atop leafless stems, **Douglas' brodiaea** also has edible bulbs. (Note that the lethal **death camas**, with creamy white flower clusters, also grows in the area—good enough reason to never sample unknown plants.)

At mile 0.4, you can find **fiddleneck**, with a draping cluster of mustard yellow flowers and hairy leaves and stems. A member of the pea family, purple **woolly vetch** blooms from tangled vines. The trail passes **western groundsel**, also known as **western butterweed**, with clusters of small, yellow ray flowers on each stem. The graceful **western blue iris** is an amazing blossom to find in this desert environment. These flowers bloom from May to early June.

Near aspen and ponderosa pine, the pink blossoms of **Nootka rose** open in early and mid-June. **Lupine** and **Nuttall's larkspur**, a member of the delphinium family also known as **common larkspur**, add a purplish blue to the sage landscape. You can hear the melodic songs of meadowlarks along much of the trail during April and June.

Beneath a low cliff on the left at mile 0.7, you'll find a great variety of wildflowers, including fiddleneck, Nootka rose, and lacy white **yarrow**. A standard of eastern Washington, **arrowleaf balsamroot** presents large leaves and yellow sunflower heads that bloom from late April to early May. Purple

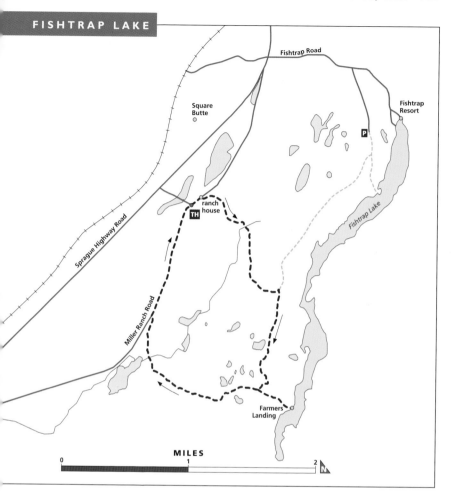

FISHTRAP LAKE

Fishtrap Road

Square
Butte

Fishtrap
Resort

P

ranch
house

TH

Fishtrap Lake

Sprague Highway Road

Miller Ranch Road

Farmers
Landing

MILES

0   1   2

N

long-plumed avens, also called old-man's whiskers, display unusual purple-red globes with five arching sepals. Pink-blossomed sticky geranium grows abundantly in eastern Washington. With spiky leaves, puccoon, or lemonweed, has clusters of pale yellow blossoms hidden in the stem-top leaves. Mid-May through mid-June is the best time to witness the blossoms in this vicinity.

Well adapted to harsh conditions, buckwheats thrive in the region. Because more than 24 kinds grow in Washington—many species with several color variations—identification can be difficult. Thyme-leaved buckwheat has twiggy stems, and its flowers are usually colored cream and pink. With sage-green leaves, cushion buckwheat's blossoms are generally cream-colored.

The trail briefly follows a fence line on the right. At the bottom of a gentle hill is a trail junction at mile 1.2. The left fork leads north along the west side of Fishtrap Lake. But stay to the right at the junction, where a small trail sign directs you through a gate in about 60 yards. After the gate, stay right again on the two-track trail, ignoring a well-beaten single track branching to the left. You'll come upon a pond on the right, ringed with bulrush, a water-dwelling reed, and **chokecherry**, a small tree with white, cylindrical flower clusters. These scabland ponds provide excellent habitat for an assortment of waterfowl, reptiles, and amphibians.

Traveling through open ponderosa pine forest, you'll see lovely **longleaf phlox**, with five-petaled, pink and lavender blossoms. **Serviceberry**, a large, prevalent shrub with white flowers, sometimes grows up to 20 feet tall.

At a marked junction near a red-barked ponderosa pine, 2.0 miles from where you started, stay left and drop down a short distance (about 0.25 mile) to Farmer's Landing on Fishtrap Lake. This is a great picnic spot. During fishing season, however, you might see weekend boat traffic on the lake. Along the lakeshore, yellow narrow-leaved desert-parsley blooms in May. In April, graceful **desert shooting star** exhibits fuchsia petals arching skyward. **Grass widow** is one of the first plants to bloom here, with purple or pink disks and grasslike leaves. Keep an eye out for **elkhorn clarkia**, with pink petals that look like lobed leaves.

Farmer's Landing is the turnaround point. From here, return to the last junction, but now stay to the left to complete the loop hike. The trail soon enters an open landscape once again, with a 1-acre pond on the left and another soon after on the right. The small, white five-petaled flowers of **prairie star** flourish here. At a rise approaching a larger lake on the left, pink-flowering phlox grows abundantly. Lupine and balsamroot brighten the trail, which leads out to a road. A right onto this road takes you back to the parking area near the farmhouse.

Bluebird

A riot of wildflowers in Turnbull National Wildlife Refuge

Easy	*Trail Rating*
3 miles round trip	*Trail Length*
Turnbull National Wildlife Refuge, near Cheney	*Location*
2,300 feet (no elevation gain)	*Elevation*
March to late July	*Bloom Season*
Late April to early June	*Peak Bloom*
Turnbull National Wildlife Refuge, (509) 235-4723	*Contact*
From I-90 southwest of Spokane, take the Cheney/ Four Lakes exit (Exit 270) and head south on WA 904, driving 5 miles to the town of Cheney. Pass through downtown and turn left (south) on Cheney-Plaza Road. Drive 4.5 miles and turn left (east) on South Smith Road, where a sign marks the entrance to Turnbull National Wildlife Refuge. Proceed east on the dirt road. It's 2 miles to the refuge headquarters and the parking area. There is an entrance fee of $3.	*Directions*

Most people come to Turnbull National Wildlife Refuge to view the wildlife—but from April through June, hikers here can witness a show of wildflowers, too. Bring your binoculars. Also be sure to stop at the Environmental Education Center, where you can pick up a brochure with a map of the Bluebird Trail.

From the parking area north of the Environmental Education Center, small trail signs direct you past an old barn with a stone foundation, some sheds, and garages. Several hundred yards beyond the headquarters buildings, the Bluebird Trail begins its trip north along the refuge's eastern border. Immediately, yellow sprays of **narrow-leaved desert-parsley** stand out like miniature fireworks. The deep blue, half-inch blossoms of **small-flowered blue-eyed Mary** open in May. You'll notice it off and on during the first half mile of trail. With clusters of horizontal, light blue trumpets on single stems, **Douglas' brodiaea** is commonly found in sage and ponderosa pine habitats. Also widespread in the region, **Nuttall's larkspur** is a purple-blue delphinium that grows 16 inches in height.

Many flowering plants in the area held an important place in the diets of American Indians. **Large-fruited desert-parsley**, or **biscuitroot**, with a dirty-white spray of flowers, is one of at least 30 lomatiums found in Washington. Their taproots were usually pounded into a flour-paste, then boiled, steamed, or roasted. The common **Hooker's onion** has clusters of sharp-pointed, pink to purple blossoms and small edible bulbs, which can be difficult to dig up with simple stone tools. Often preferring rocky areas, **bitterroot** remains inconspicuous until its rose-pink flowers open in May. At one time, a sack of its roots could be traded for a good horse. **Common camas**, which sometimes covers meadows in carpets of purple-blue, has an edible, onion-shaped bulb. With small, creamy flowers packed into a cone-shaped head, the very poisonous **death camas** fortunately looks nothing like common camas. Never sample any plants if you are in the least doubt as to their identities.

Prairie star dwells from sagebrush to ponderosa pine habitats, growing abundantly with small, white, finger-tipped blossoms. Also common, **western butterweed**, or **western groundsel**, produces clusters of small, yellow ray flowers on 20- to 30-inch stems. One of a dozen varieties of pussytoes in Washington, **field pussytoes** displays a mat of woolly leaves and soft, rounded white flower heads. Small, purple-flowered **naked broomrape** lacks leaves and is parasitic on plants such as saxifrages and stonecrops. With odd-looking, pale maroon blossoms, **old-man's whiskers**, also referred to as **long-plumed avens**, has globe-shaped flowers and five arching sepals. **Lupine's** blue flowers may bloom profusely or sparsely in the area, depending on winter rains. **Western blue iris**, one of the loveliest flowers in the area, appears even more beautiful in the wild than it does in cultivated gardens.

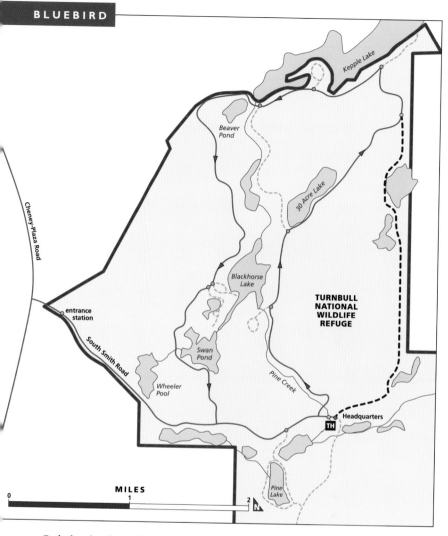

Only hardy plants thrive in the area's thin, rocky soil. With an arc of mustard yellow clusters, **round-headed buckwheat** is one of several types of buckwheat growing here. **Fiddleneck**, with small, five-lobed yellow flowers and bristly hairs on its leaves and stems, also flourishes in nutrient-poor soil. With stamens projecting from yellow petals, low and spiky **stonecrop** joins the rugged survivors along rocky sections of the trail.

Most of the flowers mentioned so far bloom in May and early June. A walk in April and early May reveals a different set of blossoms. After a wet winter, pink carpets of **grass widow** appear in April and fade in the first heat wave. The six-petaled flower ranges from pale blue to purple. **Yellow bell**, with an edible bulb, looks like its name, with usually one hanging flower per plant. Another early bloomer, **desert shooting star** produces an elegant, hanging, pink flower with petals reaching skyward above a yellow ring. With five yellow petals, **buttercup** is usually the first to bloom, often on sunny, south-facing slopes; sometimes it shows up as early as late February, before the pond ice has melted.

Late June ushers in a different grouping of blossoms. **Woolly vetch** seems to take over areas, its purple blooms sometimes covering whole hillsides. White and lacy, **yarrow** is also widespread, amazingly able to prosper in many ecosystems, from sagebrush to subalpine habitats. Sparsely leaved **brown-eyed Susan** has notched, yellow rays around a large reddish brown center. With a mass of protruding yellow stamens, five-petaled **St. John's wort** blooms from late June to late July. People have used the plant medicinally for centuries, most recently as a natural mood lifter.

STICKY GERANIUM
Geranium viscosissimum

HEIGHT: 12" to 20"
BLOOMS: May and June

As its Latin name *Geranium viscosissimum* suggests, sticky geranium has gummy, viscous little hairs on its stems and large-lobed leaves. The attractive roselike flower is pink to purple with darker veins. Found mainly east of the Cascades, sticky geranium ranges from foothill forests to low-elevation drylands. According to legend, American Indian women used sticky geranium as a love-related medicine.

At mile 0.6, the trail enters open woods with ponderosa pines and a scattering of Douglas fir. The tree rings of one large cut ponderosa showed the old-timer to be 152 years in age. Under partial shade, **western spring beauty's** small white, five-petaled blossoms poke out of pine needles. In late May and June, the pink blossoms of **wild rose** are a common sight. **Sticky geranium** blooms about the same time, in a bright rose pink. Widespread in the sagebrush and ponderosa pine habitats of the eastern part of the state, **showy** and **tufted phlox** bloom in pale shades of pink and lavender. Sporting yellow five-petaled blossoms, as well as serrated leaves with an undercoating of silver, **silverweed** is a type of cinquefoil.

At mile 1.0, you'll come upon a pond on the left—a waterfowl nesting site that also provides habitat for reptiles and amphibians. Aspen trees and white-blooming **serviceberry** scatter through the open forest surrounding the lake. **Star-flowered false Solomon's seal**, with lance-shaped leaves and tiny white stars, grows abundantly here. Found from eastern Washington to the Rocky Mountains, **alumroot's** creamy flowers congregate on leafless stems that rise above a mass of rounded basal leaves. Hidden beneath shrubs and bushes along the south end of the lake, **mountain lady's slipper** is a rare and exquisite-looking white orchid, blooming in June. Small yellow blossoms of **water butter-cup** float on the lake's surface, as the plant is able to root underwater.

At mile 1.2, you'll encounter a small lake on the right. **Early blue violet** resides here. Lacking green leaves and relying on decayed vegetation for nutrients, parasitic **pinedrops** are recognized by their stout, sticky red stems. Prairie star, Nuttall's larkspur, field pussytoes, and Douglas' brodiaea grow scattered throughout this area. **Miner's lettuce**, fine in a salad, has tiny white flowers surrounded by disk-shaped leaves.

At mile 1.5, the trail ends at a road. Traffic is light on this dirt lane, and taking a left onto the road will lead you back to the parking area near the Environmental Education Center. Otherwise, return the way you came for a 3-mile hike and the slightly different perspective you get from traveling in the opposite direction.

Sunlight filters through the fog in a forest of ponderosa pine

*Wildflower
Hike 48*

Little Spokane River

*Yellow iris
along the Little
Spokane River*

The Little Spokane River–Indian Painted Rocks Trail is one of the hiking destinations closest to Spokane, and it is a popular place on nice weekends. The nearly level trail parallels the Little Spokane River, passing through open ponderosa pine forest, small meadows, and wetlands. The trail enters the 1,993-acre Little Spokane River Natural Area, a preserve renowned for its wildlife. Many varieties of waterfowl live here or pass through, and eagles and osprey hunt in the area. Cougars have been sighted here, and you might even spy the occasional resident moose. Rattlesnake encounters have occurred here sporadically.

At the trailhead, an interpretive brochure is usually available, highlighting many of the area's features. Although the trail is not signed, the lack of side

Trail Rating	Easy
Trail Length	3.6 miles round trip
Location	Little Spokane River Natural Area, near Spokane
Elevation	1,550 to 1,620 feet
Bloom Season	March to late July
Peak Bloom	May to early June
Contact	Little Spokane River Natural Area, (509) 465-5537
Directions	From I-90 in Spokane, take the Maple Street exit north (Exit 280). Cross over the Maple Street Bridge and continue north about 4 miles. Turn left (west) onto Francis Avenue and go 1 mile to the stoplight at Indian Trail Road. Turn right (north) and drive 5 miles to Rutter Parkway. Indian Trail Road feeds into the right fork of Rutter Parkway, continuing north. Stay right and cross the Little Spokane River. The Indian Painted Rocks Trailhead is just after the bridge. Look for the parking lot, with outhouse, on the left (west) side of the road.

trails makes it difficult to get lost. Bring water, as none is available, and carry any valuables with you because break-ins have occurred at the trailhead.

The Little Spokane River valley has an intriguing human history. Near the trailhead, American Indian pictographs decorate a basalt slab now protected behind iron bars. Trappers arrived in the area in 1810, and a trading post, the Spokane House, was built near the confluence of the Spokane and Little Spokane Rivers. Trappers and American Indians bartered and socialized here.

The flower of note along this hike is the **yellow flag iris**, which blooms in late May and early June across large marshlands that border the river. An introduced species, this iris provides both waterfowl habitat and stream bank stability. Along the first half mile of the trail, you pass several overlooks where you can admire the iris. Another excellent way to view the iris and abundant wildlife found here is by canoe.

From the trailhead, hike west, passing several blooming trees and shrubs, many bearing edible fruit for wildlife. Some of the fruit was also important in the diet of American Indians, but remember never to consume wild plants without absolute certainty as to their identity. Yielding fruit similar to raspberries, **thimbleberry** has white papery blossoms and large maplelike leaves. **Serviceberry** blooms in April with clusters of five-petaled blossoms; in late summer, it produces edible berries. With black berries that can be used to make jam, **chokecherry** displays dense, hanging cylinder-shaped clusters of cream-colored blossoms.

American Indians consumed the black-purple "apples" of **black hawthorn** both fresh and dried; its blossoms are white and five-petaled. **Syringa**, or **mock orange**, dwells on hillsides along the west end of the trail, generating four-petaled white flowers.

Birds of prey nest on the high granite cliffs lining the north side of the trail. In late spring and early summer, you can sometimes hear the beautiful descending notes of the canyon wren, its song resonating off the rock walls. At mile 0.5, look for several old-growth ponderosa pines, their bark reddening with age. These amazing trees can survive ground fires as long as their crowns remain fire free. Beneath the trees, **wild rose** displays pink flowers and, later in the summer, edible scarlet roseships. Another flowering shrub, **Oregon grape** sprouts hollylike leaves and clusters of yellow blossoms. Later in the season, purple berries mature on this common evergreen plant. Watch out for a few patches of poison ivy.

Along several stretches of the trail, **yarrow** holds high its lacy white flower heads and feathery leaves. **Nuttall's larkspur**, a member of the delphinium family, exhibits deep purple to blue, winged blossoms. Another treasure, **scarlet gilia**, or **skyrocket**, reveals vivid, trumpet-shaped blossoms; it can bloom here anytime from June into October. Elegant **sticky geranium** flowers in late May or June with bright rose-pink blossoms.

In the forest, **wild strawberry** and edible **miner's lettuce** bear small white blossoms. **Long-flowered bluebell** reveals clusters of blue to pink tubular blooms. Also in the woods, **star-flowered false Solomon's seal** produces deep green, lance-shaped leaves and small white blooms. Under partial shade, **western spring beauty's** small, white five-petaled blossoms poke out of pine needles.

In several places, the trail nears the Little Spokane River, which runs clear and cold all year long from springs upstream. The water provides excellent habitat for rainbow and eastern brook trout. Three miles upstream, the Little Spokane Fish Hatchery releases 2,000 rainbows into the river each June. Steelhead, cutthroat, and Chinook salmon once inhabited the Little Spokane River; today their migration is blocked by dams, including the Grand Coulee Dam on the Columbia River.

At mile 1.4, the trail detours from the river into rolling pine-covered hills. The detour was constructed to reroute hikers away from a great blue heron rookery in black cottonwoods along the river, though the herons have since abandoned this area to nest farther upstream. From April to June, about a dozen types of flowers bloom along this detour section of trail. Several are quite diminutive. **Small-flowered blue-eyed Mary** generates tiny penstemon-like blossoms. Displaying small white, finger-tipped blossoms, **prairie star** grows in habitats from sagebrush to ponderosa pine. With an odd-looking, pale maroon blossom, **old-man's whiskers**, or **long-plumed avens**, has globe-shaped flowers and five arching sepals.

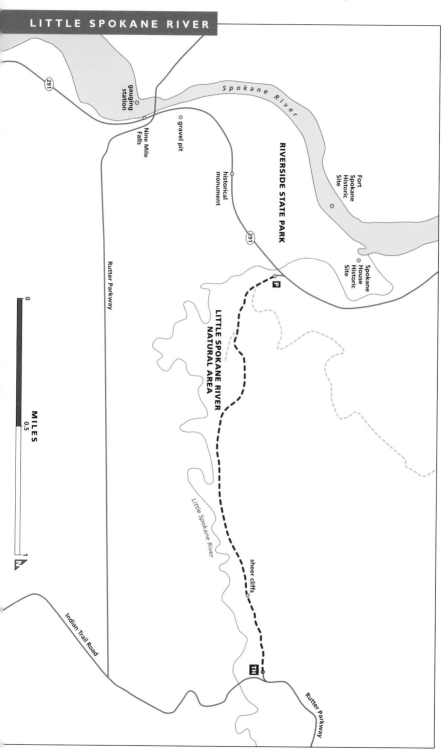

LITTLE SPOKANE RIVER

Spokane River

291

gauging station

Nine Mile Falls

gravel pit

historical monument

291

RIVERSIDE STATE PARK

Fort Spokane Historic Site

Spokane House Historic Site

LITTLE SPOKANE RIVER NATURAL AREA

Rutter Parkway

Little Spokane River

sheer cliffs

Indian Trail Road

Rutter parkway

0

MILES

0.5

1

On the conspicuous side, **arrowleaf balsamroot** generates clumps of large yellow sunflowers and sage green, teardrop-shaped leaves. Another composite, **western butterweed**, or **western groundsel**, produces clusters of small yellow ray flowers on 20- to 30-inch stems. **Narrow-leaved desert-parsley's** yellow, umbrella-shaped flower heads consist of many tiny blossoms. **Douglas' brodiaea** presents clusters of horizontal, light blue trumpets. **Lupine's** blue flowers may be profuse or sparse here, depending on winter rains. **Showy** and **tufted phlox** bloom in pale shades of pink and lavender. Also look for Nuttall's larkspur, scarlet gilia, and yarrow.

In addition to gathering edible berries, American Indians made use of many of the other flowering plants in this region. The taproots of the **large-fruited desert-parsley**, or **biscuitroot**, were usually pounded into a flour-paste and then boiled, steamed, or roasted. One of some 30 different kinds of lomatiums found in Washington, it has a dirty-white spray of flowers. The common **Hooker's onion** has small edible bulbs and clusters of sharp-pointed, pink to purple blossoms. **Sweet fennel**, a member of the carrot family, sprouts feathery leaves and yellow umbellate flower heads. Purple-blue **common camas** has an edible, onion-shaped bulb. Fortunately, the very poisonous **death camas**, with small creamy flowers packed into a cone-shaped head, looks nothing like the common camas. Again, never sample any plant without positive identification.

Most of the flowers mentioned previously bloom from

DEATH CAMAS
Zigadenus venenosus

HEIGHT: 10" to 16"
BLOOMS: April to June

As its name suggests, this plant is not to be eaten. Often called meadow death camas, this member of the lily family contains alkaloids poisonous to livestock, particularly sheep. Symptoms include lockjaw and foaming at the mouth. It can also be poisonous to humans and bees. According to folk tradition, butter or grease counteracts the poison. Coastal tribes used this plant as an emetic to induce vomiting and also applied it as a poultice to ease the pain of sprains, bruises, boils, and sore joints.

Death camas bears blossoms in dense pyramidal clusters. Each tiny, cream-colored flower contains three sepals and three similar-looking petals. Basal leaves grow straight, tall, and grasslike. Found primarily in the foothills and dry country of eastern Washington, death camas flourishes on arid slopes.

May to early June. A hike in April shows a very different scene. After a wet winter, pink to lavender **grass widow** blossoms in April, fading with the first heat wave. **Yellow bell** looks like its name, with a single hanging flower and an edible bulb. Another early bloomer, **desert shooting star** produces an elegant, hanging pink flower with petals reaching skyward from a yellow ring. With five yellow petals, **buttercup** is usually the first to bloom on the sunny, south-facing slopes—sometimes as early as late February.

The trail curves back to enter the valley again, heading west. On the left, a large open area is thick with sedges and grasses. The hillside on the right hosts **fiddleneck**, with small, five-lobed yellow flowers and bristly hairs on its leaves and stems. In June, **woolly vetch**, a member of the pea family, opens purple flower clusters on trailing vines. Also purple, **narrowleaf skullcap** displays hooded blossoms on 4- to 12-inch stems. Lavender-colored **asters** bloom here during late summer.

Toward the end of the trail, highway noise becomes apparent. At mile 1.8, you'll reach a parking area. Unless you've arranged for a vehicle shuttle, turn around here and return the way you came.

Yellow iris

*Wildflower
Hike 49* # Twin Lakes

Water buttercup thrive in the Twin Lakes BLM lands

Trail Rating	Moderate
Trail Length	8.4-mile loop
Location	West of Harrington
Elevation	1,880 to 2,120 feet
Bloom Season	March to late June
Peak Bloom	Late April to late May
Contact	Bureau of Land Management, Spokane District Office, (509) 536-1200
Directions	From Harrington, drive west on Coffeepot Road for about 14 miles. The road drops down into the Coffeepot Lake valley; look for Highline Road on the right and a sign saying, "public access to Twin Lakes." Take this road north 1.9 miles and turn right onto a small gravel road at a "public land boundary" sign. Continue 2 miles to the end of this road, where there is a parking area with an outhouse and picnic tables.

The dry scablands of eastern Washington are not known for fabulous wild-flowers. Casual observers traveling the highways see endless plains of sage-brush, and most people wouldn't consider this a place for a nature hike. But in this seemingly uninteresting landscape grow many kinds of wildflowers, mixed in among the predominant sagebrush, rabbitbrush, and bunchgrass.

A good loop hike, the Twin Lakes Trail provides a good representation of flowering plants found in this steppe ecosystem. The Twin Lakes Unit is one of the larger Bureau of Land Management units in this type of habitat, and the Twin Lakes Trail has been developed to explore it. Be sure to bring your own water and pick up a map, which is available at the Bureau of Land Management's Spokane District Office.

The landforms in this area were shaped by massive geologic events. First, vast amounts of lava were deposited across eastern Washington. Then, during the last ice age, gigantic ice dams created glacial lakes in Montana and surrounding areas. As the climate gradually warmed 10,000 to 15,000 years ago, these dams periodically broke, creating the largest known floods on earth. It is estimated that some of these floods carried a volume of water equal to the combined flow of all the planet's current rivers. These raging waters scoured the lava fields of eastern Washington, gouging out coulees and potholes and creating an area known today as the scablands.

From the parking area, near picnic tables and a boat launch, walk south-west about 100 yards and cross the footbridge over Lake Creek, the stream flowing out of the upper Twin Lake. Look for a large **serviceberry** shrub, with white blossoms in late April. Beneath it you'll find a smaller shrub, a yellow-flowering **golden currant**. From both of these shrubs, American Indians picked the autumn berries,

DAGGERPOD
Phoenicaulis cheiranthoides

HEIGHT: 8"

BLOOMS: Late May to early June

Taking its name from the shape of its seedpod, which resembles a small dagger, daggerpod grows in the rocky soils of ponderosa pine and sagebrush ecosystems. Based in a cluster of fuzzy, olive green leaves close to the ground, daggerpod has three stems per plant, each holding six or more pink or red-violet flowers. Daggerpod flourishes in Washington east of the Cascades.

rich in vitamin C. Remember never to consume any wild plant without absolute confirmation of its identity. The trail proceeds northeast along the eastern lake-shore, where serviceberry lines the stair-stepping cliffs.

Passing through a gate, the trail soon begins to curve to the right (east) past the yellow, umbrella-shaped heads of desert-parsley. Inhabiting the area are several related types, all of which are edible; American Indians harvested many of these. Most common in this area is **narrow-leaved desert-parsley**. Also growing in this area are **nine-leaf**, **fern-leaved**, and **Gray's desert-parsley**. Common along much of the trail, **large-fruited desert-parsley**, or **biscuitroot**, has dirty-white blossoms and deep, edible taproots that were valued by native peoples.

Many yellow composite members of the aster family grow in this region. Often the first noticed, **arrowleaf balsamroot** has large yellow heads with wide, flame-shaped leaves. This common resident of eastern Washington blooms in late April and early May. Several smaller yellow asters blossom at about the same time, from mid-May through June, and dwell in similar habitats. **Narrowleaf goldenweed** is a woody cushion plant with spiny leaves and six to eight rays. With 20 or more rays, **linear-leaf daisy**, or **line-leaf fleabane**, has grasslike leaves and grows 6 to 10 inches tall. Often appearing in rocky areas, **Oregon sunshine**, or **woolly sunflower**, displays petals that are usually two-toned, with lighter and darker shades of yellow.

A mainstay of the state's dry areas, purple-blue **Nuttall's larkspur**, also known as **common larkspur**, dwells along much of this trail. A small white flower with three notches in each of its five petals, **prairie star** also grows along the trail, with three slightly different varieties found here.

At mile 0.2, where the trail approaches an aspen grove, you'll see a marshy pool on the right where **water buttercup** blooms in late April and early May. Able to root under water, this plant has yellow blossoms and stems that float on the surface. Purplish-blue **common camas** fringes the edges of the pool. Also flowering in late April and early May, **hesperochiron**, with small white five-petaled blossoms, dwells in the same area.

Just beyond this wetland stands an aspen grove with an undergrowth of **wild rose** and **sticky geranium**, both with pink blossoms in late May and early June. Less than 100 yards past the grove is a spring filled with watercress and surrounded by nettles and western birch. I rousted two owls as I came through this treed desert oasis, the last terrain with shade and water for several miles.

Breaking out into the open sage, the trail climbs to a dry landscape where sun-loving flowers thrive. Of the many varieties of buckwheat found in Washington, several are found here, including **thyme-leaved**, **parsnip-flowered**, **heart-leaf**, and **round-headed buckwheat**. Buckwheats vary in flower color, even within the same species, from white to cream, yellow, or pink. Well adapted to dry conditions, buckwheats have clusters of many tiny blooms composing each umbellate flower head.

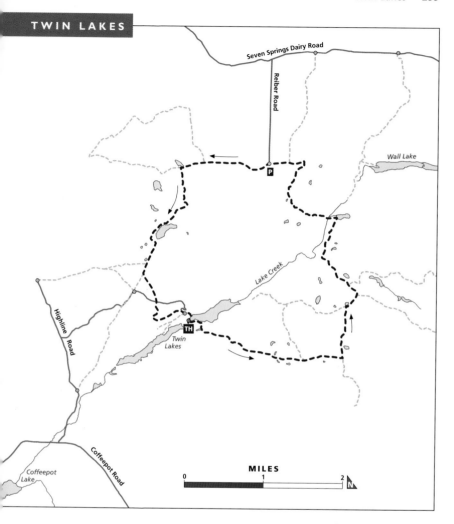

Some beautiful clumps of grass grow in the valley, reaching up to 6 feet in height. From the lake valley, the trail gently ascends. Look for arrowleaf balsamroot at the base of lichen-splattered cliffs. Resembling a miniature penstemon, the tiny blooms of **small-flowered blue-eyed Mary** have lighter upper petals and deep blue lower ones. Toward the end of the valley, stunted **hawthorn** blooms in late May. In April, listen for meadowlarks singing with melodic clarity.

The trail at last reaches high, open plains and heads eastward, where fragrant blue and white **lupine** blooms from May into June. Phlox always seems out of place in such harsh environments, but the five-petaled flowers of **longleaf phlox** and **tufted phlox** add shades of pink and lavender throughout May. You'll go through a gate and pass by springtime ponds, which dry up later in the year. Look for **puccoon**, or **lemonweed**, with pale yellow blossoms hidden in spiky leaves.

At mile 2.2, keep an eye out for a sharp left turn; take this trail north. **Western butterweed**, or **western groundsel**, a tallish plant with many yellow ray flower heads, blooms in May. At mile 3.2, you'll go to the left, heading in a northwesterly direction. At mile 3.8, the trail begins to drop into the Lake Creek valley and then parallels the stream briefly. In June, look for **blanket flower**, or **brown-eyed Susan**, a unique composite with notched yellow rays around a reddish-brown center. **Yarrow**, with lacy white blossoms, grows here, along with the furled yellow flower clusters of **fiddleneck**. Near a pond, the trail turns left to cross Lake Creek and soon begins to climb out of the valley.

Once out of the creek valley and atop open flats again, the trail curves to the north, then west to arrive at a parking area and access point off Reiber Road. Here you are halfway through the hike, at mile 4.2. To complete the loop, find the signed trail leading west from here.

Daggerpod, an interesting-looking perennial, has a thick clump of grayish green, lance-shaped leaves; its blossoms range from deep pink to reddish purple. Plants found on the east side of Lake Creek continue along the trail here. Especially showy after a wet winter are desert-parsley, cream-colored lupine, buckwheat, butterweed, and Nuttall's larkspur.

At mile 5.4, which is 1.2 miles from the Reiber Road parking area, look for a junction and turn left (south) to head back to your vehicle. In rocky areas, look for **bitterroot**, with graceful pink blossoms in May. **Rockcress** also grows here, with small tubular pink-to-lavender blossoms on nonbranching stems. You'll come upon an unnamed lake on the left, which often hosts waterfowl in the spring. Continue south to cross the Twin Lakes access road. The trail turns east to parallel this road, then drops down to the parking area at Twin Lakes. Time to soak your feet and munch on an apple!

Steamboat Rock

*Arrowleaf
balsamroot at
Steamboat Rock
State Park*

en thousand years ago, a series of colossal floods swept from Montana
across eastern Washington, gouging immense canyons into the basalt
rock and forming a huge area known as the channeled scablands. Steamboat
Rock, a 500-foot monolith, was shaped during that time. Because of difficult access, the top of this formation remains in its natural state, offering
a glimpse of what the land looked like before grazing and farming altered
much of the region.

Steamboat Rock and 3,523-acre Steamboat Rock State Park jut out
into Banks Lake like an island. With 50,000 feet of shoreline, the park
is mainly known for boating, although the hiking here is unique, with

Trail Rating	Moderate
Trail Length	5.6 miles round trip
Location	Steamboat Rock State Park, south of Grand Coulee
Elevation	1,600 to 2,280 feet
Bloom Season	March to late June
Peak Bloom	Late April to late May
Contact	Steamboat Rock State Park, (509) 633-1304
Directions	From Grand Coulee, drive south on WA 155 to Electric City. Continue south 9.0 miles to Steamboat Rock State Park and turn right (west) into the park. (You can also access the park from Coulee City by driving north on WA 155 for 26.5 miles and turning left at the park entrance.) Enter the park and continue past the campgrounds. Park near the restrooms in the second (northerly) campground. The trail begins directly across the main road from here.

cliff-top trails meandering above the sprawling lake below. To view the best flowers—and to avoid motor noise—hike on weekdays in April and May. Because no water is available along the trail, you'll need to carry it with you from the campground. Trail junctions on this route are unmarked, and the sheer cliffs and the potential for rattlesnake encounters, however rare, make this hike inadvisable for small children.

The trailhead (unmarked but easily seen) is located on the west side of the main park road, across from the second and most northerly campground. The trail leads to the top of Steamboat Rock, passing through a wide variety of spring-blooming wildflowers.

Climb the gradual first 0.4 mile to the base of the cliffs. This lower section of trail is lined with **arrowleaf balsamroot**, blooming in late April and early May with yellow sunflowers. Smaller flowers are scattered between the rabbit-brush and sagebrush, including **bulblet prairie star**, with five notched white petals. Hidden near the ground, the tiny blooms of **small-flowered blue-eyed Mary** look like a miniature penstemon.

Several common flowers grow along this first section of trail. Following a wet winter, blue **lupine** adds a sweet fragrance to the desert air in May. **Nuttall's larkspur**, also bountiful, has stems covered with delicate purple-blue blossoms. Of several desert-parsleys, or lomatiums, in the area, most common are **Gray's** and **narrow-leaved desert-parsley**, both displaying bright yellow, branching umbellate flower heads.

As you approach the cliffs of Steamboat Rock, listen for the quick, descending call of the canyon wren, summering here near its northern reach. A few stunted ponderosa pines offer the only shade on this hike. Continue toward the cliffs, where a trail-board warns hikers to watch out for rattlesnakes. A trail branching right wanders north along the base of the cliffs. However, you want to go straight. Watch for pink **longleaf phlox** along the trail.

Soon the trail begins climbing past furled **fiddleneck** and up through the only accessible route through the cliffs. **Linear-leaf daisy**, with showy low-growing yellow ray flowers that bloom in late April and early May, brighten the rocky slopes. At mile 0.7, you'll reach a bench decorated with a variety of flowers.

Thyme-leaved buckwheat, one of several buckwheats in the vicinity, has a cluster of creamy white flowers, usually pink toward the center. Like a dandelion, yellow-flowering **microseris** exhibits one flower on a single stem. Look for bright displays of green and orange lichen on the cliff face. **Serviceberry**, a large shrub, grows beneath the walls, blooming in late April. Several varieties of white and pink phlox bloom here in late April and May, including **cushion** and **spreading phlox**.

Near the top of a second climb, at mile 1.1, a smaller, more informal trail branches to the right (northeast). Note this junction, as you will return to this spot to explore the northern section of Steamboat Rock. For now, continue straight (west). The trail curves slightly to the left, past showy displays of **western butterweed**, or **western groundsel**, which grows 20 to 30 inches tall and blooms in May with bright yellow clusters of ray flowers on each stalk. In spring, the flute-like songs of western meadowlarks fill the air. Smaller than arrowleaf balsamroot,

NARROWLEAF GOLDENWEED
Haplopappus stenophyllus

HEIGHT: 3" to 6"
BLOOMS: May
Narrowleaf goldenweed resembles a short sunflower with 6 to 8 petals. The flowers grow on twiggy stems from mats of spiny, dark olive green leaves. Thriving in dry, rocky areas across the Columbia Basin, goldenweed often dwells along with buckwheats.

A close cousin, jimmyweed (*Haplopappus heterophyllus*) is toxic to livestock because of the concentrated amount of tremetol in its leaves, which causes animals to shake violently as if with chills.

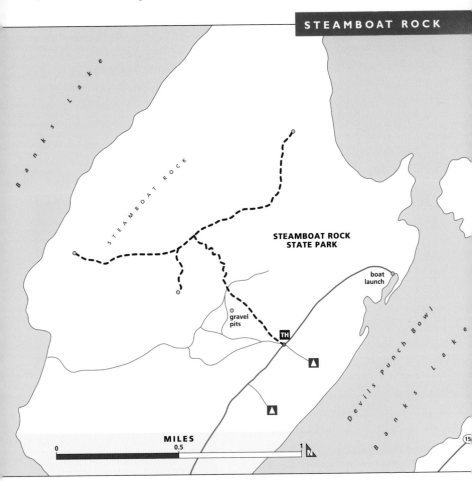

Hooker's balsamroot grows abundantly along the next section of trail. It has yellow sunflowers with deeply serrated leaves. You'll see a beautiful hillside of this flower mixed with lupine as the trail makes its final ascent toward the top of the plateau.

The trail enters a small valley with several trails heading left (south) up the steep slope. Continue straight (west), passing an area crowded with western groundsel. With pale yellow bracts posing as flower heads, **Thompson's paintbrush** also blooms in May. Early in the spring, look for the varnished yellow disks of **sagebrush buttercup**.

As the trail climbs out of the valley, the view opens to the west to the snowy peaks of the Lake Chelan–Sawtooth Wilderness, visible on the horizon 70 miles away. With edible berries in the fall, serviceberry and **squaw currant** dwell along the low cliff band on the left; remember not to consume any wild plant without positive identification. Look for the small but elegant **long-flowered**

bluebell, with clusters of blue to pink tubular flowers. The very toxic **death camas** displays a cone-shaped cluster of tiny cream-colored blossoms. An unusual white lupine, **velvet lupine** is a resident of sagebrush areas in eastern Washington.

The trail ends at the western rim of Steamboat Rock, 1.7 miles into the hike, where the stony soil supports a small, lovely yellow composite, **narrowleaf goldenweed**, which blooms in May. Another rock dweller, **bitterroot** is inconspicuous until it blooms with showy pink flowers. Its roots were an important food source for American Indians. Amazing views up and down 43,800-acre Banks Lake make this spot a great lunch site.

Return back on the same trail 0.5 mile to the junction of trails that climb the hill to the south. These trails connect at the top, and any one of them will take you south to an overlook, a 0.6-mile round-trip diversion on a spur trail. Look for death camas, narrow-leaved desert-parsley, lupine, Hooker's balsamroot, long-flowered bluebell, prairie star, and pink **shooting star**. At the top, the trail levels and continues south to the overlook, passing microseris, Nuttall's larkspur, thyme-leaved buckwheat, and the dirty-white **large-fruited desert-parsley**, or **biscuitroot**. With five mauve to lavender petals, **thread-leaved phacelia** displays several saucer-shaped flowers on each stem. Narrowleaf goldenweed decorates this southern overlook, where you can see Banks Lake stretching south for 18 miles.

Follow the spur trail back to the junction at the base of the hill and turn right (east) toward the campground. Drop down 0.1 mile to where a trail branches north from the main trail. This informal trail climbs up to access the largest section of the 640-acre Steamboat Rock plateau. Along the way, look for linear-leaf daisy, death camas, Nuttall's larkspur, thyme-leaved buckwheat, biscuitroot, and Gray's and narrow-leaved desert-parsley. The trail climbs northeast to the top of Steamboat Rock and heads north along the cliff's rim. Lupine grows abundantly here, along with yellow western groundsel and several types of phlox in shades of pink and lavender.

Once you've hiked 0.8 mile on this side trail (for a total distance of 3.7 miles), you'll see your turnaround point, an overlook above cottonwood-lined campsites for boaters. From here, you'll feel as if you're on an island in the sky as you look across the water to interesting rock formations. Return on this side trail 0.8 mile to the main trail and turn left, heading 1.1 miles downhill to the grassy shade of the campground.

APPENDIX A: *Trail Ratings and Bloom Seasons*

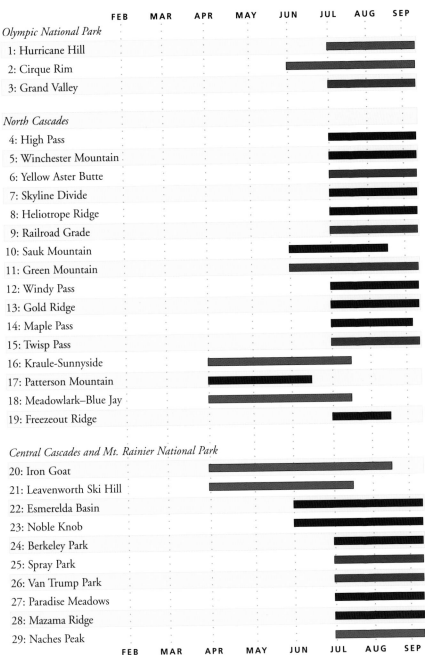

	FEB	MAR	APR	MAY	JUN	JUL	AUG	SEP
Olympic National Park								
1: Hurricane Hill								
2: Cirque Rim								
3: Grand Valley								
North Cascades								
4: High Pass								
5: Winchester Mountain								
6: Yellow Aster Butte								
7: Skyline Divide								
8: Heliotrope Ridge								
9: Railroad Grade								
10: Sauk Mountain								
11: Green Mountain								
12: Windy Pass								
13: Gold Ridge								
14: Maple Pass								
15: Twisp Pass								
16: Kraule-Sunnyside								
17: Patterson Mountain								
18: Meadowlark–Blue Jay								
19: Freezeout Ridge								
Central Cascades and Mt. Rainier National Park								
20: Iron Goat								
21: Leavenworth Ski Hill								
22: Esmerelda Basin								
23: Noble Knob								
24: Berkeley Park								
25: Spray Park								
26: Van Trump Park								
27: Paradise Meadows								
28: Mazama Ridge								
29: Naches Peak								

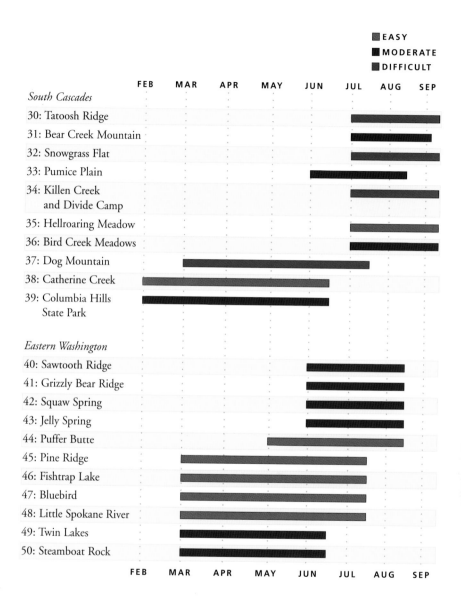

EASY
MODERATE
DIFFICULT

	FEB	MAR	APR	MAY	JUN	JUL	AUG	SEP

South Cascades

30: Tatoosh Ridge

31: Bear Creek Mountain

32: Snowgrass Flat

33: Pumice Plain

34: Killen Creek
and Divide Camp

35: Hellroaring Meadow

36: Bird Creek Meadows

37: Dog Mountain

38: Catherine Creek

39: Columbia Hills
State Park

Eastern Washington

40: Sawtooth Ridge

41: Grizzly Bear Ridge

42: Squaw Spring

43: Jelly Spring

44: Puffer Butte

45: Pine Ridge

46: Fishtrap Lake

47: Bluebird

48: Little Spokane River

49: Twin Lakes

50: Steamboat Rock

APPENDIX B: *Land-Management Agencies and Phone Numbers*

BUREAU OF LAND MANAGEMENT

Spokane District   (509) 536-1200

NATIONAL FORESTS

Gifford Pinchot National Forest

Cowlitz Valley Ranger   (360) 497-1100
District

Mt. Adams Ranger District (509) 395-3400

Mount St. Helens National (360) 247-3900
Volcanic Monument

Mt. Baker–Snoqualmie National Forest

Darrington Ranger District (360) 436-1155

Mt. Baker Ranger District (360) 856-5700

Skykomish Ranger District (360) 677-2414

Snoqualmie Ranger District (360) 825-6585

Okanogan National Forest

Methow Valley Ranger   (509) 997-2131
District

Tonasket Ranger District   (509) 486-2186

Wenatchee National Forest

Cle Elum Ranger District   (509) 674-4411

Leavenworth Ranger   (509) 548-6977
District

Naches Ranger District   (509) 653-2205

Umatilla National Forest

Pomeroy Ranger District   (509) 843-1891

NATIONAL PARKS

Mt. Rainier National Park (360) 569-2211

Olympic National Park   (360) 565-3100

STATE AND COUNTY PARKS

Fields Spring State Park   (509) 256-3332

Horsethief Lake State Park (509) 767-1159

Kamiak Butte County Park (509) 878-1869

Steamboat Rock State Park (509) 633-1304

OTHER

Columbia River Gorge   (541) 386-2333
National Scenic Area

Little Spokane River   (509) 465-5537
Natural Area

Sun Mountain Lodge   (800) 572-0493
Outdoor Center   ext. 735

Turnbull National   (509) 235-4723
Wildlife Refuge

APPENDIX C: *Suggested Reading*

Blackwell, Laird R. *Wildflowers of Mount Rainier.* Auburn, Wash.: Lone Pine Publishing, 2000.

Lyons, C. P. *Wildflowers of Washington.* Auburn, Wash.: Lone Pine Publishing, 1999.

———. *Trees and Shrubs of Washington.* Auburn, Wash.: Lone Pine Publishing, 1999.

Pojar, Jim, and Andy MacKinnon. *Plants of the Pacific Northwest Coast: Washington, Oregon, British Columbia, and Alaska.* Auburn, Wash.: Lone Pine Publishing, 1994.

Spellenberg, Richard. *The Audubon Society Field Guide to North American Wildflowers, Western Region.* New York: Alfred A. Knopf, Inc., 1979.

Stewart, Charles. *Wildflowers of the Olympics and Cascades.* Port Angeles, Wash.: Nature Education Enterprises, 1988.

Strickler, Dee. *Wayside Wildflowers of the Pacific Northwest.* Columbia Falls, Mont.: The Flower Press, 1993.

Taylor, Ronald J., and George W. Douglas. *Mountain Plants of the Pacific Northwest: A Field Guide to Washington, Western British Columbia, and Southeastern Alaska.* Missoula, Mont.: Mountain Press Publishing Company, 1995.

Taylor, Ronald J. *Sagebrush Country: A Wildflower Sanctuary.* Missoula, Mont.: Mountain Press Publishing Company, 1992.

Index

Charles Gurche is one of the country's foremost nature photographers. His large-format (4x5) images have appeared in hundreds of publications, including those of the National Park Service, as well as in such magazines as *Audubon, National Geographic,* and *Smithsonian.* As sole photographer, Gurche has completed 70 calendars and 13 books. He has received awards from the Roger Tory Peterson Institute of Natural History, the Society of Professional Journalists, and Nature's Best International Photography Awards. He lives in Spokane. For print information, please e-mail charlesgurche@msn.com or visit charlesgurche.com.